32⁵⁰

MARXISM IN ASIA

MARXISM IN ASIA

COLIN MACKERRAS & NICK KNIGHT

ST. MARTIN'S PRESS
New York

© 1985 Colin Mackerras and Nick Knight
All rights reserved. For information, write:
St. Martin's Press, Inc., 175 Fifth Avenue, New York, NY 10010
Printed in Great Britain

First published in the United States of America in 1985

Library of Congress Cataloging in Publication Data
Main entry under title: ⸜

    Marxism in Asia.
    Includes bibliographies and index.
    1. Communism—Asia—Addresses, essays, lectures.
    2. Socialism—Asia—Addresses, essays, lectures.
    I. Mackerras, Colin.   II. Knight, Nick.
    HX376.A6M38   1985   335.43'095   85-14591

    ISBN 0-312-51852-8

CONTENTS

35289

PREFACE

The decision to write and edit this book grew out of our experiences teaching an advanced undergraduate course entitled 'Marxism in Asia' in the School of Modern Asian Studies at Griffith University. It became clear to us that, while an enormous quantity of secondary literature on the various Asian Marxisms is available, no satisfactory or readily accessible text existed which could provide reasonably simple interpretations within a comparative framework. This volume is intended to fill that gap.

Marxism in Asia is thus designed primarily as an introductory reference work, suitable for senior undergraduates who have some understanding of European Marxism and who are interested in the way in which Marxist ideas have been interpreted in different Asian contexts. We hope, nevertheless, that the judgements and interpretations that appear in this book will also be of some interest to the specialist. We believe that an objectivist account of the various Asian Marxisms is not possible; we are dealing here with the nebulous world of ideas, and the interpretations we have rendered are unlikely to coincide in all essential details with previous interpretations. The study and analysis of ideas proceeds through constructive argumentation and debate, not through the continued reiteration of time-honoured commentaries. We would not, therefore, deem it as negative if our readings of Asian Marxisms were challenged by the specialist in a spirit of positive intellectual inquiry. Similarly, we invite the students for whom this work is primarily intended to read it critically, extending their capacity to respond in a critical vein by studying the more detailed interpretations referred to in the select bibliographies appended to each chapter.

The focus of this volume is the Marxisms of East and Southeast Asia. However, we were forced, even within this restricted sphere, to exclude certain Asian Marxisms. There is, for example, no reference to the theoretical doctrines of the New People's Army of the Philippines, of the Malay or Thai Communist Parties, or of the Pathet Lao of Laos. Their exclusion was dictated by the requirements of brevity rather than a failure to appreciate the important role that such Marxist-derived ideas have played in their respective social contexts. Consequently, it was our duty as editors to select for consideration those Marxisms which appeared to us to have exercised the greatest influence both domestically and within the international communist movement.

We hope that this selection of essays will prove a useful introduction to the study of Marxism in Asia, and contribute to a clearer understanding of the process of differentiation which Marxism has undergone to accommodate itself to the particular characteristics and needs of different Asian societies.

Many people have contributed their time and energy to the production of this book. Kerrie Gibbon did a splendid job typing and coding the original manuscript. Jeff Russell and Geoff Dow provided much-needed criticism of Chapter 1. Barry Mather and Richard Blundell provided technical advice on the problems associated with producing a photo-typeset camera-ready manuscript. And Jeff Russell laboured mightily to transform a mass of inchoate scribblings into a finished camera-ready copy suitable for publication; he also produced the index. To these people, and others who have encouraged us in this project, we offer our sincere gratitude.

Nick Knight
Colin Mackerras.

Contributors

Robert Cribb is a lecturer in Indonesian politics and history in the School of Modern Asian Studies, Griffith University. His research interests include the regional politics and economics of Indonesia's national revolution (1945-9) and the development of Asian political ideologies.

Sean Kelly is in the Australian Department of Foreign Affairs, Canberra, and is doing a Ph.D. degree on Vietnam at Griffith University, Brisbane.

Ben Kiernan is a Postdoctoral Research Fellow at the Centre of Southeast Asian Studies, Monash University, Melbourne. His current research is on the Pol Pot regime, and his main publication is *How Pol Pot Came to Power*, 1985.

Nick Knight is a lecturer in the School of Modern Asian Studies at Griffith University. He has research interests in Chinese Marxism and Chinese politics.

Colin Mackerras is Foundation Professor in the School of Modern Asian Studies, Griffith University Brisbane, and was the School Chairman from June 1979 to June 1985. His research interests include modern Chinese history, society and ideology. He has written widely on these topics, his main book being *Modern China, A Chronology*, 1982.

Alan Rix is Professor of Japanese, University of Queensland. He has written numerous articles on Japanese politics and foreign policy, Australia-Japan relations and is author of *Japan's Economic Aid*, 1980. He has worked at the Australian National University, the Australian Department of Foreign Affairs, and Griffith University.

INTRODUCTION: MARX AND EUROPE, MARXISM IN ASIA

Nick Knight and Colin Mackerras

In the century since Marx's death, there has been a profusion of interpretations by Marx's critics, adherents and scholars as to what constitute the essential elements or themes of Marxism. This continuing process of differentiation within the Marxist tradition has involved theoretical disagreements over key concepts of Marxism and how Marxism should best be employed in the analysis of social and historical development. It has also involved disagreements which have sprung from the national differences among the various societies in which Marxism has become an ideological force of political importance.

The differentiation of a doctrine or ideology in this manner is of course not without precedent. The 2000-year history of Christianity is a good example of a doctrine which has experienced schism and fragmentation to produce a multiplicity of creeds and organisations all claiming allegiance to a common source of inspiration. While Marxism is a much younger doctrine than Christianity, its history suggests an even more volatile predisposition to manifest very varied formulations concerning 'true' or appropriate interpretations.

The differentiation of Marxism along national lines and the hostility which has resulted between rival national interpretations of its political implications is one of the great ironies of history. One of the dominant themes of Marx's thought has usually been considered to be internationalism, a hope that common class interests could unite individuals across national boundaries and that the parochialism of the nation would be transcended by the strength of common identification of members of the same class.

In Marx's view, the modern working class (proletariat) was the 'universal class', the class which possessed an international character because of the common condition of exploitation shared by its members regardless of national origins. This presumption of shared class interest would, Marx hoped, constitute the basis for the decline and eventual disappearance of the nation and the establishment of an international socialist order. [1] Class identification was, from this perspective, a more powerful force than national identification.

Marxism has also been perceived and proclaimed as a universal theory by its adherents. Marx wrote extensively on a wide variety of subjects for more than four decades, but his interest focussed primarily on countries dominated by the capitalist mode of production which had emerged in Western Europe with the decline of feudalism, allowing the onset of the Industrial Revolution. This intense interest in the development and internal dynamics of capitalist society did not, however, lead Marx to ignore other modes of production which have characterised human societies. Nevertheless, many of Marx's followers believe his analysis of capitalism represented the centrepiece of Marxism, and that the conclusions Marx arrived at through intensive study of capitalism and its development bore implications for the development of human society in general. Marx's analysis of capitalist society was perceived, therefore, as having an application over and above the specific historical context which Marx had analysed. In other words, the generalisations which emerged from Marx's study of Western European capitalism came to be regarded as a 'universal' theory of history and society.

Several such generalisations were to bear important implications for the forms of Marxism which emerged in the various national contexts of Asia. Firstly, and perhaps most importantly, was Marx's analysis of the dominant structure of class relations which characterised capitalism. As capitalism emerged from the disintegration of the feudal order, the bourgeoisie replaced the land-owning aristocracy as the owning or ruling class, and the industrial proletariat replaced the peasantry as the principal producing class. In this relationship between the bourgeoisie and the proletariat, the proletariat was economically dependent upon the bourgeoisie for it possessed nothing except its own labour power. It was precisely this which the bourgeoisie required, and within the context of industrial production, the bourgeoisie proceeded to extract surplus value from the proletariat, this being achieved by paying the workers far less than the value they had actually produced. It was this discrepancy which was the origin of an entirely new category of income—capitalists' profit. With the displacement of feudal rent as the dominant form of unearned income, the capitalist mode of production came into existence. From his analysis of the nature of capitalist society and especially the sociological conditions under which the industrial proletariat worked and lived, Marx suggested that this class would eventually rise in revolution, overthrow the bourgeoisie and establish a socialist society. Marx gives several accounts of how this might happen. His major claim is that on economic grounds a society dominated by a capitalist mode of production cannot last indefinitely. Market relations need eventually to be replaced by more explicitly political ones—thus undermining capitalist social relations. This process presumably would take place over a long term but would not on that account cease to be a revolutionary one. The emergence of a conscious political struggle to usher in a socialist society was understood by Marx to be both desirable and inevitable.

Marx's predictions were not, he believed, based on wishful thinking. On the contrary, several important characteristics of capitalist society suggested to him that the proletariat was the 'universal class' whose task was the abolition of all classes. [2] These characteristics included:

(i)The cooperative form characterising labour under the capitalist system. The nature of labour at the point of production under capitalism involved a division of function which necessitated cooperation and organisation to produce a finished commodity.

(ii)This could lead to the possibility of an increased unity and class identification by the industrial proletariat. The fact that its mode of work brought members of the working class into close contact (both geographically and occupationally) suggested that a greater unity of class outlook could be achieved. [3]

(iii)The advanced forces of production which characterised capitalism could potentially, under the control and guidance of the working class, serve to liberate rather than enslave mankind.

(iv)A concomitant of the advanced forces of production was the scientific nature of modern inquiry which could for the first time indicate to the working class the true nature of society. The knowledge which resulted from such scientific social investigation could inform the working class about its own condition, and the way out of the impasse of class society. In practical terms the most significant example of this development of working class knowledge would be the seizure by it of the right to determine the content of production and thereby the direction of societal development. Control over production is the means by which any class stamps its impression upon society and helps to create an accepted complex of understanding and social behaviour.

The second generalisation that Marx believed he had isolated concerned the internal mechanisms within capitalist society which would lead to the socialist transformation by means of which the working class would displace the bourgeoisie from its position of political and economic dominance. Marx asserted that the development of capitalism was characterised by the incessant accumulation of capital under the control of the bourgeoisie, a process which was accompanied by increasingly fierce economic competition. The consequence of this competition would be the liquidation of inefficient capitalists and members of intermediate classes such as the petit-bourgeoisie who would be forced into the ranks of the working class. The concentration of capital in the hands of fewer and fewer capitalists would be thus accompanied by a growth in the size of the working class. As the numbers of the working class swelled, so its bargaining position with the bourgeoisie would worsen, because of increased competition for the available number of jobs. This competition would be exacerbated by the creation of a large body of unemployed who could not obtain work. (Marx referred to periodically produced unemployed groups as the 'industrial reserve army'.) The effect of competition for employment within the working class would be a lowering of wages for labour. The growth in the numbers of the working class and the lowering of wages means that the working class would become progressively more 'immiserated' as the bourgeoisie became a smaller and wealthier class. [4] This increasing polarisation between the working class and the bourgeoisie would lead to a point at which the contradiction between the antagonistic classes would reach an extreme level, one which could be resolved only through a process of social revolution in which the proletariat would become the dominant class, and the bourgeoisie no longer a constraint upon further social and economic progress. From his fragmented comments on the subject of socialism it seems that Marx believed that in the wake of such a successful socialist revolution, the working class would establish a 'dictatorship of the proletariat' whose function would be the prevention of counterrevolution and the administration of the needs of society during the transitional period between capitalism and communism. Following this transitional period, society would enter the higher phase of communism whereby class divisions would disappear and in which there would be an equitable distribution of society's wealth and resources on the basis of need.

As already indicated, Marx's suggestions concerning the eventual demise of capitalism were only incompletely formulated. The most reasonable interpretation seems to be his expectation that the full maturity of capitalist economic development would portend such immense pressure on the underlying social arrangements that a very different basis for political and economic progress, one based on post-bourgeois or socialist principles of allocation of resources for production, would be necessary. Hence a proletarian revolution to displace bourgeois hegemony seemed to Marx to be, in the long run, very likely. Such a process would be revolutionary, no matter how long it took.

Despite the manifest ambiguities in his incomplete scenarios, Marx unambiguously assigns to the industrial proletariat a key role in this transformation from capitalism to socialism; hence the sometimes vulgarised accounts of socialist revolution that are associated with Marxist thought and the often repeated idea that a future era of socialism could be ushered in only by a revolution led by the proletariat. As Marx was to point out in his 'Conspectus of Bakunin's "Statism and Anarchy"' (1874),

> A radical social revolution depends on certain definite historical conditions of economic development as its pre-condition. It is also only possible where with capitalist production the industrial proletariat occupies at least an important position among the mass of the people. [5]

For both objective and subjective reasons, then, revolutionaries would need to take cognizance of the stage of social and economic development reached in their particular society.

Revolutionary consciousness is not enough. Marx is referring to the more active role the working class can be expected to play in capitalist production decisions at some stages of capitalist development compared with other stages where this involvement is likely to be less emphatic.

The centrality of the proletariat in Marx's schema of revolution and social change was accompanied by a general lack of enthusiasm for the revolutionary potential of the peasantry. The peasants were, Marx believed, unable to constitute the class vehicle for radical change because of the conditions of existence which characterised their class. In Marx's view, any society which retained a significant peasant population would be unlikely to possess a developed industrial economy; the forces of production would probably not be well developed. These conditions would not be propitious for any revolutionary transition to the higher mode of production which was Marx's conception of socialism. In *The Eighteenth Brumaire of Louis Bonaparte,* Marx was to assert a relationship between these conditions of existence and the peasantry's inability to produce a unity of class consciousness or organisation:

> The small peasant proprietors form an immense mass, the members of which live in the same situation but do not enter into manifold relationships with each other. Their mode of operation isolates them instead of bringing them into mutual intercourse. This isolation is strengthened by the wretched state of France's means of communication and by the poverty of the peasants. Their place of operation, the smallholding, permits no division of labour in its cultivation, no application of science and therefore no diversity of development, variety of talent, or wealth of social relationship...In so far as these small peasant proprieters are merely connected on a local basis, and the identity of their interests fails to produce a feeling of community, national links, or a political organisation, they do not form a class. They are therefore incapable of asserting their class interest in their own name... [6]

Elsewhere, Marx was to refer scathingly to the 'idiocy of rural life' [7] and the 'crudity of the peasants'. [8]

This low estimation of the peasantry as a class and Marx's

emphasis on the revolutionary potential of the proletariat were to create significant problems for the employment of Marxism in Asia where the peasantry constituted the large bulk of the population and where the proletariat was often diminutive in size or even non-existent. How were Asian Marxists to resolve this dilemma? Should they attend patiently on the development of modern industry and the gradual growth of a working class which might lead a socialist revolution? Should they ignore the rural unrest engendered by problems of land ownership, poverty, rural unemployment, and the economic dislocation which accompanied imperialism? Or should they adapt this fundamental element of Marxism to conform more closely to the social realities of their own societies?

In five of the countries examined in this book - China, Kampuchea, Korea, Vietnam and Indonesia - the size of the peasant population has constituted a considerable stumbling block to the ready employment of Marxist ideas in their undiluted European form, and has necessitated certain innovative theoretical formulations to specify the role of the peasantry vis-a-vis the working class in the process of revolution and socialist construction in a largely peasant society. The attempt to adapt this aspect of Marxism to a form of class society very different from that about which Marx wrote will constitute one of the themes explored in this book.

A feature of Marx's analysis which necessarily must have important implications for Marxism in Asia was the role he ascribed to the various modes of production through which Western European society had progressed prior to its capitalist stage. Marx concentrated in particular on the feudal mode of production from which capitalism had emerged in an attempt to isolate the factors which had given rise to the new mode of production while the old one was still in existence. It is clear from Marx's writings that he perceived tensions and transformations within the feudal economy and society as giving rise to a capitalist form of production; likewise certain features of capitalist society suggested to Marx that the dynamic of class relationships within capitalist society would eventually produce contradictions whose resolution would help to usher in more non-bourgeois relations of production and eventually contribute to a socialist society. There thus appeared a general progression of modes of production which would successively characterise social formations—each providing material conditions for further transformation to successively higher stages of development and implying different patterns of surplus extraction and different patterns of class domination. Marx loosely assumed that communist society would be characterised by universal abundance and a complete absence of class oppression.

It is widely accepted that a central feature of Marx's philosophy of history (historical materialism) was the belief that society developed through different stages characterised and dominated by different modes of production. Marx did not insist however on a *fixed* order of such stages. Eric Hobsbawm, for example, has argued that 'the general theory of historical materialism requires only that there should be a succession of modes of production, though not necessarily any particular modes, and perhaps not in any particular predetermined order.' [9] A close reading of Marx's writings shows that he did not perceive in history a fixed and undeviating series of stages through which all societies must progress. Marx's analysis of Russian society is a case in point. Marx made no assumption that Russia would necessarily follow the path trodden by its European neighbours. To the contrary, his analysis indicated a dualism within the form of land ownership evident in the Russian village community (land held in common but farmed separately) which might permit a form of development in which the collective element might prevail over private forms of ownership; Russia might thus be able to avoid a capitalist epoch similar to that experienced elsewhere in Europe. 'Everything depends', Marx wrote in a letter to Vera Zasulich (1881), 'on the historical environment in which it occurs'. [10]

Despite Marx's apparent sensitivity to the various patterns of historical development which different societies might pursue, many of his critics and followers were quick to perceive in his philosophy of history a theory of historical progression which imputed a uniformity of development to very different forms of society. Marx was aware of this and was concerned to deny authorship of such an all-embracing theory of historical development. In an unpublished letter to the Russian journal *Otechestvenniye Zapiski* (written in 1877), Marx was to take issue with a reviewer who attributed to him the formulation of just such a blue-print for historical development:

The chapter on primitive accumulation does not pretend to do more than trace the path by which, in Western Europe, the capitalist order of economy emerged from the womb of the feudal order of economy.

But that is too little for my critic. He feels he absolutely must metamorphose my historical sketch of the genesis of capitalism in Western Europe into a historico-philosophical theory of the general path every people is fated to tread, whatever the historical circumstances in which it finds itself, in order that it may ultimately arrive at the form of economy which ensures, together with the greatest expansion of the productive powers of social labour, the most complete development of man. But I beg his pardon. He is both honouring and shaming me too much...Thus events strikingly analogous but taking place in different historical surroundings led to totally different results. By studying each of these forms of evolution separately and then comparing them one can easily find the clue to this phenomenon, but one will never arrive there by using as one's master key a general historico-philosophical theory, the supreme virtue of which consists in being super-historical. [11]

However, despite Marx's denunciation of such a 'general historico-philosophical theory', it remains a fact that many influential Marxists have perceived in Marxism just such a theory. The Bolsheviks under Lenin, for example, adopted a theoretical framework for understanding historical development which incorporated a largely unilinear progression of all societies through five fixed stages: primitive communism, slave society, feudalism, capitalism, and socialism. [12] Lenin had come to the conclusion very early in his career that Russia was not, as some of his Menshevik opponents claimed, an Asiatic mode of production. The concept of an Asiatic mode of production, which was alluded to in Marx's writings on India and China, suggests a society in which the fragmentation of the economy into countless isolated and self-sufficient villages would be likely to prevent the emergence of intrinsic factors for historical change. Their presumed stagnation not only indicates a pattern of historical development very different to that experienced by European societies, but implies that some extrinsic factor (such as imperialism) would be necessary to initiate change. The acceptance of this means of analysing Asian societies thus bore the critical implication that such societies were backward and outside the mainstream of world (European) history and that changes within them would be dependent upon developments within the historically advanced countries of Europe. To admit that Russia possessed a predominantly Asiatic mode of production would consequently have threatened the possibility that it might in the near future undergo a socialist revolution, and would have given credence to the Menshevik counsel that patience and restraint were essential during the long period in which Russia's productive forces had to develop and mature. Lenin therefore insisted that Russia had, during the latter half of the nineteenth century, transformed itself from a largely feudal society into one in which the forms of production and social relationships were essentially capitalist. Lenin thus insisted that Russian society, despite its specific characteristics, could be accommodated within the orthodox Marxist schema of historical development. [13] As the general experience of capitalist development which Marx had studied in Europe was not to be repeated in Russia, Lenin, by interpreting and reinterpreting Marx's theories to provide a guide to revolutionary political action in Russia, was creating a theory and prognosis of his own.

Like Lenin, Stalin too was to regard Marxism as a general or universal theory of history which imputed a rigid pattern of development to all societies, and the five-stage schema of historical development was to gain the ultimate imprimatur in Stalin's *Dialectical and Historical Materialism* (1938):

In conformity with the change and development of the productive forces of society in the course of history, men's relations of production, their economic relations also changed and developed.

Five *main* types of relations of production are known to history: primitive communal, slave, feudal, capitalist and socialist. [14]

For many Asian Marxists, this rather mechanical unilinear schema of historical progression represented orthodox Marxism, which purported to describe the historical evolution of all societies regardless of their specific characteristics. This type of Marxism was to have important consequences for Asian Marxists both in terms of theory and the formulation of revolutionary strategies and tactics. What were the possible consequences of orthodox Marxism? The unilinear conception of historical development presumes that a socialist revolution would be likely only following the large-scale development of the forces of production under capitalism. The forces of production and the class relations in a capitalist society are seen as essential foundations from which any socialist society could be created. This suggests that any socialist revolution within a feudal or semi-feudal context in which the development of capitalism was extremely limited or non-existent would encounter immense difficulties for which Marx's writings and theories would offer little help. If this was the case, what course of action should aspiring Marxist revolutionaries follow in societies in which the predominant mode of production was still pre-capitalist? Should they forgo their revolutionary activity and passively wait for the inevitable dynamic of historical development to produce a capitalist society and hence the social conditions for a socialist revolution? Or should they give their support to what would be the progressive class in an emergent capitalism, the bourgeoisie, in an effort to hasten the development of a capitalist society? Or should they, while giving a perfunctory nod in the direction of this orthodoxy, pursue a revolution with socialist objectives and based on the specific characteristics of their own societies? Whichever course was followed (and there are historical examples of all of these alternatives), the concept of a unilinear progression of historical development through five fixed stages represented for many Marxists the ideological straitjacket within and around which their revolutionary responses were formulated. It is thus clear that any Asian Marxism must be an interpretation of Marxism. Insofar as a successful political strategy inspired by Marx's own work is derived, the credit must accrue as substantially to the modifying forces as to the original work of Marx himself.

We now move to consider some particular doctrines enunciated by Marx and Engels which have recurred in the works of Asian Marxist thinkers, whether by affirmation, differing emphasis, or even specific negation. These include dialectical materialism and the materialist conception of history (or historical materialism). There have been significant disagreements over the meaning and applicability of historical materialism, for it is not self-evident what stress should be placed on the role of the productive forces as opposed to the class relations of production or 'superstructure' in analysing the historical process and formulating strategies for revolution and socialist construction. As we shall observe in Chapter 2, Stalin premised his strategy for socialist construction and the attainment of communism on a single-minded development of the forces of production. Other Marxists, Mao Zedong included, have been inclined to perceive this as mistaken, and have stressed the role of the relations of production and superstructure in bringing about social change. By social relations of production, Marx meant the arrangement peculiar to each mode of production by which ruling classes ensured surplus labour is performed and surplus value appropriated from the labour of the majority of the population. The superstructure is generally taken to be a metaphor alluding to the institutional and ideological practices which one way or another help to sustain the favoured social relations of production. Emphasis on the historical role of the forces of production in an underdeveloped society would signify the necessity of a lengthy wait for the maturation of the objective economic conditions for revolution. The activist temper of most Asian revolutionaries made them disinclined to choose such a path, but to oppose class domination, social oppression and backwardness by more immediate political or ideological strategies. By stressing class relations and the role of superstructural factors such as political organisation and ideology within the theory of historical materialism, Asian revolutionaries could address themselves to the task of rapid social change while still claiming adherence to Marxism.

There has been by and large little disagreement over dialectical materialism. Most Asian Marxists have accepted that embracing Marxism has meant accepting the materialist philosophy underpinning Marxism. Consequently, apart from discussions of Stalin's *Dialectical and Historical Materialism* which appear in Chapters 2 and 9, the doctrine of dialectical materialism does not figure very largely in this book. The deepest philosophical tenets of Marxism are not in themselves powerful levers for change, although some of their implications are. A political movement cannot be based upon an appeal to dialectical materialism or any other abstract philosophical principles alone. Indeed, Marx himself is on record as declaring: 'The philosophers have only *interpreted* the world, in various ways; the point, however, is to *change* it'. [15]

What has concerned the overwhelming majority of Asian Marxists has been social change, the overthrow of the immensely powerful, longstanding, oppressive and inegalitarian traditions which have characterised Asian countries, and their replacement by relatively egalitarian and progressive societies. Asian Marxists have also been greatly preoccupied with the emancipation of their own peoples from colonial or imperialist bonds and subsequent development of extremely backward economies toward national strength and prosperity.

Consequently, it has been historical materialism's stress on revolution and class struggle that has interested Asian Marxists. It was part of the materialist conception of history that 'at a certain stage of their development, the material productive forces of society come in conflict with the existing relations of production', resulting in 'an epoch of social revolution' which would bring about a radical transformation of all aspects of society. [16] Marx and Engels declared in their most famous rhetorical work that 'the history of all hitherto existing society is the history of class struggles'. [17] What this doctrine of class struggle appeared to offer the oppressed peoples of Asia was that the poor and humble masses would be able to rise up against the rich and lordly few, overthrow them and build a better, more equitable and just society on the ruins of the old. An Asian revolutionary, sensitive to the poverty and backwardness of the people, could not but be impressed with the peroration of *The Communist Manifesto* which declared that the Communists 'openly declare that their ends can be attained only by the forcible overthrow of all existing social conditions. Let the ruling classes tremble at a Communistic revolution. The proletarians have nothing to lose but their chains. They have a world to win. Working men of all countries, unite!' [18]

Marx laid no claim to have been the first to describe the development of class struggle in history. But in a letter he wrote to his friend the German Communist Joseph Weydemeyer (1818-66) in 1852, Marx does suggest three of his central ideas as 'new':

(1) that the *existence of classes* is only bound up with *particular historical phases in the development of production,* (2) that the class struggle necessarily leads to *the dictatorship of the proletariat,* (3) that this dictatorship itself only constitutes the transition to the *abolition of all classes* and to a *classless society.* [19]

This promise of a golden future inevitably held a strong appeal for the wretched of the Asian earth.

Curiously enough, despite its importance even for Marx, the expression 'dictatorship of the proletariat' appears only seldom in his works and never in documents he intended for publication. David McLellan has suggested also that Marx held an understanding of the word dictatorship different from that current in the second half of the twentieth century. He associated it mainly with the ancient Roman office of *dictatura* 'where all power was legally concentrated in the hands of a single man during a limited period in a time of crisis'. [20] The dictatorship of the proletariat was but a transitional 'moment' pending the emergence of a system of social production without class subjugation or class conflict. Marx and Engels have very little to say about the nature of the society which they believed would follow a socialist revolution. However, they do list in *The Communist Manifesto* ten measures which will be 'pretty generally applicable' despite variations in different countries. These include the abolition of property in land and of all right of inheritance, the centralisation of credit and of the means of communication and transport in the hands of the state, equal liability of all to labour, and free education for all children in public schools. [21] While it is true that Marx and Engels specify the most advanced countries as the places where the preconditions are such that these measures are most susceptible to implementation, Asian Marxists could well see them as adaptable and appropriate to their own situations as well.

Marx also refers to the administration of the society which follows the proletarian revolution in his discussion of the famous Paris Commune which lasted some two months in 1871. On 30 May, just two days after its final defeat, he gave a speech to the General Council of the International Workingmen's Association in London which 'amounted to an obituary' for the

Commune. [22]

In his address Marx praised the Commune highly and, in particular, listed several features of its administration which he believed should be copied. Firstly, the municipal councillors were chosen by universal suffrage and subject to recall at short terms; secondly, control of the Commune was in the hands of workers or their representatives; thirdly, all officials of the administration, which was at once executive and legislative, were subject to recall at all times; and finally, all public service was carried out at workmen's wages. [23]

Marx also commended the Commune for its attempts to get rid of three evils of the old society: the standing army, the police and 'parson power'. The magistrates and judges were to become elective, and their appointments revocable. They were to lose 'that sham independence which had but served to mask their abject subserviency' to former governments. The Church would be disestablished and lose its property, while priests would become private persons and mendicants, like the Apostles. [24] Marx drew attention to a problem later to become very familiar to Asian Marxists, people who sneak into the revolution for opportunistic reasons, and who do not support it or turn against it. Marx refers to them as 'an unavoidable evil', adding that 'with time they are shaken off; but time was not allowed to the Commune'. [25] The problem he omits to face is how to distinguish the reliable and unreliable revolutionaries.

It should be noted that Marx retreated from his enthusiasm for the Paris Commune. In a letter to the Dutch anarchist Ferdinand Domela-Nieuwenhuis (1822-91), dated 22 February 1881, Marx wrote that 'the majority of the Commune was in no wise socialist, nor could it be'. He even accused it of a lack of common sense in the strategy it followed. [26] However, this does not invalidate the use of his effusive description of its administrative structures in 1871 as a guide to Marx's political thought. Certainly, when Engels wrote a long introduction to Marx's speech to commemorate the twentieth anniversary of the Commune, his ringing climax was 'look at the Paris Commune. That was the dictatorship of the proletariat.' [27]

The dictatorship of the proletariat is a concept developed to deal with problems of transition in a post-revolutionary situation. In 1875, the two wings of the German socialists, one of which was led by Marx's disciple and friend Wilhelm Liebknecht

(1826-1900), met in Gotha in central Germany and decided on unity based on a common programme. Marx wrote his 'Critique of the Gotha Programme' to Liebknecht, expressing his disapproval. A major criticism was the programme's failure to consider the transition period between capitalist and communist society, 'in which the state can be nothing but the revolutionary dictatorship of the proletariat'. In this connection Marx raises the crucial question of distribution and inequalities in the transition period which he considers the first phase of communist society. This is equivalent to what later Marxists know as socialist society, before the arrival of 'communist' society or, as Marx referred to it, 'a higher phase of communist society'.

Marx envisaged that during the transition period, distribution would still be based on the principle of remuneration according to the amount of work contributed by the worker to society. There would continue to be deductions to cover the cost of administration, social welfare, funds for those unable to work, and most importantly, that share of social product directed to accumulation. Consequently the harder the workers collectively toil, the more they would receive from society, collectively. Bourgeois allocation would be transcended:

> In a higher phase of communist society, after the enslaving subordination of the individual to the division of labour, and therewith also the antithesis between mental and physical labour, has vanished; after labour has become not only a means of life but life's prime want; after the productive forces have also increased with the all-round development of the individual, and all the springs of co-operative wealth flow more abundantly - only then can the narrow horizon of bourgeois right be crossed in its entirety and society inscribe on its banners: From each according to his ability, to each according to his needs! [28]

Marx thus clearly recognised and accepted that there would continue to be inequalities in socialist society. However those forms of inequality which derived from bourgeois property ownership, the social relations of capitalist production and the class structure would cease to be the basis of social inequality. He did not condemn residues of post–revolutionary inequality, but he did see them as phenomena which would and should disappear eventually.

Unlike Marx himself, Marxist political leaders and practitioners have frequently had to face problems raised in nations where serious inequalities have survived the triumph of revolution. Marx's ideas on the subject have been duly influential. However, the fact remains that Marx was primarily concerned with analysing the capitalist West of his own time, especially Britain, France and Germany. He did not consider the problems of implementing a socialist revolution in an Asian country. Some of his ideas have thus posed quite serious obstacles to those who would carry out social transformation on the basis of a national tradition, and in particular an Asian one. This complex of problems, conceptual and practical, gives to Asian Marxism its specific character.

We have already raised the problem of Marx's disenchantment with the revolutionary potential of the peasantry, and the difficulties this has posed for the adoption of Marxism by Asian revolutionaries. Other aspects of Marx's thought which have complicated the application of Marxism in an Asian context are the family and nationalism.

In theoretical terms Marx and Engels saw the origin of the family certainly not as natural but simply as an aspect of the division of labour and property relations. Through the division of labour the husband deploys of the labour-power of his wife and children. In the family, they claim, 'wife and children are the slaves of the husband', and this crude latent slavery is 'the first form of property'. [29]

Marx and Engels were thus extremely critical of the oppression which the family caused in feudal and bourgeois society, especially as regards women. Yet Marx is on record as claiming that, even under capitalism, large-scale industry can create 'a new economic foundation for a higher form of the family and of relations between the sexes'. This is because it assigns women, young people, and even children, a role in production outside the home. [30]

The dissolution of the social slavery which Marx and Engels believed the family represented is discussed in *The Communist Manifesto*. 'Abolition of the family! Even the most radical flare up at this infamous proposal of the Communists'. This provocative statement introduces a feigned dialogue between the

Communists and the bourgeoisie.

In the dialogue the bourgeoisie accuses the Communists of planning to introduce education by society and of breaking down the relationship of parent and child; and, most of all, of introducing a community of women to replace the one-husband one-wife system. The Communists retort that bourgeois education is also social, that family ties have been torn asunder among the proletarians in bourgeois society and their children changed into 'simple articles of commerce and instruments of labour'. As for the community of women, the *Manifesto's* wording suggests such indeed is the communists' intention, but it is not new and the bourgeoisie have been practising it, hypocritically, for a long time. But their main point is that the real aim of the communists is 'to do away with the status of women as mere instruments of production'. [31]

Possibly the most difficult problem of all for Asian Marxists was Marx's quite clear contempt for the nation and nationalism despite his recognition that it was within such contexts that capitalist development and capitalism's crises occurred. Marx himself died stateless and never became British, even though he lived in England, with only brief interludes elsewhere, from August 1849 to the end of his life.

One of the charges which *The Communist Manifesto* puts in the mouth of the bourgeoisie against the Communists is of wishing to abolish countries and nationality. The response begins as follows:

> The working men have no country. We cannot take from them what they have not got. Since the proletariat must first of all acquire political supremacy, must rise to be the leading class of the nation, must constitute itself *the* nation, it is, so far, itself national, though not in the bourgeois sense of the word. [32]

Marx and Engels also hoped that national differences and antagonisms would vanish with the supremacy of the proletariat. 'In proportion as the antagonism between classes within the nation vanishes', they conclude, 'the hostility of one nation to another will come to an end'. Clearly problems for nationally based socialist politics would dissipate to the extent that genuine internationalism developed.

Marx was quite caustic about nationalism itself. He stated flatly that it had ruined Rome and Greece, not to mention the French Revolution. He equated it to pure egoism. [33] For him revolution has nothing to do with nationalism. The Paris Commune was the 'true representative of all the healthy elements of French society', but he still declared it 'emphatically international'. [34]

Asian Marxists may wish to shatter the bonds which the feudal family system has inflicted upon society, especially women. But very few indeed have tried seriously to abolish the family. Nationalism may have ruined Rome and Greece, but every Asian Marxist knows that to ignore it is tantamount to political suicide. The history of twentieth-century Asia has not confirmed the expectations that the supremacy of the proletariat would hasten the disappearance of national differences and antagonisms.

In addition to theoretical issues that cause some difficulty, there are others which Marx and Engels did not confront in detail sufficient to provide guidelines to a potential Asian revolutionary. One example is how to bring about the revolution, how the proletariat should organise its political victory. Marx was actively involved in politics for some of his life and took a founding and leading role in the International Workingmen's Association, or First International, which lasted from 1864 to 1872. But he was in no sense a politician or statesman like many of his later followers, especially in Asia. He was never really forced to find concrete methods for leading a revolution, and it was left to Marxist thinkers like Lenin and Mao to provide Marxism with a strategy for political action and organisation which could be effective.

Despite the problems and lacunae in Marx's thought, it is clear that he developed a theory of history and social change of outstanding brilliance and originality upon which others could build useful experience and ideas. Towards the end of his life, he became quite sanguine for a successful proletarian revolution in Russia, and in his last published writing even states that 'Russia forms the vanguard of revolutionary action in Europe'. [35] But just as he did not live to see the full development of capitalist economies in Europe, neither could he have imagined the successful implementation of essential parts of his philosophy in the countries of Asia.

In the chapters which follow, analysis will be offered of the types of Marxism which have developed in certain countries of

East and South East Asia. The object of this analysis is to investigate the manner in which a nineteenth-century European theory of history and social change has been interpreted, modified or applied in twentieth-century Asian societies. Attention will focus on the theoretical problems and consequences of these applications of Marx's views to the largely pre-capitalist societies of Asia. The themes within Marxism which have occupied the attention of Asian Marxists include the status of the industrial proletariat in relation to other potentially revolutionary classes and the degree of emphasis accorded to the peasantry in revolutionary struggle; the extent to which class struggle and national struggle could and should be harmonised; the problem of devising strategies for resisting the encroachments of imperialism and colonialism; and the formulation of organisational principles capable of facilitating mass mobilisation and social change. The manner in which Asian Marxists have addressed the difficulties of employing Marxism as a theoretical tool for the analysis of an Asian society will also be considered. Such difficulties have included the extent to which a Marxist-derived class analysis can provide an understanding of Asian social reality; the difficulties involved in applying orthodox Marxism's periodisation of history to Asian societies – in particular whether such societies were predominantly feudal after the pattern of European feudalism or in certain important respects distinctively Asian; and the problems that the limited development of capitalism in many of these societies posed for a revolutionary seizure of power and construction of socialism. Analysis will also be offered of the theoretical formulations devised by those Marxist leaders who have attempted to create the conditions for socialism following attainment of political power. In several of the countries considered in this book—China, Korea, Kampuchea, and Vietnam—the problems encountered in the attempt to implement socialist strategy on the basis of the fragmentary references to it in Marx's own writings have led to both innovative and idiosyncratic results in terms of both the development of theory and practical consequences.

What is under consideration, then, is the way in which Asian Marxists have interpreted, reinterpreted and applied an originally European ideology to facilitate social change in non-European societies. It is beyond the scope of this text to provide a comprehensive coverage of all the different interpretations of

Marxism which have evolved even within particular Asian societies. Examination will be restricted to the views and policies of those Asians whose interpretations of Marxism have been most influential in revolutionary struggle and in subsequent attempts to construct a post-revolutionary socialist society. This process of selection is, we believe, unavoidable, and highlights a methodological dilemma which confronts the student of Asian Marxism. Does any Asian revolutionary or politician claiming adherence to Marxism automatically qualify as a Marxist? Or is it necessary to construct a set of objective criteria by which the credentials of a self-proclaimed Marxist can be evaluated? By and large, we have chosen to avoid the latter, accepting instead claims of allegiance to Marxism at face value. Our major concern is not so much to judge the authenticity or validity of various Asian Marxisms, but to investigate the manner in which important themes occurring originally in the writings of Marx have been interpreted and utilised in social contexts far removed from their original formulation. It is hoped that these essays will facilitate an enhanced understanding of the ways in which Marxism has become a powerful ideological force for change in Asia.

NOTES

1.See Karl Marx, *The Revolutions of 1848* (Penguin, Harmondsworth, 1973), p. 84.

2.See Karl Marx, *Capital Volume 1* (Penguin, Harmondsworth, 1976), p. 98.

3.See, in particular, Marx's description of this process in *The Poverty of Philosophy* (Progress Publishers, Moscow, 1955), pp. 144-52.

4.See *Capital Volume 1*, pp. 659, 799; also Karl Marx, *Early Writings* (Penguin, Harmondsworth, 1975), pp. 285, 322. For an alternative interpretation of the 'immiseration thesis', see Ernest Mandel's Introduction to *Capital Volume 1*, pp. 63, 66-71.

5.Karl Marx, *The First International and After* (Penguin, Harmondsworth, 1974), p.334.

6.Karl Marx, *Surveys From Exile* (Penguin, Harmondsworth, 1973), pp. 238-9.

7. *The Revolutions of 1848*, p.71.

8.Karl Marx and Frederick Engels, *The German Ideology* (Lawrence and Wishart, London, 1974), p. 71.

9.See Eric Hobsbawm's Introduction to Karl Marx, *Pre-Capitalist Economic Formations* (Lawrence and Wishart, London, 1964), pp. 19-20. See also Umberto Melotti, *Marx and the Third World* (Macmillan, London, 1977), pp. 8-9.

10. *Pre-Capitalist Economic Formations*, p. 145.

11.Quoted in Shlomo Avineri, *The Social and Political Thought of Karl*

Marx (Cambridge University Press, Cambridge, 1968), pp. 151-2.

12. See in particular V.I. Lenin, *Collected Works* (40 vols., Lawrence and Wishart, London, 1964), vol. 29, pp. 475-6.

13. Ibid., vol 3, esp. pp. 172, 181, 312, 381, 435 and 484.

14. J.V. Stalin, *Problems of Leninism* (Foreign Languages Press, Peking, 1976), p. 862. Emphasis in original.

15. Thesis XI, 'Theses on Feuerbach', *Karl Marx and Frederick Engels Selected Works* (3 vols., Progress Publishers, Moscow, 1969-70), vol. 1, p. 15.

16. Preface to 'A Contribution to the Critique of Political Economy', *Selected Works,* vol. 1, pp. 503-4.

17. 'Manifesto of the Communist Party', *Selected Works,* vol. 1, p. 108.

18. Ibid., p. 137.

19. *Selected Works,* vol. 1. p. 528. Italics in original.

20. 'Politics' in David McLellan (ed.), *Marx The First Hundred Years* (Fontana, Great Britain, 1983), p. 155.

21. 'Manifesto of the Communist Party', *Selected Works,* vol. 1. pp. 126-7.

22. David McLellan (ed.,), *Karl Marx Selected Writings* (Oxford University Press, Oxford, 1977), p. 539.

23. 'The Civil War in France', *Selected Works,* vol. 2, p. 220.

24. Ibid., pp. 220-1.

25. Ibid., p. 229.

26. McLellan (ed.,), *Selected Writings,* p.594.

27. *Selected Works,* vol. 2, p.189.

28. 'Critique of the Gotha Programme', *Selected Works,* vol. 3, p. 19.

29. 'The German Ideology', *Karl Marx Frederick Engels Collected Works, Volume 5* (Lawrence and Wishart, London, 1976), p. 46.

30. Karl Marx, *Capital Volume I,* pp. 620-1.

31. 'Manifesto of the Communist Party', *Selected Works,* vol. 1, pp. 123-4.

32. Ibid.,p.124.

33. 'The Holy Family', *Karl Marx Frederick Engels Collected Works, Volume 4,* (Lawrence and Wishart, London, 1975), p. 120.

34. 'The Civil War in France', *Selected Works,* vol. 2, p. 226.

35. 'Preface to the Russian Edition of 1882' 'Manifesto of the Communist Party', *Selected Works,* vol. 1, p. 100.

SELECT BIBLIOGRAPHY

Avineri, Shlomo, *The Social and Political Thought of Karl Marx* (Cambridge University Press, Cambridge, 1968). An elegant analysis which questions many of the conventional interpretations of Marx's social and political thought.

Karl Marx Frederick Engels Collected Works (Lawrence and Wishart, London, 1975 -). The standard attempt to compile and collect the complete works of Marx and Engels, translated into English. The project is jointly undertaken by Lawrence and Wishart and Progress Publishers of Moscow. The works are given chronologically. Vol. 1 was published in 1975; as of 1983 the project had reached vol. 18, as well as Vols. 38 & 39.

Karl Marx and Frederick Engels Selected Works (3 vols., Progress Publishers, Moscow, 1969-70). A standard edition in English of the most famous and important of the shorter works of Marx and Engels.

Marx, Karl, *Pre-Capitalist Economic Formations,* edited and introduced by Eric

Hobsbawm (Lawrence and Wishart, London, 1964). Hobsbawm's introduction provides an excellent discussion of the problem of historical periodisation in Marx's thought, and contests orthodox Marxism's insistence on a unilinear five-stage schema of historical development.

McLellan, David, ed., *Karl Marx Selected Writings* (Oxford University Press, Oxford, 1977). A selection of Marx's shorter works, with brief introductory explanations, by one of the foremost contemporary scholars of Marx and his thought.

McLellan, David, ed., *Marx, The First Hundred Years* (Fontana, Great Britain, 1983). Excellent summative articles, by many of the world's leading authorities, on the life, thought and influence of Karl Marx, published in commemoration of the centenary of Marx's death in March 1883.

Melotti, Umberto, *Marx and the Third World* (Macmillan, London, 1977). In this most interesting analysis, Melotti challenges the unilinear schema of historical development of orthodox Marxism and posits a multilinear schema based on Marx's later writings.

LENINISM, STALINISM AND THE COMINTERN
Nick Knight

LENINISM

The view of historical development derived by Marx from his analysis of the capitalist societies of Western Europe appeared to suggest that the possibilities for revolution and the transition to socialism were limited to those societies which had already made the transition from feudalism to capitalism. The development of capitalism had been based upon the large-scale development of machinery and technology, and a parallel transformation in class structure and relationships. Under capitalism, the producing class (the proletariat) was characterised by certain shared sociological features (physical concentration, cooperative production, common identification, shared perceptions of exploitation) which indicated that it would be this class which would rise in revolution to overturn the age-old cycle of class exploitation and oppression, and lead mankind forward into the era of socialism and eventually communism. In order for socialism to be achieved, it was therefore necessary that the proletariat constitute, if not a numerical majority of the population, at least a significant proportion of it. The peasantry, because of its fragmentation, lack of class consciousness, and essentially atavistic outlook, was not capable of performing this historic mission, and in those societies which were still predominantly peasant, the realisation of socialism remained a distant goal. Marx appeared to be suggesting that a lengthy period of economic and social development would be necessary in such peasant societies before the objective conditions for a transition to socialism could be achieved.

As a doctrine for change, Marxism (in its pre- Leninist form) appeared therefore to have little relevance for those Asian revolutionaries who were impatient to commence the task of transforming and modernising their largely peasant societies. The paradox is that Marxism eventually was to create a far greater impact as a doctrine for social and political change in these peasant societies of Asia than in Europe. The reasons for this are complex, but can be explained in part by the contributions made to Marxist theory by the leader of the Russian revolution, V.I. Lenin. The ideas of Lenin, or Leninism, came to represent a bridge forged between European Marxism and a Marxism relevant to the peasant societies of Asia. When Marxism came to be adopted by Asian revolutionaries, it was therefore frequently in its Leninist guise. Such revolutionaries did not perceive themselves as just Marxists, but as Marxist-Leninists. In order to gain any comprehension of Marxism in Asia, it is consequently necessary to have some understanding of Leninism and why this ideology appealed to those facing the urgent tasks of revolution and reconstruction in Asian societies.

Lenin on Historical Development

There is something of a paradox in the manner in which Lenin interpreted the Marxist conception of history. On the one hand, he accepted it as virtually self-evident that the general schema of historical development through different stages suggested by Marx was correct. All societies, regardless of their specific characteristics, followed an historical path which was clearly laid out through certain fixed stages. Human society, from this perspective, was destined to pass from a state of primitive communism into and through certain forms of class society; from slave society to feudalism based on the enserfdom of the peasants; from feudalism, society developed certain patterns and relations of production which were essentially capitalist; and eventually capitalism would supersede the feudal society out of which it had grown and by virtue of the class antagonisms inherent within it, would give rise inevitably to a transitional socialist society which preceded mankind's final goal—the attainment of a communist society. The pattern of human society was therefore fixed, and there were only a very limited number of stages through which society would travel during its historical development. By accepting the correctness of this five-stage schema of historical development, Lenin was accepting that there was a large measure of inevitability in the manner in which history unfolded. We could describe this as a rather deterministic view, one which believes in the inevitability that certain historical goals will be realised, which implies in turn that the realisation of historical goals is not a function of conscious human action. Whether men like it or not, are passive or active, those goals will eventually be realised.

On the other hand, it is clear that there is a very strong activist theme evident in Lenin's writing and thinking. He refused to be beguiled by the passivity implied in the determinist interpretation of Marxism. To the contrary, Lenin was the exponent and masterful practitioner of the art of political organisation and action. Far from passively allowing the historical process to take its own course, Lenin constantly urged the judicious utilisation of political means to achieve historical goals.

How is this paradox to be resolved? How was it possible for Lenin to subscribe to a seemingly deterministic view of history while at the same time urging the need for political action to achieve goals adjudged as inevitable by that view of history?

There are several possible solutions to this apparent paradox. Firstly, although it is quite evident that Lenin accepted as correct Marxism's categorisation of historical development as being through fixed stages towards inevitable goals, it is also quite evident that he was very sensitive to the possibility of variations existing within this general plan of history. All societies would conform to the general pattern described by Marxism, but the way in which individual societies progressed through that pattern would vary as the characteristics of those societies varied. There was thus a degree of variation among societies as they progressed through history. This concession to the particularities of individual societies did not extend to the point where societies could develop at variance with the general trends of historical development. Lenin's insistence on the existence of a pattern in world history to which all societies must conform is clearly demonstrated in his speech of 1919 entitled 'The State': 'The development of all human societies for thousands of years, in all countries *without exception,* reveals a general conformity to law, a regularity and consistency'. [1]

Yet, this rather deterministic perception of historical development is modified in an article of 1923 entitled 'Our Revolution':

> ...while the development of world history as a whole fol-
> lows general laws it is by no means precluded, but, on the
> contrary, presumed, that certain periods of development
> may display peculiarities in either the form or the sequence
> of this development. [2]

It can be seen from this quote that Lenin was prepared to
concede a degree of variation within the general pattern of the
development of world history. The fact that the potential for
variation existed, promoted the possibility that conscious human
effort and adroit political action and organisation could play an
important role in the realisation of historical goals. As the situation varied, so would the means necessary to attain those goals.

Secondly, although Lenin accepted without question the
Marxist assertion that it was class struggle which constituted the
central and determinant feature of historical development, he interpreted the concept of class struggle in a manner which stressed
its political aspect. Lenin of course recognised clearly that class
struggle was rooted in the material conditions of existence within
society; that is, that there was an economic foundation to classes
and class struggle. However, such struggles at the economic level
eventually gave rise to a political struggle, and it was at this level
that conscious political action could influence the outcome of
that struggle. Lenin's tendency to interpret class struggle from a
political perspective emerges clearly in his article on the life and
doctrine of Karl Marx (1913):

> ...Marx gave brilliant and profound examples of materialist
> historiography, of an analysis of the position of *each* indi-
> vidual class, and sometimes of various groups or strata
> within a class, showing plainly why and how 'every class
> struggle is a political struggle'. [3]

This political perspective of class struggle helps explain Lenin's insistence on the necessity for conscious political action to
achieve historical goals. Such goals were inevitable, but their
realisation depended in part at least upon political action; political action thus became a factor in the determination that certain
goals would be inevitable. Moreover, the conscious utilisation of

politics could accelerate the historical process, and for those (like Lenin) imbued with an impatience to witness the rapid emergence of inevitable historical goals in the shape of a socialist society, there was great attraction in the thesis that political organisation and activity could shorten the time it would take for those goals to be realised.

Thirdly, and related to this emphasis on the political aspect of class struggle, was Lenin's insistence that Marxism was not 'a dogma, but a guide to action'. [4] For political action to have any utility, it had to defer to the constraints of the objective situation. Activity which was not predicated on a correct analysis of the situation was bound to come to grief, and it could fall into one of two traps; that of underestimating the potential for political action and overestimating the limitations imposed by the objective situation, a fault which could lead to a failure to act when decisive action was necessary; and that of underestimating the constraints of the objective situation and as a consequence taking rash or adventurist actions which would be crushed. According to Lenin, the only way of arriving at a correct interpretation of the objective situation was to employ the methodology for social analysis supplied by Marxism. Only through the utilisation of Marxism as a methodology could the specific features of particular historical contexts be laid bare:

> ...the task consists in learning to apply the general and basic principles of communism to the *specific relations* between classes and parties, to the *specific features* in the objective development towards communism, which are different in each country and which we must be able to discover, study and predict. [5]

And for Lenin, the most important feature of this methodology was the tool of class analysis which could disclose the class structure of a society and the degree of class struggle between classes; 'Marxism has provided the guidance, i.e. the theory of the class struggle, for the discovery of the laws governing this seeming maze and chaos.' [6]

Lenin's acceptance of a seemingly deterministic view of the historical process was thus modified by his insistence on the possibility of some variation between societies within this general pattern of world history, through his emphasis on the political aspects of class struggle, and through his insistence that the nature of specific concrete historical contexts could not be presumed but had to be disclosed by utilising Marxism as a methodology for the analysis of society.

Let us now turn to an examination of the type of political organisation which Lenin advocated for use by those who constituted the vanguard of the proletariat.

Lenin on Party Building

Lenin's theory of party building grew out of his analysis of the limitations on open revolutionary activity in Russia just after the turn of the century. The possibility of carrying out agitational and propaganda work was severely limited by the repressive nature of Russian society, and the ever present danger of arrest and exile by the czar's secret police. Under such conditions it was ludicrous, Lenin claimed, to talk as the Mensheviks did about building a mass political party which would be premised on the spontaneity of the masses. Such a view did not recognise the absolute necessity of building a party which could undertake conspiratorial and illegal activities.

Lenin was to set out his views on the problem of party organisation in *What is to be Done?* (written in 1902). In this document, Lenin criticises the view that revolutionaries should rely on and wait upon the development of the spontaneous revolutionary action of the masses. Such a view was closely associated with the Menshevik position which believed it necessary for there to be a lengthy development of Russia's productive forces before there could be any chance of a realisation of socialist revolutionary goals. This deference to 'economism' and to the spontaneity of the masses was a fundamental mistake, for this 'worshipping of spontaneity' as Lenin termed it, would have the effect of preventing the emergence of coherent leadership of the mass movement. [7] Rather than leading the mass movement, those revolutionaries who deferred to mass spontaneity would be left behind; such revolutionaries were therefore guilty of 'tailism'. Lenin's rejection of the spontaneity of the masses as the foundation upon which a revolutionary party should be built grew out of his conviction that without strong leadership from outside its ranks the working class could never give rise to anything except a trade union consciousness which was essentially reformist rather than revolutionary. This propensity to give rise to a trade union consciousness was a function of the inability of the members of the working class to see beyond the confines of their immediate economic struggle. Because their goals were limited, there did not arise a wider and long-term perspective which was premised upon the objective conditions of the working class as a whole. That perspective could only be gained by those whose vision was not constrained by the immediate economic struggle and who were in a position to gain a more general and complete view of the condition and objective interests of the working class. As Lenin was to point out:

> We have said that *there could not yet be* Social-Democratic consciousness among the workers. It could only be brought to them from without. The history of all countries shows that the working class, exclusively by its own effort, is able to develop only trade union consciousness, i.e., the conviction that it is necessary to combine in unions, fight the employers and strive to compel the government to pass necessary labour legislation, etc....in Russia, the theoretical doctrine of Social Democracy arose quite independently of the spontaneous growth of the working-class movement, it arose as a natural and inevitable outcome of the development of ideas among the revolutionary socialist intelligentsia. [8]

Lenin's distrust of mass spontaneity and the belief that revolutionary consciousness could only be brought to the working class 'from without', is closely related to his conception of the party organisation which revolutionary intellectuals should construct in order to lead the masses. The revolutionary party needed to be constructed of a tightly-knit and highly organised body of professional revolutionaries whose task was to formulate immediate and long-term goals (the 'minimum' and 'maximum' programme), and to devise a strategy and tactics capable of realising those goals. Lenin insisted that secrecy was essential given the repressive activities of the czarist police. The party had to be an organisation capable of carrying out revolutionary propaganda and agitation in a situation in which open and legal activities were impossible. The party thus had to be capable of conspiratorial operations. The structure of this party would be consequently hierarchical, with a strong central leading body.

There would be an emphasis on leadership within such a party. Lenin had no time for the mass-based party proposed by the Mensheviks precisely because it would lack strong central leadership. As Lenin was to argue, 'such an organization must of necessity be not too extensive and as secret as possible'. [9] Leadership was essential, both because of the conditions prevailing in Russia, and because of the inability of the working class to perceive its own objective interests. The leadership of the party would be constituted largely of revolutionary intellectuals who would be capable of bringing a revolutionary consciousness to the working class 'from without'. Lenin's emphasis on strong leadership emerges continually throughout *What is to be Done?*, for without the 'dozen tried and talented leaders (and talented men are not born by the hundred), professionally trained, schooled by long experience and working in perfect harmony, no class in modern society can wage a determined struggle'. [10]

Lenin had a rather particular way of viewing the operation of democracy within such a party organisation. Lenin would make no concession to mass-based or 'grass-roots' democracy which would make the party organisation more vulnerable to attack. Democracy was of necessity a feature of internal party life which had to be balanced by the need for centralism; through the combination of the concept of democracy and the concept of centralism, Lenin was to provide the party with an operational principle for organisation which is still utilised by many Marxist parties. Under the system of democratic-centralism, full and frank discussion of an issue is permissable before the final decision has been taken by the party centre. Once that decision has been made, the discipline of the party dictates that all members unhesitatingly and unquestioningly carry out the centre's decision. In Lenin's view of party organisation there is therefore a strong emphasis on intra-party discipline, and a belief that centralisation of decision-making would increase the efficiency and chances of survival of the party.

Lenin on Imperialism

Lenin's views on political organisation and party-building were regarded very favourably by many Asian revolutionaries. In the cloak of Lenin's ideas, Marxism appeared to speak directly to the activist inclinations of those who wished to change the social and political landscape of Asia. Yet, political action by itself was not enough. What was needed was a general theory of how the revolutionary struggle of the colonies and semi-colonies could be regarded as part of the world revolution. Such a theory was forthcoming from Lenin in the shape of his theory of imperialism. In *Imperialism, the Highest Stage of Capitalism* (written in 1916 and published in 1917), Lenin set out to establish that capitalism had developed since Marx's time. [11] This development comprised most importantly the transition from a capitalism based largely on competition, which was the basic feature in its early stage, to a capitalism based on monopoly in which free competition had largely been eradicated by the ever-increasing concentration of economic power in the hands of fewer and fewer enterprises and industries. The tendency of capitalist enterprises to grow in size in order to survive (a tendency which Marx himself had noted) had reached the stage at which such enterprises took on a monopolistic form; there was thus an advanced concentration of capital. At this stage, the domestic markets in the capitalist countries were not sufficiently large to permit the continued growth of those capitalist enterprises at the required rate; neither could the capitalist countries themselves find adequate raw materials for this expansion. Consequently, it became necessary for markets, raw materials and investment possibilities to be found abroad, amongst the underdeveloped countries of Asia, Africa and South America. Capitalism was thus exported. The important consequence of this development of monopoly capitalism was the fierce competition for colonies which emerged between the capitalist countries as they struggled with each other to establish outright control or spheres of influence within which their own capitalist monopolies would have untrammelled access to labour and resources. Lenin argued (quite convincingly) that World War I had been largely an imperialist war fought over that very issue; who would control the colonies of the third world. By 1914, the European capitalist powers had reached the point of domestic and external expansion at which no further growth could occur without making serious inroads into the empires of other European powers. The consequence was a global and bloody struggle which was fought out for all sorts of high-sounding reasons ('for king and country'), but which in actuality was nothing more than a ruthless tug-of-war over which capitalist nations would control and exploit the colonies.

Lenin believed that the emergence of this form of imperial-

ism was an important reason why the European industrial proletariat had not risen in revolution. By utilising the profits and
resources of the colonies, European capitalism had been able to
'buy off' its proletariat, to improve its living standard, and so
defuse the potential for revolution which Marx had noted. This
process usually took the form of detaching the most organised
sections of the working class from that class through the grant-
ing of special privileges by the bourgeoisie. This privileged section of the working class was now characterised by what Lenin
termed 'opportunism', a willingness to compromise and collude
with its bourgeoisie. Consequently, the most important section of
the working class became 'bourgeoisified', and perceived the interests of the working class as inextricably intertwined with the
interests of its national monopoly capital. The leadership of the
working class thus came to approve of the exploitation of the
colonies in its own interest and those of its own working class.
Lenin claimed to see irrefutable proof of this opportunism in the
actions of the working class movements at the outbreak of
World War I. Many of the socialist parties of Europe, rather
than refusing to become involved in an imperialist war, scram-
bled in unseemly haste to declare their allegiance to their countries, and to commit themselves to backing the nationalist claims
of their political leaders. [12]

Lenin came to believe that nationalist revolutions in the colonies were a consequence of imperialism and were thus an
integral feature of the world revolution; after all, if imperialism
constituted an international economic system, any revolutionary
uprising which disrupted it contributed to its weakening and final
collapse. However, while Lenin was prepared to allow that colonial revolutions must be regarded as an important part of the
world revolution, he was not prepared to allow that the locus for
revolution had shifted from Europe to the colonies. Rather, the
revolution in the 'advanced countries' was still central to the final victory of the world revolution. As Lenin was to point out in
1919:

It is self-evident that final victory can be won only by the
proletariat of all the advanced countries of the world, and
we, the Russians, are beginning the work which the British,
French or German proletariat will consolidate. But we see
that they will not be victorious without the aid of the work-

ing people of all the oppressed colonial nations, first and foremost, of Eastern nations. [13]

Nevertheless, it is clear that Lenin perceived the important contribution which revolution in the colonies could make to the final victory of the world revolution. Lenin recognised, of course, that such revolutions in the colonies would not be of the classic Marxist type. In the colonies, the working class was virtually non-existent, and where it did exist was insignificant in proportion to the peasantry, which was the largest class in terms of sheer numbers. Moreover, the impulse for revolution often came from the newly-emergent bourgeoisie within the colonies; the grievances of this class were directed against the imperialist powers precisely because of their monopoly over economic activity. This monopoly prevented the full development of native capitalism, and this led to resentment on the part of the domestic colonial bourgeoisie against the imperialist power. This resentment found articulation as an emergent nationalism which grew in response to the repression of imperialism. Revolution in the colonies thus often took the form of bourgeois-nationalist revolutions.

Lenin's reformulation of Marxism to incorporate the development of monopoly capitalism and imperialism provided the theoretical foundation for revolutionary strategies in the colonies. These strategies could claim to be Marxist by invoking the authority of Lenin's theory of imperialism, even though the revolutions they described were very different to that envisaged by Marx.

Lenin on the National Question

Lenin's theory of imperialism provided a Marxist sanction to the national revolutions in the colonies and semi-colonies. However, this theoretical endorsement of revolutionary struggles based on nationalism appears as something of a paradox when it is remembered that Marxism laid claim to being an internationalist doctrine.

The manner in which Lenin resolved this paradox was to argue that the liberation of subject nations and peoples from colonial exploitation had to precede the historical stage during which true internationalism would be achieved. [14] It was not possible to talk of an international order or world government while so many nations laboured under the colonial yoke. It was first necessary that the self-determination of the colonies and semi-colonies be achieved. This would come about through the establishment of the right of such oppressed nations to secede politically from their colonial masters. Only after a genuine equality of nations had been accomplished would it be possible to realise the ultimate goal of an international world order in which the division of mankind into nations would disappear.

As with other forms of political action, it was not possible to attempt to achieve the final goal of complete internationalism at one stroke; such a course was impractical and would lead to mistaken tactics and disaster. Rather, it was necessary to act to achieve those goals which were realisable in the short term; this was what Lenin referred to as the 'minimum programme'. In terms of achieving the long-term objective or 'maximum programme' of an international order, it was first necessary to raise as one's minimum programme the right of oppressed nations to secede from the colonial powers. Such a position did not endorse nationalism as such, but was based on the premise that only after national equality had been achieved would a progression to the maximum programme be possible. It is important to note that Lenin perceived this maximum programme as the 'inevitable merging of nations.' [15]

Lenin's view that the struggle for national self-determination for the colonies and semi- colonies was not only an integral part of the world revolution but the first step on the road to the establishment of a truly internationalist order clearly made Marxist theory of immediate relevance to revolutionaries in the Asian context. Far from being portrayed as purely local nationalist struggles, anti-colonial revolutions could now be incorporated into the corpus of Marxist theory and given theoretical legitimacy.

Lenin on the Peasants

Marxism had traditionally been interpreted as being rather hostile to the peasantry. Lenin's approach to the peasants, while reflecting this Marxist bias, also incorporated a lucid political assessment of the revolutionary potential of the peasantry as a class. While the peasantry might be 'frightfully scattered, backward and ignorant', [16] it was highly unrealistic to exclude the peasantry from any proposed revolutionary scenario in those societies whose populations were predominantly peasant. Lenin's sensitivity to the possibility that the peasantry might constitute a revolutionary ally for the proletariat derived from his analysis of the socio-economic conditions of the Russian peasantry and from his first-hand experience of the peasant uprisings which accompanied the Russian revolution of 1905. The deterioration in the economic position of much of the peasantry as a result of ejection from the land and loss of traditional rights to farm communal land was sufficient to provide the peasantry (or at least sections of it) with a revolutionary potential. The proletariat and its vanguard party could not afford to ignore that potential and it was essential that efforts be made to harness it in a combined assault upon the power structures of czarist Russia. Such a revolutionary assault must, however, remain under the guidance of the proletariat, and under no circumstances would the peasantry be allowed to displace the proletariat as the 'advanced class' whose task was to lead the revolution. [17] As Lenin was to point out: '...the proletariat must be sufficiently class conscious and strong to rouse the peasantry to revolutionary consciousness, to direct its attack, and thereby to pursue the line of consistent proletarian democratism independently.' [18]

Following the revolution of 1905, Lenin raised as his party's minimum programme the 'revolutionary-democratic dictatorship of the proletariat and the peasantry'. [19] Lenin did not, of course, believe that the achievement of such a political system constituted the final goal of the proletariat. It represented rather a stage in the revolution, and a rallying cry which would bring the peasantry to the side of the proletariat as its ally and for which the peasantry would fight. Once such a goal had been achieved, however, the proletariat would then begin to strive for the achievement of its next goal—the dictatorship of the proletariat. It would appear that, as with his theory of imperialism and his views on the national and colonial question, Lenin's sensitivity to the revolutionary potential of the peasantry was to have the effect of increasing the palatability of Marxist theory in colonial societies with large peasant populations. Once again, Lenin was asserting the relevance of Marxism in socio-economic contexts very different from that of Western Europe. It is interesting to note that, in promoting the peasantry to the role of ally of the proletariat in the revolutionary struggle, Lenin was extending considerably the class basis of the revolution; and in so doing was asserting the right of the proletariat (and especially its vanguard party) to speak in the name of, not just the proletariat itself, but all revolutionary classes. It is no coincidence that following the revolution of 1905 Lenin was to talk of 'the people's revolution' in order to describe this extension of those for whom the revolution was being fought:

> Yes the *people's* revolution. Social Democracy ...divides the 'people' into 'classes', not in order that the advanced class may become shut up within itself, confine itself to narrow aims and emasculate its activity for fear that the economic rulers of the world will recoil, but in order that the advanced class, which does not suffer from the halfheartedness, vacillation and indecision of the intermediate classes, may with all the greater energy and enthusiasm fight for the cause of the whole of the people, at the head of the whole of the people. [20]

It is important to note that Lenin's use of the term 'the people' did not denote an undifferentiated social category, and assumed that 'the people' could be divided into classes. Nevertheless, Lenin was, by laying claim to the right of the proletariat to speak in the name of 'the whole of the people', commencing a shift away from narrow class conceptions which perceived the revolution as being the sole prerogative of the proletariat. This tendency of Lenin's to talk on behalf of 'the whole of the people' was to have an important sequel in Mao Zedong's constant references to 'the people' (*renmin*) and 'the masses' (*qunzhong*). Like Lenin, Mao made no assumption that 'the people' was an undifferentiated category free of class divisions, and like Lenin was prepared to include in this category all of those who would support the aims of the revolution, whatever their class background. At certain times during the Chinese revolution, the concept of 'the people' was extended to include not only the proletariat, but the peasantry, the petit-bourgeoisie, and the national bourgeoisie—a far remove from expectations of revolution which would be carried out not only by, but mainly for, the proletariat.

Lenin's Theory of the State: the Dictatorship of the Proletariat

Lenin set out his views on the state most clearly and forcefully in an important document of 1917 entitled *The State and Revolution*. In this document, Lenin begins his analysis by restating the Marxist class theory of the state, and by stressing that the state is the political creature of the dominant economic class:

> The state is a product and a manifestation of the *irreconcilability* of class antagonisms. The state arises where, when and insofar as class antagonisms objectively *cannot* be reconciled. And, conversely, the existence of the state proves that the class antagonisms are irreconcilable... According to Marx, the state is an organ of class *rule,* an organ for the *oppression* of one class by another; it is the creation of 'order', which legalises and perpetuates this oppression by moderating the conflict between the classes.[21]

In Lenin's analysis, the state emerges as an organ of class rule which pursues its function through the active oppression of the exploited class(es). There is far greater emphasis in Lenin's thinking on the coercive and repressive features of the state (police, prisons, the military) than there is on the state's employment of ideology to elicit consent and to minimise the necessity for naked compulsion. As Lenin pointed out, 'The state is a special organization of force: it is an organization of violence for the suppression of some class.'[22]

Marx had suggested that following a successful proletarian revolution it would be necessary for the proletariat to create a state power and to wield it in order to prevent a counterrevolution; the repressive apparatus of the state would now, however, be directed at the former exploiting class. This period of authoritarian rule would be known as the dictatorship of the proletariat, but it would exist only during the transitional socialist period during which the foundations would be laid for a communist society. Marx did not frequently refer to or elaborate on the nature of this transitional state, but the concept of the dictatorship of the proletariat was to become a major feature of Lenin's political thought. In fact, Lenin was to assert that the dictatorship of the proletariat was a central feature of Marxist theory and that it could be utilised as a key criterion to determine those who were genuine Marxists and those who were not:

> Only he is a Marxist who *extends* the recognition

of the class struggle to the recognition of the *dictatorship of the proletariat*. This is what constitutes the most profound distinction between the Marxist and the ordinary petty (as well as big) bourgeois. This is the touchstone on which the *real* understanding and recognition of Marxism should be tested. [23]

It is important to remember, however, that Lenin believed that the dictatorship of the proletariat would exist only during the transitional period following a socialist revolution. An important corollary of the belief in the class-determined nature of the state was the belief held by Lenin (and many other Marxists) that the state must inevitably 'wither away' when a classless society had been achieved. If the state is a product of the antagonism between classes and is an agency produced by the ruling class to suppress the other classes within society, it follows logically that the state must disappear (or 'wither away') as the antagonism between classes also disappears as society gradually becomes classless. This is the type of logic used by Lenin to demonstrate the inevitability of the disappearance of the state at some point in the future.

STALINISM

The rise of Stalin to power in the Soviet Union following Lenin's death in 1924 and his approach to the theory and practice of Marxism were to have very far-reaching implications for the development of Marxism in Asia. Stalin was able, through his unchallenged control of the Bolshevik Party and the Comintern, to influence and direct the various revolutionary struggles being waged in Asia. Also, the policies for economic development pursued in the Soviet Union under Stalin came to constitute the model for socialist construction to be followed after the successful seizure of power. Stalin's interpretation of Marxism and his policies for socialist construction were to become the orthodoxy which communist parties in Asia were obliged to acknowledge for fear of losing Moscow's support. It was to be within and around this Stalinist interpretation of Marxism that Asian Marxists like Mao Zedong attempted to establish a form of Marxism relevant to the particular characteristics and needs of their own societies.

Stalin's Marxism

Stalinism incorporates far more than formulations of a purely theoretical nature. Indeed, any discussion of Stalinism necessarily incorporates aspects of Soviet practice in the economic, political and ideological realms during the Stalinist era. However, while practice constitutes an important element of Stalinism, it would be wrong to assume that it lacked any sort of theoretical or philosophical basis, and indeed Stalin was responsible for codifying and formalising the philosophical premises of the orthodox version of Marxism.

Stalin's views on Marxism were most comprehensively set out in a document of 1938 entitled *Dialectical and Historical Materialism*. [24] Marxism was constituted, according to Stalin, of two related theories of philosophy and history. The first of these, dialectical materialism, was a philosophy which was capable of explaining the nature and behaviour of all phenomena. All aspects of nature and society conformed to certain fundamental laws described by dialectical materialism. The first premise of dialectical materialism was ontological; that is, it made assumptions about the existential status of phenomena. Everything in the world is composed of matter, and there is an objective world which exists outside of man's consciousness of it. There is no fundamental (ontological) difference between objects external to thought, and the nature of thought itself; for thought too is composed of matter, or more accurately, matter in movement, and it is the task of thought to provide a reflection of the external world in the mind of the observer. Dialectical materialism thus opposed itself to branches of idealist philosophy which either perceived the external world as a function of thought (the external world only had existence and meaning because of thought) or which admitted the existence of an external world but insisted on the non-materiality of thought and the inability of thought effectively to bridge this ontological dualism and subsequently apprehend the true or essential nature of the phenomena of the external world.

Dialectical materialism therefore asserts the materiality of thought, and this then allows the assertion that all phenomena (including thought) must obey certain laws which govern their existence, change and development. Firstly, all things are inter-connected and the development of any phenomenon can only be understood through a comprehension of the total matrix of relationships in which that particular phenomenon is embedded. Secondly, all things in nature are in a state of constant change and development; nothing is static, and things emerge, develop, then decay and disappear. Thirdly, the development of any phenomenon is not even, and cannot be assumed to be a simple process of growth. Rather, development proceeds through a series of changes as quantitative development proceeds to a point at which there is a qualitative transformation of the phenomenon. Any phenomenon is thus characterised by a progression through certain stages, and this progression is not random, but a development from lower to higher, from simple to more complex forms. Fourthly, within each phenomenon there are contradictions, and it is the struggle between these contradictions which gives rise to the transformation of quantitative into qualitative change; the tension created within a phenomenon by its constituent contradictory elements is the fundamental reason for the development and change of that phenomenon.

Historical materialism, the second of the theories which constituted Marxism, was the application of dialectical materialism specifically to the study of society and its development (in other words, to the study of history). Historical materialism commenced from the assumption that man's material (productive) activities were the locus from which originated all other forms of human activity. The nature of any society was conditioned by the mode of production of material life which existed in that society. The mode of production was constituted of the productive forces (of which the instruments of production—such as the type and level of technology—were the most important aspect) and the relations of production (class relations). The relations of production were influenced by, and in turn influenced the productive forces. For Stalin, the forces of production represented the most 'revolutionary' feature of the mode of production, for they constituted the aspect of economic activity with the greatest capacity for creating change and development in other areas of society. This emphasis on the centrality of the forces of production in the process of historical development has come to be regarded as an important identifying characteristic of Stalinism. It was these 'conditions of the material life of society' which gave rise to all other elements of society, such as ideas, theories, and political institutions; these non-material elements found their origin in the material conditions of social life. Stalin stresses, however, that these non-material elements of society (superstructural elements) can have an influence on the development of society once they have been created:

> Thus social ideas, theories and political institutions, having arisen on the basis of the urgent tasks of the development of the material life of society, the development of social being, themselves then react upon social being, upon the material life of society, creating the conditions necessary for completely carrying out the urgent tasks of the material life of society, and for rendering its further development possible. [25]

Stalin was to repeat and develop this formulation in his articles of 1950 entitled *Marxism and Problems of Linguistics:*

> Further, the superstructure is a product of the base, but this by no means implies that it merely reflects the base, that it is passive, neutral, indifferent to the fate of its base, to the fate of classes, to the character of the system. On the contrary, having come into being, it becomes an exceedingly active force, actively assisting its base to take shape and consolidate itself, and doing its utmost to help the new system to finish off and eliminate the old base and the old classes. [26]

This seeming flexibility in permitting an historical role to superstructural elements did not, however, prevent Stalin from applying a rather rigid and mechanical class interpretation to such superstructural elements as the state and culture. While Stalin might have been prepared to suggest (at a theoretical level) that the state could pursue an active role in assisting its economic base to develop, he was not prepared to concede that the state was anything but a class state, and a political creature of the dominant economic class. There was, in this conception, a rigid and mechanical relationship between the dominant economic class and the apparatus of the state, and the function of the state was the domination of the class or classes in society which opposed the ruling class. Stalin's Marxism consequently insisted that a comprehension of the state and its activities could only derive from an analysis of the ruling class; for as was the ruling class, so would be its state. An explanation of the state was thus completely reducible to a class explanation.

Likewise, in the field of culture (art, literature, ideology) there was a similar reductionist approach which asserted that culture was necessarily class culture. While it might be true that class factors do play an important role in influencing the nature of culture, Stalinist Marxism asserted a rigid correlation between class and culture, and imputed an unrelenting homogeneity to the culture of a particular class. There was, therefore, such a thing as a 'working class culture' which could be defined with precision, and which permitted of no variations or subtle differentiation. The working class represented a homogeneous social category; the culture it produced was necessarily as uniform. The problem of course was that the definition of what constituted 'working class culture' became a prerogative, not of the working class itself, but of its vanguard party of which Stalin was the leader.

This economic reductionism of Stalinist Marxism is indicative of a general lack of appreciation of the variability which appears to characterise social reality. Society might well be complex and its development difficult to fathom, but by utilising a rigid and all-embracing formula an easy explanation of any historical context could always be produced. Marxism, in Stalin's hands, thus came to represent something of a closed system which could, because of the presumptions upon which it was premised, always produce the 'right' answer; in other words, the answer which was expected could always be arrived at through an unimaginative application of a class analysis. This lack of sensitivity to the complexity and possible variability characterising different societies and their development is also clearly evidenced by Stalin's canonisation of the theory of a unilinear progression of development of all societies through five fixed stages. No matter what its specific characteristics, a society had necessarily to follow the historical path which had been trodden by the societies of Western Europe. [27] There appeared to be no dispensation from this pattern of development; the many peasant societies of the East were regarded by Stalin as basically feudal (or weakly differentiated variants of European feudalism). There was no

concession that Asian societies might pursue alternative and differing patterns of historical development, let alone the concession that each particular society (because of its uniqueness and
specific historical background) might have its own particular
historical path to tread. Marx's denial of having created a 'super-historical' philosophy of history was thus to fall on deaf ears
during the formulation of Soviet Marxism by Stalin. Marxism
was, under Stalin's direction, to become the new dogma, with
iron-clad laws which did not just describe the nature and development of phenomena, but *governed* them. This formalisation
was an important feature of the fate of Marxism at Stalin's
hands.

Stalin and the Party

Stalin's rise to power was achieved through his adroit manipulation of the party discipline which had become a hallmark of party life under Lenin. In 1922, Stalin had become head of the party secretariat, and consequently had it within his power to
transfer party cadres. Stalin was thus able to control the destiny
of the personnel within the party; those he recognised as allies
and supporters were concentrated around him in key areas of
policy formulation and strategic organisational posts; those perceived as potential rivals were divided and moved from possible
sources of power.

By 1929, Stalin found himself in a virtually unassailable position within the party. The generation of revolutionaries who
had carried through the revolution of 1917 found themselves cast
aside as Stalin packed all sensitive or strategic administrative positions with career party bureaucrats who were loyal, not to the
ideals of the revolution, but to Stalin himself. Stalin ensured the
loyalty of subordinates by two different methods, the dispensation of privilege, and the use of terror as a political weapon. The
dispensation of privilege was to become an important feature of
party life under Stalin. It might be thought that members of a
communist party would be committed to an egalitarianism in
which extra benefits and perquisites did not accrue to certain sections of the community in positions of influence; similarly, one
might expect that wage differentials be kept as small as possible
to prevent the emergence of a privileged group. This, in fact, is
quite the opposite of the views held by Stalin and his supporters
within the party. Stalin himself denounced those who

believed in egalitarian policies, and it became a deviation branded as 'petit-bourgeois egalitarianism'. Those in positions of influence within the party not only received far greater financial
remuneration than those outside the party, but were able to aug-
ment their incomes through varying forms of administrative corruption. These seemingly unsocialist practices were rife under
Stalin as he bound officials and bureaucrats to himself in a relationship of personal loyalty.

A concomitant of Stalin's policy of dispensing privileges to
trusted subordinates was his harsh treatment of those of an independent turn of mind. There is clearly an anti-intellectualism in
Stalin's recruitment and promotion of party bureaucrats able to
think only within the narrow confines of party orthodoxy. Those
perceived as questioning this party orthodoxy not only found
their advancement blocked, but were also subject to physical har-
rassment and arbitrary arrest. During the Stalinist years a rigid
conformism descended on the intellectual world within the Soviet
Union. In all spheres of intellectual life (from the natural sciences through the social sciences and history to arts, literature and
drama), a rigid prescription of the truth prevented the untrammelled formulation of innovative ideas; there was only one line,
and this covered all aspects of thought. In art and literature, the
needs of Soviet industrialisation dictated that all compositions
conform to the criterion of 'socialist realism'. Such 'socialist
realism' did not mean that art and literature had to depict life as
it really was in the Soviet Union; on the contrary, the concept of
'socialist realism' dictated the depiction of society as it would be,
an idealised version of life in a socialist utopia. All other forms
of artistic and literary expression were proscribed. Writers with
inclinations different from those acceptable to this socialist realism found that their works were not accepted for publication, all
publication being at the sole discretion of the Union of Soviet
Writers which was, of course, packed with Stalin's own men.
This conformism imposed on art and literature was replicated in
all other areas of intellectual life. In history and historical studies, a rigid form of historical materialism choked off the independent formulation of historical hypotheses or conclusions at
variance with that doctrine. Indeed, history writing during the
Stalinist era not only had to conform to the dictates of a rigid
and mechanical view of history and historical development, it also was employed as a cloak to disguise the aspects of the past

and present which did not conform to the current party line.

This policy of stifling the independence of intellectuals must not, however, be viewed as an isolated and extreme policy. On the contrary Stalin's treatment of intellectuals was just one aspect of a broad policy of imposing conformism on all aspects of public life, this imposition backed up by a ruthless willingness to employ terror as a political weapon should that conformism be flouted. The use of terror in this manner had its origins, so claim some analysts (Solzhenitsyn amongst them), in the policies of Lenin himself and the harsh policies he pursued during the chaotic years of the civil war following the revolution (1917-21). The exigencies which the Bolsheviks faced (foreign invasion, internal subversion, food shortages, civil turmoil) necessitated a tough line. What democracy there had been within the Bolshevik Party was virtually stifled after 1921 with the banning of opposition factions. However, Stalin was to take this tactic born of necessity and develop it into a dominant feature of his own political style and of the Soviet political system. First evidence of Stalin's inclination to employ terror emerged in his struggle with the 'left' (Trotskyist) opposition during the years 1924-27. Members of this opposition were hounded and persecuted, subjected to arbitrary harassment, and were eventually arrested and exiled, many (like Trotsky) suffering summary execution at the hands of Stalin's assassins. Stalin did not, however, limit the application of terror to intellectuals and members of the opposition. Indeed, the use of terror became so widespread during the 1930s and 1940s (and especially during the great purges of 1936-38) that it came to be employed against many of Stalin's own supporters. Anyone even remotely suspected of a deviation from the current line was liable to suffer arbitrary arrest; anyone connected with or related to such a person was also liable to suffer the same fate.

It seems clear that the widespread use of terror during the Stalinist years could not have been just an unfortunate aberration inflicted on the Soviet population by a handful of over-zealous party cadres. On the contrary, it appears that the employment of terror was a systematic policy used to thwart the emergence of any opposition within the party or in society at large. This fact suggests that it is necessary to regard the systematic use of terror as a characteristic feature of Stalinism, and indeed for many the concept of Stalinism has a connotation of ruthlessness and arbitrariness in the utilisation of terror to coerce compliance with policy directives.

Stalin also violated intra-party norms instituted by Lenin by dispensing with the collective or collegiate style of leadership which Lenin had by and large observed. Stalin chose to rule, not through the constitutionally recognised organisational network of the party, but through personal fiat. As a result, the Central Committee of the party was transformed into a virtual rubber stamp whose task was to approve the decisions made executively by Stalin himself. This arrogation of power by Stalin and his contempt for party norms was accompanied by his encouragement of a cult of personality which projected an image of Stalin as an infallible leader possessed of a god-like vision in whose sole hands rested the safety of the Soviet Union and the future of socialism. Stalin's personality cult was to reach extreme heights, and it was not to be dismantled until the XXth Congress of the party in 1956, some three years after Stalin's death. In his 'Secret Speech' to this congress, Khrushchev attacked the cult of the individual which had surrounded Stalin, declaring that it is 'foreign to the spirit of Marxism-Leninism to elevate one person, to transform him into a superman possessing supernatural characteristics akin to those of a god.' [28]

'Socialism in One Country'

Stalin differed with Trotsky on the question of whether it was possible to establish socialism in Russia alone. Trotsky maintained (in the spirit of internationalism he perceived as central to Marxism) that the revolution in Russia could not succeed in the absence of revolution in neighbouring countries in industrially advanced Western Europe. Russia might, it was thought, provoke those revolutions through its own revolution; Russia was the weakest link in the chain of Western imperialism, and a revolution here might cause the onset of revolution in the heartland of capitalism, Western Europe itself. This perspective of the international dimension of the revolution seemed to find firm footing on Lenin's theory of imperialism. Moreover, Trotsky argued (as Lenin had done in 1906 at the Unity Congress) that the nature of Russian society, with its backwardness and enormous peasant population, made it essential that Russia's revolution not occur in isolation. Without the assistance of a postrevolutionary Western Europe, Russia might again degenerate into the quagmire of despotism and absolutism which had characterised political life under the czars. Russia could not go it alone, according to Trotsky, for the contradictions of Russian society necessitated a supportive international environment for their resolution. Although there had been revolutionary uprisings in various parts of Europe after World War I (and especially in Germany), none of these had succeeded, and by the mid-1920s it was evident that there was, on the international front, a retreat from the high tide of revolutionary fervour which had marked the immediate postwar years. Because of this retreat it was, in Stalin's opinion, necessary for Russia to brace itself for the shock of existence and development in a hostile international environment; Russia had no option but to go it alone, to build a socialist nation on the foundations laid by the October Revolution of 1917. Stalin therefore raised the concept of 'socialism in one country' in opposition to Trotsky's emphasis on world revolution.

This emphasis on building 'socialism in one country' was to be an important motivating factor in the economic policies which eventually unfolded and became characteristic of the Stalinist era. For 'socialism in one country' presumes that the process of industrialisation and modernisation will proceed within a hostile international environment, and that in consequence it must proceed at a rapid pace in order to furnish the industrial and military strength sufficient to counter threats from abroad.

Stalin and Agricultural Policy

The most important aspect of Stalin's policy towards the agricultural sector was his decision late in 1929 to collectivise Russian agriculture rapidly. Stalin had already indicated his willingness to use violent and harsh methods to achieve his goals in the Russian countryside; the forced requisition of grain which occurred in 1927-8 foreshadowed the type of approach which Stalin intended to follow in responding to the problems of Russian agriculture. Stalin perceived the countryside as posing two fundamental problems for the Soviet government. Firstly, there was the political problem of the *kulaks* (or rich peasants). In the early 1920s and under the policies favoured by Bukharin, this rich peasant class had been encouraged to 'get rich' (in Bukharin's words). Yet Stalin recognised that the emergence and existence of a class of rich peasants posed a political threat to the stability and effective rule of the Bolsheviks. The stronger this class became economically, the more likely was it that its political strength would grow. Another feature of the political problem of Russia's countryside was the lack of complete control which the Bolsheviks enjoyed in rural areas. In order to implement the massive and rapid industrialisation programme necessary to bring Russia into the modern age, all forms of potential or actual opposition had to be eliminated; the need to impose a disciplined uniformity on the countryside was thus perceived as a precondition for the success of the nationwide mobilisation for industrialisation. Industrialisation depended on generating sufficient capital from the countryside in the form of grain; any resistance to this process of grain procurement consequently represented a threat to industrialisation. Secondly, there was the economic problem of Russia's primitive agriculture. The technology utilised in Russia's agriculture was primitive and productivity was low. Much of the grain and livestock produced was consumed in the countryside by the Russian peasantry whose existence was only moderately above subsistence. Moreover, productivity was kept low by the fact that Russia's arable land was fragmented into numerous small holdings—the land was actually divided into narrow strips—and these small holdings created an almost insuperable barrier to the modernisation of agriculture. A peasant farming a narrow strip of land might be able to afford a horse and wooden plough, but it was out of the question that he might produce sufficient to finance a tractor, other modern farm machinery, fertiliser or improved seed. The problem was essentially a problem of scale. Both primitive technology and the fragmentation of land usage and ownership provided ceilings for productivity, constraints which limited the amount of grain which could be produced. If the agricultural sector was to produce the surplus in grain which would capitalise industrial development, it appeared necessary to confront these related problems of technology and fragmentation of the land; and of these, the fragmentation of the land was the most pressing.

There were, therefore, given the objectives of the Bolsheviks under Stalin, both political and economic factors perceived as necessitating a more radical rural policy than that which Bukharin had been pursuing. However, while there may have been economic and political factors justifying the collectivisation of agriculture, there seems little justification for the haste with which this transformation of the rural areas occurred. There was virtually no ideological preparation of the peasantry (Stalin seems to have concluded that force would be the only means of persuasion necessary), and neither was there any detailed consultation or planning within the party bureaucracy itself. The scope of the changes envisaged can be discerned from an article by Stalin published in *Pravda* on 7 November 1929. In this article, Stalin presented figures which predicted that the amount of collectivised rural land would grow by about 375 per cent (from 4 million hectares to 15 million hectares) in just one year. [29] The extensiveness of this projected collectivisation would seem to suggest the necessity for careful planning and painstaking education and persuasion of the peasantry; but these did not occur. As a result, when the collectivisation drive got underway in 1930, it was met with stubborn resistance by Russia's peasants. This resistance was met with brutal repression as the peasants were coerced into joining the collectives. Not only was land collectivised, but also livestock. This led the peasants to slaughter livestock on a massive scale. [30]

The principal effect of this rapid collectivisation was to create dislocations in the Russian countryside of such magnitude that famine was the result. The years 1930-34 were marked by the effects of collectivisation; production of grain was low, food scarce, and prices high. Despite the resistance of the peasantry, Stalin persisted with his policy of collectivisation, and by 1934 the campaign was virtually completed. Although agriculture had been collectivised, the peasants were allowed to maintain a small private plot and some livestock; much of the effort of the peasantry was channelled into these private plots for they contributed a significant proportion of the peasant household's income. Compulsory grain delivery was imposed on the collectives themselves, and the prices for grain and other produce were kept very low. At the same time the land was being cooperativised, the mechanisation of Russian agriculture proceeded, and tractor stations owned and operated by the state were established.

In summary, it is possible to discern in the agricultural policies pursued by Stalin the drive to accumulate the necessary capital for industrialisation through the exploitation of the agricultural sector. Once the decision had been made to squeeze the capital out of agriculture, certain policies such as collectivisation and mechanisation (the tractor stations) appeared as 'logical' corollaries; for under traditional farming practices and land ownership patterns, the amount of capital which could be procured from the countryside would remain limited. Only by raising the ceilings imposed by these factors could productivity be increased, and thus the capacity of Russia's agriculture to finance the capitalisation of a rapid programme of industrialisation.

Stalin and Industrial Policy

In the field of industrial policy, certain features characterised the Stalinist approach. Firstly, there was a heavy concentration on centralised planning, and all areas of economic activity were to be dictated from the centre. This was an essential aspect of 'revolution from above'; the conditions for socialism and a rapid advance to industrialisation may not have existed, but they would be created through close control over the deployment of economic resources and the dictation of priorities. The economy would not be left to the vagaries of supply and demand, but would proceed according to the norms established by a central planning organisation. Given the rapidity with which industrialisation was to be achieved, this form of centralised control of the economy may seem to be a logically necessary step. However, close central control of the economy requires that virtually all details of supply, production, distribution and pricing for every area of the economy have to be formulated in advance, and moreover, that the requirements of the various sectors of the economy be coordinated. This in turn necessitates that the planners have access to very accurate information for all productive enterprises. In reality, the heavy emphasis on centralised control led to severe dislocations and bottlenecks, for the central planning agencies were not able to produce a comprehensive programme which would cover every aspect of economic activity. Moreover, the monopoly over decision making by the centre resulted in a reduction of the initiative displayed by management at the level of the enterprise.

This policy decision to direct all aspects of economic activity from the centre was formalised in the first five year plan which ran from 1929-34. The overriding concern of the first five year plan was to transform the Soviet Union into a modern and industrialised nation in a period of five years. This would be achieved by sacrificing investment in all other sectors of the economy to the needs of heavy industry; for the establishment of a modern industrial sector would create the basis for a modernised society with the capacity to defend itself from external aggression. Reviewing the progress of the first five year plan in 1933, Stalin commented on the centrality of heavy industry to the success of Russia's attempts to modernise:

> The main link in the five-year plan was heavy industry with machine building as its core. For only heavy industry is capable of reconstructing both industry as a whole, transport and agriculture, and of putting them on their feet. It was necessary to begin the fulfilment of the five-year plan with heavy industry. Consequently, the restoration of heavy industry had to be made the basis of the fulfilment of the five-year plan. [31]

A second and related feature of this centralised direction of industry and the economy was the growth of bureaucracy under Stalin. The very fact that all details of the economy had to be planned and supervised from the centre necessitated an army of administrators whose function was the performance of those tasks. This bureaucratisation of Soviet society developed with Stalin's blessing, for the bureaucrats and the cadres represented the instrument by which Stalin would translate his economic plans into action. Stalin's famous phrase 'cadres decide everything' is indicative of his approval of this growth in bureaucracy. According to some analysts, bureaucracy and bureaucratism were central characterising features of Stalinism. Stalin gained his support and found his power base in the bureaucracy, and the bureaucracy was subsequently accorded special privileges.

A third aspect of Stalin's policies in the industrial and economic area was the manner in which remuneration was accorded for work done. There was no deference to egalitarianism, and there was a conscious manipulation of material rewards and incentives to elicit maximum effort from the workforce; as Stalin was to point out, 'The principle of socialism is that in a socialist society each works according to his ability and receives articles of consumption, not according to his needs, but according to the work he performs for society.' [32] An aspect of this emphasis on material incentives was the Stakhanovite movement. This movement was based on the popularisation of the work experiences of advanced workers, those who had greatly overachieved the production targets set them. These advanced workers were held up as models for emulation, and they were shown to have received greatly improved rewards for their ability to achieve beyond the expected norm. Another aspect of remuneration policy was the utilisation of piece-work rates. Under this system workers were paid on the basis of the amount which they actually produced, rather than on the time spent producing it. This discriminated in favour of the more productive workers and penalised those not able to produce to the expected norm.

In industrial and economic policy, then, Stalinism came to connote several important features: an emphasis on heavy industry which would be capitalised through the exploitation of the agricultural sector; the utilisation of planning to determine in advance the priorities for economic development and the targets to be achieved within a certain period; central control and direction of the economy; the growth of a bureaucracy whose task was the administration and supervision of the economy; and an emphasis on material incentives to elicit the maximum productivity from the workforce.

THE COMINTERN

Marxism had clearly undergone significant development and change at the hands of Lenin and Stalin. The orthodox form of Marxism which emerged in the Soviet Union under Stalin was to have a profound influence on the form of Marxism which came to inform and inspire revolutionary Marxist parties in Asia. The organisational medium for the dissemination of this orthodox Marxism was the Third Communist International (or Comintern).

The Formation of the Third International

Lenin's opposition to the actions of the socialist parties of the Second International was motivated by a belief that World War I had been prompted by the imperialist motives of the European powers, and that through their actions the socialist parties had identified themselves as unwitting supporters of the cause of imperialism. Lenin's interest in the formation of a Third International stemmed from 1914 and this abandonment of internationalism by the Second International. [33] At the Foundation Congress of the Third International in March 1919 a platform was adopted which set out the international nature of the organisation and its goals:

> The International, which subordinates so-called national interests to the interests of the international revolution, will embody the mutual aid of the proletariat of different countries, for without economic and other mutual aid the proletariat will not be in a position to organize the new society. On the other hand, in contrast to the yellow social-patriotic international [that is, the Second International] international proletarian communism will support the exploited colonial peoples in their struggles against imperialism, in order to promote the final downfall of the imperialist world system. [34]

Two points which arise from this platform and the general activities of the Foundation Congress are of interest. Firstly, the Comintern pledged itself to internationalism. Yet, at this very Foundation Congress, the Bolsheviks were able to establish a clear dominance over the proceedings and personnel of the fledgling international organization. [35] The very fact that the Comintern had perforce to assemble in Moscow and that the initiative for its establishment had come from the Bolshevik Party itself, paved the way for this Bolshevik dominance. Virtually all of the theses, declarations and platforms passed at this Conference were drawn up by members of the Bolshevik Party (Zinoviev, Lenin, Bukharin, Trotsky); moreover, it was resolved that the Executive Committee of the Comintern, of which Zinoviev became the President, would have its headquarters in Moscow. It is clear that neither Lenin nor Zinoviev perceived the function of the Comintern as a loose federation of fraternal socialist parties. On the contrary, both men brought to the organisation of the Comintern the experience of discipline, hierarchy and leadership which had been the experience of the Bolsheviks in terms of party-building. The influence of this experience is evident in Zinoviev's proposals for the organisational structure of the Comintern; 'a strong guiding center must be established, which will be able to lead, in ideas and organisation, the movements in all countries.' [36] It was not to be long before Lenin, Zinoviev and Stalin were making use of this 'strong guiding centre' to enforce their views on fraternal socialist parties. Bolshevik control of the Comintern, which was to increase dramatically as time went by, can thus be traced to this Foundation Congress at which Bolshevik goals and organisational principles predominated. This Bolshevik dominance of the Comintern was in due course to vitiate its declared internationalist intentions.

Secondly, the platform of the Foundation Congress singled out the 'exploited colonial peoples' for Comintern support. This interest in assisting the peoples of the colonies and aiding them in their revolutionary struggles was a clear application of Lenin's thesis on imperialism. Revolution could be sparked off in the colonies, creating the conditions under which revolution in Europe might thus occur; this in turn would lead to the disintegration of the entire imperialist system. Interest in the possibilities for revolution in the colonial context increased in the Comintern as it appeared the postwar revolutionary upsurge in Europe was receding. During the 1920s, the question of revolution in the Far East was a major preoccupation of the Comintern; and it was at the First Congress that the theoretical basis was laid for Comintern interest and support for revolutionary struggles in the colonies.

From the very beginning of the history of the Comintern, therefore, it is possible to discern two important features which were subsequently to become of considerable importance in its history; an interest in promoting revolution in the colonial context; and a tendency for the activities of the Comintern to be dominated by the Bolsheviks who gradually came to perceive the Comintern as an agency for pursuing particularly Soviet interests.

The Second Congress of the Comintern: the Lenin-Roy debate

One of the key debates at this Second Congress in July 1920 concerned the appropriate policy communist parties should adopt towards the bourgeoisie and bourgeois parties in the colonial context. The communist parties in the colonies were obviously diminutive (if they existed at all), and it appeared improbable that they would be able to lead an anti-imperialist revolution independent of the national bourgeoisie which was for the most part a stronger political force. Yet, such an admission implied that the communist parties (the vanguard parties of the proletariat) would be obliged to enter into alliances with what was essentially their principal class enemy. Should the communist parties enter such alliances with all the risks which that entailed, or should they go it alone with the possible consequence of remaining isolated from the main current of the anti-imperialist nationalist movement? Lenin's response was that communist parties would have to give qualified support to what he called the 'bourgeois-democratic liberation movement'. Such support extended to the forming of an alliance between the communist parties and such 'bourgeois-democratic' parties, but such alliances were to be operated so as not to deflect the proletariat from its final goal of overthrowing the bourgeoisie, or allow a dilution of its ranks. Lenin's thesis was:

> The Communist International must support the bourgeois-democratic national movements in colonial and backward countries only on condition that, in all backward countries, the elements of future proletarian parties, parties communist not only in name, shall be grouped together and educated to appreciate their special tasks, *viz.,* to fight the bourgeois-democratic movements within their own nations; the Communist International must enter into a temporary alliance with bourgeois democracy in colonial and backward countries, but must not merge with it and must under all circumstances uphold the independence of the proletarian movement even if in its most rudimentary form. [37]

Lenin's position therefore sanctioned a united front in which the communist party would give its support to the 'bourgeois-democratic movement' in its struggle against imperialism; however, the communist party had to maintain an awareness that the party with which it was temporarily allied would one day revert to being the target of its revolutionary activities. Such an alliance with 'bourgeois-democracy' would be one of convenience only, the purpose of the alliance being to further the development of those historical forces which would eventually bring about the conditions for a proletarian revolution.

Lenin's position on the forming of alliances with 'bourgeois-democracy' was attacked by the Indian Communist M.N. Roy who attended the Second Congress as a delegate. Roy argued that the term 'bourgeois-democracy' was too vague, and would lead to confusion between revolutionary and reformist bourgeois movements; moreover it was not the task of the Comintern to be advocating collaboration with the class enemy, but rather the development of a purely communist movement which would not have to rely on unreliable partners in the revolutionary venture. [38]

In the debate which followed, Lenin relented to the extent that the term 'bourgeois-democratic' was replaced by 'revolutionary-liberation'. This was, however, only a change in name, and Lenin's basic position remained unaltered. Finding itself unable to resolve the contradiction between Lenin's position and that of Roy, the Comintern finally adopted a resolution which effectively incorporated both positions. The slight rewording involved could not disguise the fact that this important Comintern resolution contained a significant contradiction. This contradiction was to remain a source of confusion and indecision, legitimising varying and sometimes opposed policy positions, and providing fuel for the wrangles and recriminations which were to characterise the later history of the Comintern.

However, the point remains that the Comintern had effectively given its blessing to the concept of a 'united front' in which communists formed alliances with the political parties of the bourgeoisie. This was to have far-reaching implications for the history of communist parties in Asia, and was to constitute a significant influence on the development of Marxism in Asian countries such as China and Vietnam.

The Comintern and Soviet Foreign Policy

The Comintern was established with the explicit intention of creating an international agency whose principal function would be the fomenting of revolution on a world-wide scale. Its intentions were therefore internationalist and it was deemed to be an organisation open to all bona fide communist parties between which would occur a dialogue of equals concerning the most propitious way to achieve the goal of international revolution. This assumed that the fraternal parties which constituted the Comintern would disregard the purely national interests of any of the states from which those parties came, and in so doing, avoid the 'opportunistic' patriotism and nationalism which had characterised the behaviour of the Second International in its final days.

The practice of the Comintern turned out, however, to be

rather different from this ideal in theory. We have noted already the tendency of the Bolshevik Party to dominate the proceedings of the Comintern from its very beginning. Many of the leaders of the Bolshevik Party held positions of leadership and influence within the organisational apparatus of the Comintern, and it is not overly surprising therefore that the views of the Bolsheviks were readily transferred from their own party (with its Russian concerns) to this international association of communist parties. Many of these communist parties were naturally enough prepared to defer to the policies and views of the Bolsheviks; after all, was it not the Bolshevik Party which had led the first successful socialist revolution and established against great odds the first socialist state? The views of leading Bolsheviks like Lenin, Bukharin, Zinoviev and Stalin, consequently carried great authority with those parties still struggling to realise revolutionary aspirations in their own countries.

The fact that the Bolsheviks had carried out their own socialist revolution and succeeded in setting up a socialist state meant, however, that their concerns were not solely with the problem of generating a world revolution. At the same time Bolshevik leaders spoke of the need for world revolution, they were heavily preoccupied with the problem of defending and consolidating their hold over state power in Russia itself. Being a state, the newly created Soviet Union was able to establish diplomatic relations with other states (even with those not entirely sympathetic to the Bolshevik cause), and like other states before it, use those diplomatic relations and channels of communication to further the interests of the Soviet Union as a nation. The problem was, of course, that the interests of the Soviet Union were not always best served by a policy of constantly fomenting revolution, especially in those countries with which the Soviet Union had established, or hoped to establish, diplomatic relations at a state-to-state level. There was in consequence a strong possibility that the national interests of the Soviet Union and the international objectives of the Comintern would come into conflict.

It was in fact a frequent embarrassment for the Soviet Government to be associated (through the Comintern) with communist parties which were attempting to overthrow national governments which it was courting at a diplomatic level. This potential source of embarrassment to the foreign policy aims of the Soviet Union could be removed, however, if the Bolshevik Party used Comintern discipline to regulate the activities of member parties in such countries. Such a development would necessitate that the national goals of the Soviet government be portrayed to the member parties as equivalent to those of the world revolution. This is in effect what occurred, and there was a fairly rapid transformation of the motivation underpinning Comintern activity from an unbridled encouragement of revolution to a course of action designed to facilitate the demands of Soviet foreign policy.

This correlation between Comintern activities and the needs of Soviet foreign policy was to increase during the years of Stalin's accession to power. Between 1928 and its dissolution in 1943, the Comintern virtually ceased to have any real autonomy and it became largely an agency for the pursuit of the foreign policy objectives of the Soviet Union. This helps explain the often dramatic policy changes pursued by its member parties as the foreign policy objectives of the Soviet Union shifted during the 1930s in response to the rise of fascism in Europe. The domination of the Comintern by Stalin also facilitated his control over the interpretation of Marxism adopted by its member communist parties and this in turn functioned to curb the development of forms of Marxism suited to the particular national conditions of Asian societies.

NOTES

1.V.I. Lenin, *Collected Works* (40 vols., Lawrence and Wishart, London, 1964), vol. 29, pp. 475-6. Emphasis added.

2.V.I. Lenin, *Selected Works* (3 vols., Progress Publishers, Moscow, 1975, 1976), vol. 3, p. 712.

3.Lenin, *Collected Works,* vol. 21, p. 59. Emphasis in original.

4.Lenin, *Selected Works,* vol. 3, p. 336.

5.Ibid., p. 351. Emphasis in orignal.

6.Lenin, *Collected Works,* vol. 21, p. 57.

7.V.I. Lenin, *What is to be Done?* (Foreign Languages Press, Peking, 1975), p. 25. For a useful analysis of the importance of the Party to Leninism, see Marcel Liebman, *Leninism under Lenin,* translated by Brian Pearce (Jonathan Cape, London, 1975), pp. 25-61.

8.Ibid., p. 37. Emphasis in original.

9.Ibid., p. 138.

10.Ibid., p. 149.

11.V.I. Lenin, *Imperialism, The Highest Stage of Capitalism* (Foreign Languages Press, Peking, 1969). See also Alfred G. Meyer, *Leninism* (Frederick A. Praeger, New York, 1957), pp. 235-56.

12.Ibid., pp. 128-30.

13.Lenin, *Selected Works,* vol. 3, p. 250.

14.V.I. Lenin, *Lenin on the National and Colonial Questions: Three Articles* (Foreign Languages Press, Peking, 1967).

15.Ibid., p. 6.

16.V.I. Lenin, *Two Tactics of Social Democracy in the Democratic Revolution* (Foreign Languages Press, Peking, 1970), p. 53.

17.Ibid., p. 122.

18.Ibid., p. 57.

19.Ibid., p. 56.

20.Ibid., p. 122. Emphasis in original.

21.Lenin, *Selected Works,* vol. 2, pp. 241-2. Emphasis in original.

22.Ibid., p. 254.

23.Ibid., pp. 261-2. Emphasis in original.

24.J.V. Stalin, *Problems of Leninism* (Foreign Languages Press, Peking, 1976), pp. 835-73.

25.Ibid., p. 852.

26.J.V. Stalin, *Marxism and Problems of Linguistics* (Foreign Languages Press, Peking, 1972), p. 5.

27.Stalin, *Problems of Leninism,* pp. 653-4, 862.

28.Dan N. Jacobs (ed.), *From Marx to Mao and Marchais* (Longman, New York and London, 1979), p. 161.

29.Stalin, *Problems of Leninism,*p. 437.

30.For details of the effects of the cooperativisation of agriculture, see Alec Nove, *Stalinism and After* (George Allen and Unwin, London, 1975), pp. 44. See also Roy Medvedev, *Let History Judge: The Origins and Consequences of Stalinism* (Spokesman Books, London, 1976), pp. 70-109.

31.Stalin, *Problems of Leninism,* p. 591.

32.Ibid., p. 778.

33.James W. Hulse, *The Forming of the Communist International* (Stanford University Press, Stanford, 1964), p. 1.

34.J. Degras, *The Communist International, 1919-1943* (3 vols., F. Cass, London, 1971), vol. 1, p. 23.

35.Hulse, *The Forming of the Communist International,* p. 20.

36.Ibid., p. 21.

37.Lenin, *Lenin on the National and Colonial Questions,* p. 27.

38.H. Carrère d'Encausse and Stuart R. Schram, *Marxism and Asia* (Allen Lane, The Penguin Press, London, 1969), pp. 150-2.

SELECT BIBLIOGRAPHY

Degras, Jane (ed.), *The Communist International 1919-1943: Documents* (3 vol.¦ F.Cass, London, 1971). A rich source of information about the history and policies of the Comintern.

Hulse, James W., *The Forming of the Communist International* (Stanford University Press, Stanford, 1964). An interesting analysis which traces the early emergence of Russian domination of the Comintern.

Liebman, Marcel., *Leninism under Lenin,* translated by Brian Pearce (Jonathan Cape, London, 1975). A sympathetic yet critical analysis of the evolution of Leninism. Liebman argues that Lenin's chief contribution to the theory and practice of revolution was the creation of the Bolshevik Party, but that he failed to solve the vital problems of the dictatorship of the proletariat and socialist democracy.

Medvedev, Roy A., *Let History Judge: The Origins and Consequences of Stalinism* (Spokesman Books, London, 1976). A passionate but carefully documented denunciation of Stalin and Stalinism. Medvedev argues that Stalin manipulated party discipline and the cult of personality to facilitate his many abuses of power.

Meyer, Alfred G., *Leninism* (Frederick A. Praeger, New York, 1957). A standard scholarly work which pays particular attention to those aspects of Leninism which have had implications for the political activities of the Communist Party of the Soviet Union and the Soviet state.

Nove, Alec., *Stalinism and After* (George Allen and Unwin, London, 1975). A very useful introduction to the theory and practice of Stalinism.

3

MAO ZEDONG AND THE 'SINIFICATION OF MARXISM'
Nick Knight

A recurring theme in Chinese Marxism has been the attempt to make an ideology born of the social conditions of nineteenth century industrialised Europe into an ideology of practical significance in an unindustrialised context with a predominantly peasant population. The disparity between these two social contexts was so great that it appears as something of a paradox that Marxism should have had any appeal to Chinese revolutionaries intent on transforming their country into a modernised nation. That paradox can only be resolved by an understanding of the manner in which Marxism was perceived and interpreted by Chinese revolutionaries, for Marxism in its traditional form had to find some modification before it could function as a guide to action in the context of Chinese society.

Early Radical Tendencies in China

Many of China's early radicals perceived in Marx's writings a doctrine which was too historically specific to be of any utility in the Chinese context. Marxism was perceived as a theory grown out of European conditions. As such, it appeared to have little to say about the sort of problems which confronted young Chinese radicals and intellectuals passionately concerned with China's plight—her humiliation at the hands of the West, the poverty and backwardness of her people, and the corruption and ineptitude of her political rulers. Although there was some interest demonstrated in Marxism in the first decade of this century, by 1907 this interest had given way to a growing commitment to the ideals and practices of anarchism. As Martin Bernal has demonstrated, those Chinese radicals attracted to socialism were also drawn to some form of anarchism. This interest in anarchist solutions to China's problems came as a result of an increased interest by Japanese student circles in the activities of Russian anarchists, the Social Revolutionaries. Chinese students studying in Japan were exposed to this intellectual current, and it made sufficient impression on them to make the theories of Marx and European socialism seem 'very tame and uninteresting'. [1] As a result, in the years after 1907 radical practices tended to adopt the methods of anarchism, and there was a spate of bombings and attempted assassinations. Such direct action seemed preferable to a Marxist theory which reached Japan and China in a largely Menshevist guise, stressing the necessity of a capitalist phase of development prior to the achievement of socialism, and indicating the lengthy nature of such social transformations.

This early failure of Marxism to win Chinese converts was to result in a lack of interest in Marxist theory for the next decade. During that decade, however, certain historical events intervened to create an environment in which Marxism came to be perceived by an important and influential group of Chinese intellectuals as having a clear relevance to the resolution of China's social and economic problems. After 1915, intellectual opinion and debate underwent a dramatic transformation. As a result of China's inability to resist the predations of an emergent Japanese imperialism, Chinese intellectuals renounced their Confucian heritage and began to search for alternatives outside the Chinese tradition. This act of renunciation was accompanied by a revolution in literary styles in which the classical style of writing (*wen-yan*) was rejected in favour of a more colloquial form of writing (*baihua*) intelligible to the ordinary Chinese. In 1915, an influential journal entitled *Xin Qingnian* (*New Youth*) was founded by Chen Duxiu (later to lead the Chinese Communist Party) which became a focal point for the expression of dissent and the formulation of new ideas. An iconoclastic atmosphere prevailed in which numerous beliefs and ideologies competed in criticising Confucianism and in suggesting the means whereby China's parlous situation could be reversed. The impact of the May Fourth Movement, as it came to be known, cannot be overestimated, for it constitutes an important watershed in modern Chinese history, a watershed which created an intellectual climate in which a foreign doctrine such as Marxism might gain acceptance and adherence. A second important event which served to change

Marxism's low fortunes in China was the Russian revolution of 1917. Although the impact of the Russian revolution was not immediate throughout Chinese intellectual circles, it greatly influenced certain Chinese intellectuals whose writings attracted a mass following. The Russian revolution was seen as having obvious implications for Chinese society; Russia's society was predominantly agrarian and her population largely peasant, her economy backward and largely traditional like China's. Moreover, through the act of revolution, Russia appeared to have wiped the slate clean, allowing a fresh start to the creation of a fair and just society based on an equitable distribution of the material rewards which would flow from industrialisation and modernisation. Those who had successfully prosecuted and led this revolution claimed adherence to Marxism, and asserted that this doctrine was indeed relevant to the problems encountered in a colonial and semi-colonial context.

The Marxism of Li Dazhao

Of the early Chinese Marxists, none was quicker to hail the victory of the Russian revolution than Li Dazhao. For Li, the Russian revolution represented a stirring example of the possibilities for radical change in a context of underdevelopment. In an article entitled 'The Victory of Bolshevism' (15 November, 1918), Li exuberantly welcomed the revolution in Russia and indicated that he perceived its relevance for other nations. [2] Li perceived in the Russian revolution the first and most important wave of revolution which would sweep before it the forces opposed to the realisation of mankind's common goals. However, Li's biographer, Maurice Meisner, has argued that Li's positive response to the Russian revolution does not signify an instantaneous conversion to the fundamental views of Marxism. Rather, Li was attracted by the Russian revolution because it signified the onset of a tidal wave of revolution which would carry all before it, an irresistible force which would sweep all corrupt and reactionary regimes from the stage of history. This imagery of 'mighty rolling tides' of revolution was an expression of a view of history which perceived global categories within the march of history, and which talked in terms of the 'spirit of the times', terminology more Hegelian than Marxist. The attraction of the Russian revolution did not therefore immediately convert Li into a materialist who perceived history as a process of struggle between antagonistic classes. [3]

Despite the rather unMarxist categories in which Li portrayed the Russian revolution and its implications for world history, his conversion to Marxism was to be an important event in the development of Chinese Marxism. Not only did Li's writings reach a large audience (often through the pages of *Xin Qingnian*), but Li was, in his capacity as librarian of Peking University, to influence other young radicals (Mao Zedong among them) who were later to occupy strategic positions within the Chinese Communist Party (CCP). [4] Certain ideas characteristic of Li's Marxism were to appear subsequently in the writings of Chinese Marxists, and especially Mao Zedong. Firstly, Li indicated a close intellectual affinity with the populist ideas of the Russian *narodniks* and Social Revolutionaries. This affinity was demonstrated by Li's emotional attachment to the peasantry and the belief that the Chinese revolution would be an essentially peasant revolution. Li was amongst the first of the Chinese Marxists to perceive the importance of the peasantry to the revolution. However, the peasants would not be able to raise a revolutionary demand for their own liberation without the prompting of the educated youth of China who were urged by Li to 'go to the villages' and rouse the peasants to revolution. This call to youth to forsake the cities and go to the villages was inspired both by a belief in the revolutionary potential of the peasantry, and by a suspicion of the values which were fostered by city life; virtue resided in the countryside, and by arousing the peasants the educated youth could also distance themselves from the deleterious effects of the 'mire of the city'. [5]

There are clear parallels between this populist sentiment in Li's ideas and the views expressed by Mao at a later stage in the Chinese revolution. Not only did Mao come to stress the importance of the peasantry in the Chinese revolution, he also indicated a bias against urban life which was reflected in his call to youth to 'go down to the countryside' to learn from the peasants. Mao, like Li, admired the virtues of the countryside and was suspicious of the cities in which the soft life and 'sugar-coated bullets' could sap the revolutionary vitality of communists and lead to a degeneration of the revolution.

A second aspect of Li's populism which is paralleled in Mao's thought is the belief that backwardness constituted a virtue in revolutionary terms. Li was convinced that China would avoid a capitalist future with all its attendant evils, and this conviction was premised on the backwardness of Chinese society. China's backwardness, rather than suggesting (as orthodox Marxism did) that a socialist revolution was out of the question, suggested instead that Chinese society had abundant 'surplus energy' which had not been tapped. Through the exploitation of this 'surplus energy', China would be able to bypass the capitalist stage of development, building socialism directly through a reorganisation of society and premised on the virtues inherent in the primitive simplicity of the Chinese rural community. [6] While Mao too came to believe that China might avoid a capitalist future, [7] he also argued on several occasions that China was well placed to achieve socialism because she was 'poor and blank'; backwardness here deemed as virtue, for it increased the attractiveness of revolutionary change to China's largely peasant population. [8]

However, while it appears clear that there are certain parallels between Li's populism and elements of Mao's thinking, it is important to highlight the important distinction between the two strands of populism. Li tended to view 'the people' as a largely undifferentiated entity in which differentiations resulting from class cleavages were not prominent. In contrast, Mao's conception of 'the people' presumed a category which was necessarily riven by class cleavages—-between the various strata of the peasantry, between landlords and the peasants, between working class and peasantry, between bourgeoisie and workers, and so on. What distinguished 'the people' as a category was not a lack of class differentiation, but a unity of common purpose which could extend across class boundaries to unite various classes and strata. Here we can perceive an essential distinction between Mao's populism, which began from a Marxist presumption of class differentiation and class struggle as the fundamental aspects of social organisation, and that of Li which was premised on the essential unity of the Chinese as a people.

The Marxism of Chen Duxiu

Chen's initial conversion was not to Marxism at the start of the May Fourth Period, but to 'democracy' and 'science'. Chen did not respond to the victory of the Russian revolution as did Li Dazhao, and it was not until 1920 that he announced his conversion to Marxism. However, having once converted to Marxism,

Chen (unlike Li) immediately adopted virtually all aspects of a largely orthodox interpretation of Marxism and historical materialism. [9] This adoption of an orthodox (this is, largely European) form of Marxism by Chen was to have important implications for the early Chinese Communist Movement, for it introduced historical ideas and political categories which were often unsuited to the realities of Chinese society, and which were often utilised in an uncritical manner by Chen's followers within the CCP.

Let us look briefly at some of these aspects of Chen's Marxism. Firstly, Chen adopted a concept of 'dual revolution' to signal that the Chinese revolution could not lead China immediately into socialism. Rather, the bourgeois-democratic revolution (then in process) was quite a distinct revolution from the socialist revolution which would follow it. Because the current revolution was bourgeois-democratic in nature, Chen believed that the bourgeoisie would lead it. The Chinese economy was underdeveloped, its industrialisation hardly begun; consequently, the proletariat constituted only a very diminutive class incapable of leading the revolution at that stage. Only as industrialisation proceeded and the size and importance of the proletariat grew, could it assume leadership of a socialist revolution. This view in fact incorporated a rather Menshevist notion of the historical process, perceiving in it an inexorable development which could not be accelerated by human volition. There could be no possibility of skipping stages of historical development, and socialism could only come through the development of the objective conditions, most importantly through industrialisation and the growth in the size of the proletariat. [10]

Secondly, and related to Chen's rather mechanistic Marxist doctrine of the 'dual revolution', was the low opinion he held of China's peasantry. This low opinion stemmed from Chen's adoption of the traditional Marxist view of the peasants as essentially conservative, with a poorly developed class consciousness, and unable to lead a progressive revolution. [11] As Stuart Schram points out, 'for Chen, the Chinese countryside was a remote and murky realm, apprehended in outline from documents, but never directly experienced or vividly present in his mind'. [12] A consequence of Chen's low estimation of the peasantry was his belief that the centre for political struggle resided in the cities and industrial areas in which the proletariat was represented. Political strategy had to be based on the proletariat, building up the labour unions, and employing strikes and industrial disruption to achieve political ends.

It was Chen's adoption of a rather orthodox European form of Marxism which led him initially to oppose the entry of the CCP into a united front with the Guomindang (GMD, Nationalist Party). Chen believed that a united front of the sort advocated by the Comintern agent Sneevliet (Maring) contravened a basic tenet of Marxism—-that of class struggle. In order to establish the united front, the proletariat and its party would have to enter an alliance with what was the enemy of the proletariat, the bourgeoisie. Prior to 1923, Chen's position was rather like that of M. N. Roy who had argued (at the Second Congress of the Comintern in 1920) that it was the task of communists in the context of colonialism to build up an independent communist organisation in preparation for the inevitable struggle with the bourgeoisie. However, after the February Seventh (1923) Incident in which a communist-led strike of railway workers was smashed by the warlord Wu Peifu, Chen's resistance to the united front weakened; for the vulnerability of the young communist party was made patently obvious. Nevertheless, Chen remained less than sympathetic to the united front. Therefore it is rather ironical that Chen was made a scapegoat by Stalin for the failure of the united front in 1927, and dismissed from his position as Secretary-General of the party.

It is also somewhat ironical that, while Chen's Marxist ideas were influential at the level of doctrine within the party, actual direction of the political strategy of the CCP was never entirely in his hands. Throughout the almost six years that Chen was Secretary-General of the CCP, he was forced to defer to the views of Comintern agents, and to directives formulated in Moscow by Stalin. These strategies formulated by the Comintern for the CCP prevented Chen from fully following his own political intuition, and led eventually to disaster. By the same token, however, it remains probable that, in the absence of Comintern interference in the internal affairs of the CCP, Chen's rather mechanical Marxist views would also have led the party to grief; for given his rather Menshevist conception of the historical process and his antipathy towards China's peasantry, it is unlikely that Chen would have been able to devise a strategy in full accord with the realities of Chinese society which would have led the communists to victory.

This paradox is resolved when we realise that both Chen's own Marxism and the Marxist political strategy forced upon the CCP by the Comintern had one important feature in common—they were both foreign brands of Marxism which had not been adapted to the particularities of Chinese society. Chen's emphasis on the proletariat in a largely peasant society is clear evidence that his rather Europocentric Marxism was actually concealing (rather then revealing) an essential feature of China's potential for revolution. Likewise, Comintern Marxism was a foreign ideology in that it derived strategies not from a concentration on the characteristics of Chinese society, but from a preoccupation with the needs of Soviet foreign policy and from a presumption that Stalin possessed an infallible insight into the manner in which the world revolution should be conducted.

The Marxism of Mao Zedong

In the years between 1927 and Mao's rise to power within the CCP in 1935, Comintern directives continued to lead the CCP from one crisis to another, and from one defeat to another. Under Li Lisan, the CCP attempted through military means to capture and control large cities in southern China. When this policy ended in failure, Li Lisan was removed (and like Chen Duxiu, blamed for the failure) and leadership of the CCP fell into the hands of the Twenty-eight Bolsheviks (or Returned Students' Faction). This group had lived and studied in the Soviet Union, and was thoroughly imbued with Soviet Marxism. Wang Ming and Bo Gu who led the Returned Students' Faction quickly found themselves in conflict with Mao Zedong. Mao's opposition to the Returned Students' Faction was premised on the belief that a dogmatic adherence to a foreign brand of Marxism could not but hinder the cause of the Chinese revolution. Rather than leading to a strategy based on China's particular characteristics, the Marxism of the Returned Students' Faction attempted to impose on the CCP a blueprint for revolution based on foreign models and experience. By 1930, Mao had come to the conclusion that the Chinese revolution was characterised by several distinctive features, and that failure to take account of these would lead to mistaken tactics in the revolutionary struggle. [13]

Of these specific characteristics, several stand out. Firstly, Mao stressed the importance of the peasantry to the Chinese revolution. Unlike many of his comrades within the CCP, Mao appears to have grasped very early on that the Chinese revolution was essentially a peasant revolution. By the mid-1920s, Mao was attempting to employ a Marxist class analysis to unravel the nature of social stratification in the Chinese countryside, [14] and in 1927, Mao spent a month investigating the peasant movement in his native Hunan province; his findings there led him to assert in no uncertain terms the revolutionary potential of China's peasants:

> All talk directed against the peasant movement must be speedily set right. All the wrong measures taken by the revolutionary authorities concerning the peasant movement must be speedily changed. Only thus can the future of the revolution be benefited. For the present upsurge of the peasant movement is a colossal event. In a very short time, in China's central, southern and northern provinces, several hundred million peasants will rise like a mighty storm, like a hurricane, a force so swift and violent that no power, however great, will be able to hold it back. They will smash all the trammels that bind them and rush forward along the road to liberation. They will sweep all the imperialists, warlords, corrupt officials, local tyrants and evil gentry into their graves. [15]

However, while Mao stressed the importance of the peasantry to the Chinese revolution, he did *not* in the 1920s or subsequently allow that leadership of the revolution would pass into the hands of the peasantry. Leadership of the revolution remained the prerogative of the proletariat and its vanguard party. Mao was aware that the peasantry without extra-class leadership could not lead a modernising revolution; the danger of a purely peasant revolution lay in the possibility that it might degenerate into a traditional atavistic peasant rebellion. So while Mao frequently referred to the peasantry as the 'main force' of the Chinese revolution, he insisted that the peasantry required the leadership of the proletariat.

Mao's emphasis on the peasantry raises an important question concerning his integrity as a Marxist. Is it possible for a revolutionary to place as much emphasis on the revolutionary potential of the peasantry as did Mao, and remain a Marxist? Is it not the case that Marxism regards the proletariat as the agency by which revolution will be carried out, and that the peasantry by its very nature as a class is prevented from participating in any meaningful way in revolution? Stuart Schram, after looking in detail at Mao's writings of the mid-1920s on the peasant question, came to the following conclusion:

> ....he [Mao] diverged sharply from orthodoxy, and from the essential logic of Marxism, not only by the sheer importance he accorded to the countryside, but by attributing to the peasants both the capacity to organize themselves, and a clear consciousness of their historical role. [16]

Such a judgement, however, makes a presumption about the nature of Marxism. It presumes that Marxism is indissolubly linked to the historical and socio-economic context from which it emerged, and which it analysed. To Marx, the most observable feature of capitalism was the antagonistic class relationship which existed between the proletariat and the bourgeoisie; and it was on a sociological analysis of the proletariat and the dynamic of capitalist society that Marx made tentative predictions about the possibility of a socialist revolution. Under the conditions obtaining in Europe, Marx did not concede that the peasantry constituted a revolutionary force of any significance. While it might be true that the conclusions drawn from this class analysis represent a central element of Marx's analysis of capitalism in Europe, do they therefore represent the essential and defining characteristic of Marxism?; or do the conclusions drawn from this class analysis constitute an aspect of the *content* of Marx's analysis, an aspect which needs to be separated from Marx's *methodology* which represents rather the essential feature of Marxism? If the former, then Mao did depart from the 'essential logic' of Marxism; if, however, the latter, Mao can still be regarded as having maintained a genuinely Marxist position while not adhering rigidly to the content of Marx's analysis of European capitalism. Therefore, whether one interprets Mao's emphasis on the peasantry as a departure from the 'essential logic' of Marxism depends largely on the definition one gives to Marxism itself.

It should be noted however, that Mao appeared to regard class analysis (rather than a particular class structure or relationship) as 'the fundamental viewpoint of Marxism.' [17] Only by employing a class analysis of Chinese society to disclose its specific characteristics could one claim to be a true Marxist. If such a class analysis disclosed the revolutionary potential of the peasantry, then a Marxist would have to take that important factor into account when formulating a political strategy. Not to do so but to stick unswervingly to conclusions derived from a class analysis of a very different historical and social context, would (in Mao's opinion) have constituted a dogmatic and essentially unMarxist approach to the interpretation of social reality.

A second important characterising feature of the Chinese revolution perceived by Mao in 1930 was the existence and development of an armed force under the control of the CCP. This development of an independent armed force had been made necessary by the clearly demonstrated danger of relying on the armed forces of another political party. Up to 1927, the CCP had possessed no armed force of its own, and relied entirely on the military under the control of the GMD. The Shanghai Massacre of April 1927 shattered the illusion that the CCP could achieve political power (or even survive) without its own military force. Mao Zedong had been amongst the first of the Chinese Communists to grasp this fact, and immediately after the Shanghai Massacre had set about establishing the Red Army and creating rural soviets under the control of the CCP. Once the CCP had established its own military force, an important principle also needed to be established; that is, that the military would remain subordinate to party direction and control. Mao's concern in this direction can be perceived in his 1929 article 'On Correcting Mistaken Ideas Within the Party' in which he castigated those who had adopted a 'purely military viewpoint' and who had forgotten that the aim of military struggle was to facilitate the realisation of the party's political objectives. [18]

In these two areas, the role of the peasantry in the Chinese revolution and the manner in which the Red Army should be deployed, Mao found himself in conflict with the Returned Students' Faction which controlled the Party during the early 1930s. The Returned Students' Faction continued to employ a Soviet brand of Marxism with its emphasis on the proletariat and the struggle in urban areas; it also tended to look down on Mao's guerilla strategy which questioned the wisdom of attempting to defend rural soviets as though they were sovereign states. Mao perceived in the sort of Marxism advocated by the Returned

Students' Faction a dogmatic adherence to the Europocentric aspects of Marxism and a refusal to come to grips with the realities of Chinese society.

It was not to be until the debacle of the Fifth Encirclement Campaign which drove the Communists from the Jiangxi Soviet and onto the Long March that Mao was to gain a position of authority which would allow his brand of Marxism to influence the strategy pursued by the CCP. At the Zunyi Conference in January 1935, the strategy followed by the Returned Students' Faction was rejected and Mao elevated to a leading post within the Party. [19] In the years which followed (frequently called the Yan'an period, 1936-47), Mao set out in earnest to forge a Marxism which was well suited to the particular needs and characteristics of Chinese society and the Chinese revolution, and which would contribute to the victory over Japanese imperialism. Let us look at some of the specific elements of Mao's Marxism during the Yan'an period before moving on to an examination of the logic which underpinned this 'Sinification of Marxism' at Mao's hands.

During the early Yan'an period, Mao penned several important theoretical texts which were to become extremely influential in the development of Chinese Marxism. In the first of these texts, *On Contradiction* (parts of which were written in August 1937), Mao elaborated a theory of contradictions which would facilitate the analysis of the concrete contradictions within Chinese society and consequently lead to a strategy appropriate to the resolution of those contradictions. [20] Mao commenced from the premise that all phenomena are characterised by contradictions; that is, contradiction exists in every thing or process. By contradiction, Mao meant the inevitable division of a phenomenon into two opposing aspects; no phenomenon could be a unified entity, but was divided and thus possessed a 'contradictory' characteristic. Because all phenomena were characterised by contradictions, there was what Mao called a 'universality of contradiction'. However, knowledge of the universality of contradiction was only of utility if one mobilised this knowledge to comprehend the 'particularity of contradiction', and Mao's stress on the particularity of contradiction constituted a critique of the Returned Students' Faction which was, Mao believed, ignoring the particular contradictions which characterised Chinese society. Mao argued that contradictions manifest themselves differently in different phenomena. It was therefore necessary to mount a concrete empirical analysis of each phenomenon in order to comprehend the particular configuration of the contradictory aspects within that phenomenon. Of the two opposing aspects of the contradiction within a phenomenon, one would be dominant, the other secondary; similarly, in a complex phenomenon or process, there might be more than one contradiction of which one would be the principal contradiction. Analysis of social reality thus had to grasp the contradictions present in that social reality, determine which was the principal contradiction, and use the principal contradiction in the determination of political priorities.

Let us take a concrete example. During the early stages of the anti-Japanese war, Mao argued on many occasions that the principal contradiction of Chinese society was not that between the CCP and the GMD, but that between Chinese society and the forces of Japanese imperialism. He also argued that the principal aspect of this principal contradiction was Japanese imperialism. This did not signify that no contradiction existed between the CCP and the GMD, but that it was secondary and of less importance than the principal contradiction. Consequently, the hostility between the CCP and the GMD had to be put aside in order to allow a united front between the two parties against Japanese imperialism; in this case, the principal contradiction determined the relative priority of the other contradictions characterising society. However, as the situation altered, so might the configuration of its contradictions; on the cessation of the anti-Japanese war, the principal contradiction once again became the antagonism between the CCP and GMD, and this laid the theoretical basis for the civil war of 1946-9.

Even a cursory reading of Mao's writings reveals that he invariably interpreted history and society through the intellectual framework of his theory of contradictions. His emphasis on contradictions has had a lasting impact on Chinese Marxism, and although contemporary Chinese leaders might now disagree with Mao's evaluation of the intensity of the contradictions which characterised Chinese society during the 1960s and 1970s, their objections are couched in terminology easily recognisable as deriving from Mao's theory of contradictions.

Similarly, Mao's theory of knowledge (or epistemology) has exercised a lasting influence on Chinese Marxism. In *On Practice*

(1937) Mao argued that knowledge of the real world only came through concrete investigation and empirical analysis. [21] Mao's hostility to book learning for its own sake or intuitive theorising was based on his conviction that knowledge only derived from actively seeking out the 'facts' of empirical reality; if one wanted to unearth the 'laws' of Chinese society, one had to mount an analysis of the 'facts' of Chinese society—its class structure, patterns of ownership, the influence of imperialism on domestic economic activity, and so on. Here again, Mao's emphasis on 'seeking truth from facts' represented a criticism of the Marxism of the Returned Students' Faction which Mao felt put too much emphasis on theory at the expense of empirical investigation; without the latter, one could never know if one's theory was correct, and this could well lead to inappropriate political tactics. Theory, without continual reference to empirical reality, became 'dogma', and the members of the Returned Students' Faction were 'dogmatists' because they attempted uncritically to apply a foreign brand of Marxism without sufficient reference to the particularities of Chinese society.

Another important aspect of Mao's thought was the concept of the 'united front'. Mao had been introduced to the potentialities and dangers of the united front in the period 1924-7 during which time the CCP had entered a 'bloc within' form of united front with the GMD (members of the CCP actually joining the GMD). While that particular united front had ended in disaster for the CCP, Mao did not reject the possibility of again exploiting the tactic for political gain. For Mao, the united front was a largely temporary alliance between partners who might have very different long-term objectives but who perceived a common interest in the short term. On many occasions, Mao decidedly rejected the notion that the CCP should as a matter of principle always go it alone without help and assistance from other quarters. [22] Depending on the historical situation, the CCP needed to make alliances of convenience which would increase its ability to pursue the resolution of the principal contradiction. Such united fronts did not indicate that the CCP was abandoning its long-term objectives when it entered alliances with partners such as the GMD. Rather, such alliances would increase the ability of the CCP to achieve its short-term objectives, at which point the differences between the erstwhile allies would reassert themselves and a struggle for dominance would again commence.

The united front strategy has been employed frequently by Mao and the Chinese leadership in the formulation of both domestic and foreign policy; domestically, to broaden the basis of their support by establishing alliances with various non-party sections of the Chinese population (such as intellectuals, or the national bourgeoisie); and internationally, to avoid isolation and to increase China's ability to resist the enemy defined as the principal contradiction in the arena of foreign relations.

In terms of orthodoxy, Mao was clearly following in Lenin's footsteps by manipulating the united front tactic to achieve political objectives. Lenin had shown no patience with those communists who misguidedly put principle first at all cost and isolated themselves from potential allies. Such communists were guilty, in Lenin's estimation, of an 'infantile disorder' and the consequence of their actions could only be isolation and defeat. [23]

Mao also drew on his Leninist heritage in interpreting the historical stages through which China had and was passing. The orthodox Marxist view of historical development suggested five major stages or modes of production in the development of society; also, that capitalism was the stage which preceded the socialist transition to communism. The Chinese instance obviously posed problems for those who, like Mao, largely accepted this orthodox view of historical progression. Firstly, had traditional China been a feudal society, or had it been an Asiatic mode of production with socio-economic characteristics very different from the classical European form of feudalism? Secondly, how was Chinese society since 1840 to be categorised? Was it still feudal, or was it becoming a predominantly capitalist society? Mao's reaction to these questions was to pursue an orthodox Leninist line. Traditional China had been a feudal society which became, with the intervention of Western imperialism, a 'semifeudal, semi-colonial' society. This society clearly contained a mixture of various modes of production (feudalism, domestic capitalism, compradore capitalism, even socialism), but the feudal mode of production remained dominant. [24]

Mao incorporated the whole of modern Chinese history into what he termed the 'bourgeois-democratic' revolution. The basic characteristic of this 'bourgeois-democratic' revolution was the struggle against imperialism and Chinese feudalism, and Mao believed that it was made up of two distinct stages with the May

Fourth Movement of 1919 representing the historical watershed. Between 1840 and 1919, the revolution had been led by the bourgeoisie, this being the period of 'Old Democracy' according to Mao. With the May Fourth Movement, leadership of the 'bourgeois-democratic' revolution had passed from the bourgeoisie to the proletariat and its vanguard party, the CCP. Mao perceived the distinction between the new and old stages of the 'bourgeois-democratic' revolution as resulting from the changed domestic and international situation, particularly World War I with its ramifications in China and the Russian revolution of 1917. With the change of leadership following the May Fourth Movement, the 'bourgeois-democratic' revolution, entered the period of the 'new democratic' revolution, and only following the realisation of New Democracy could China turn its attention to the realisation of socialism. [25]

Mao was to equivocate over the necessity of a capitalist stage in China's historical development. In his Yan'an writings, Western imperialism is portrayed as the agency which disrupted the long period of feudal stagnation in China's history. However, with the revision of Mao's *Selected Works* in the early 1950s, the following sentence was added to increase the orthodoxy of Mao's position:

> As China's feudal society had developed a commodity economy, and so carried within itself the seeds (*mengya*) of capitalism, China would of herself have developed slowly into a capitalist society even without the impact of foreign capitalism. [26]

As we have observed, Mao did not concede that China would have to pass through a fully developed capitalist society to achieve socialism, and he believed that the development of the forces of production which had accompanied the rise of capitalism in Europe could come about in China under the direction of a New Democratic government. Nevertheless, China had had to experience at least some development of capitalism to permit the realisation of New Democracy and eventually socialism.

Mao was aware that an important ingredient of the Chinese revolution during its 'bourgeois-democratic' stage was the growth of nationalism inspired by hostility of the imperialism of Japan and the Western powers. However, he perceived no contradiction

between the fostering of Chinese nationalism and the internationalism of Marxism, and he harmonised his appeal to these
two seemingly divergent themes in orthodox Leninist fashion (see
Chapter 2). Chinese Marxists *were* internationalists, Mao insisted, but their first task was the ejection of the imperialists and
the establishment of an independent China; only when this had
been achieved could attention be turned to the creation of an international order. The following passage, written in 1938, is typical of Mao's position on the question of nationalism and
internationalism:

> Can a Communist, who is an internationalist, at the same
> time be a patriot? We hold that he not only can be but
> must be...Chinese communists must therefore combine pa-
> triotism with internationalism. We are at once interna-
> tionalists and patriots and our slogan is, 'Fight to defend
> the motherland against the aggressors.' For us defeatism is
> a crime and to strive for victory in the War of Resistance is
> an inescapable duty. For only by fighting in defence of the
> motherland can we defeat the aggressors and achieve na-
> tional liberation. And only by achieving national liberation
> will it be possible for the proletariat and other working
> people to achieve their own emancipation. The victory of
> China and the defeat of the invading imperialists will help
> the people of other countries. Thus in wars of national li-
> beration patriotism is applied internationalism. [27]

During the Yan'an period, Mao developed distinctive approaches to several important problems of political organisation
and leadership. Of these, the concepts of the 'mass line' and
'party rectification' have had a lasting effect. Like Lenin, Mao
accepted the necessity of a vanguard party which would lead the
revolution and facilitate increased class consciousness amongst
the proletariat. However, Mao attempted to temper the elitism
implicit in the Leninist conception of party organisation by insisting that party leadership had to maintain constant links with
the masses, and allow a constant flow of information on attitudes and opinion amongst the masses to reach the leadership
and education and advice on leadership policies to be widely
communicated amongst the masses. Mao referred to this principle as the 'mass line', and he was to refer to it in June 1943 as

follows:

> In all the practical work of our Party, all correct leadership is necessarily 'from the masses, to the masses'. This means: take the ideas of the masses (scattered and unsystematic ideas) and concentrate them (through study turn them into concentrated and systematic ideas), then go to the masses and propagate and explain these ideas until the masses embrace them as their own, hold fast to them and translate them into action, and test the correctness of these ideas in such action. Then once again concentrate ideas from the masses and once again go to the masses so that the ideas are persevered in and carried through. And so on, over and over again in an endless spiral, with the ideas becoming more correct, more vital and richer each time. [28]

Although Mao believed in constant reference to the attitudes of the masses, he did not allow that leadership must always defer to those attitudes; that would lead to 'tailism', an excessive deference to the wishes of the masses at the expense of the long-term objectives of the party. By the same token, Mao was opposed to 'commandism', the propensity of leadership to dictate orders and push through policies for which the ideological and educational groundwork had not been laid. Leadership thus had to pilot a sensitive course between these two 'deviations', and the mass line was the principle of organisation which could achieve this in practice.

The Leninist principles of party organisation were also tempered in Mao's thought by his belief that the Communist Party itself needed to undergo periodic rectification to eliminate ideological deviations and to educate cadres on the policies and strategies of the party. The first major rectification campaign (*zhengfeng*) was held in Yan'an between 1942-4. During the war years, the party had grown rapidly and the ideological level of many new cadres was low. Moreover, the contingencies faced by the CCP necessitated that party cadres be able to flexibly apply policies at a local level while remaining within the spirit of party directives issued at the centre. The balance between discipline and personal initiative could only be achieved through cadre comprehension of the long-term objectives of the party and an understanding of the type of Sinified Marxism which the party advocated under Mao's leadership. Hence the need for a party rectification.

There was thus, from Mao's perspective, no guarantee that the vanguard status of the party ensured the ideological level or purity of its cadres. Consequently, rectification campaigns were periodically necessary. Such campaigns could take two basic forms; 'closed door' rectification which restricted the campaign to the confines of the party itself; and 'open door' rectification which allowed non-party individuals to participate in the criticism and education of party cadres. This latter type of rectification is obviously a political tactic at some remove from pure Leninism, and Mao was later to employ it at several critical junctures in the party's history.

While Mao's views on party organisation and activity may have strayed some distance from Lenin's, his perception of the state as the political instrument of the dominant class within society was orthodox Leninism. Moreover, his refusal to contemplate a too-rapid establishment of a dictatorship of the proletariat in China paralleled Lenin's belief of 1905 that the form of state system appropriate to contemporary Russian conditions was one which reflected the composition of classes within the revolutionary movement; Lenin had advocated a 'revolutionary dictatorship of the proletariat and the peasantry' (see Chapter 2). Mao believed that the 'semi-feudal' conditions of China precluded a dictatorship of the proletariat as practised in the Soviet Union under Stalin. In 1940 he called for the establishment of a 'new-democratic republic', a transitional form of state under the joint dictatorship of several classes, [29] and in 1945 he proposed 'a state system which we call New Democracy, namely, a united-front democratic alliance based on the overwhelming majority of the people under the leadership of the working class'. [30] With the victory of the revolution in 1949, the form of state system to adopt ceased to be an academic question, and became a pressing political concern. At that time, Mao returned to the concept of a state system based on an alliance of classes under the leadership of the proletariat. He referred to this state system as a 'people's democratic dictatorship', and the classes it would incorporate were the working class, peasantry, urban petty bourgeoisie, and the national bourgeoisie:

These classes, led by the working class and the communist

party, unite to form their own state and elect their own government; they enforce their dictatorship over the running dogs of imperialism...Democracy is practised within the ranks of the people, who enjoy the rights of freedom of speech, assembly, association, and so on. The right to vote belongs only to the people, not to the reactionaries. The combination of these two aspects, democracy for the people and dictatorship over the reactionaries, is the people's democratic dictatorship. [31]

While Mao did not advocate a dictatorship of the proletariat, he believed that the future industrialisation and socialisation of the economy would eventually create the social conditions under which the dictatorship of the proletariat would constitute the appropriate state system for China.

Mao on Culture and the Family

Mao's views on the family, marriage and the role of women had been influenced by those intellectual currents of the May Fourth Movement strongly opposed to the traditional feudal family and the oppression of women through such practices as arranged marriages. His insistence on the need to liberate women from male domination within the feudal family dates from that time and emerges frequently in his subsequent writings. [32] With his conversion to Marxism, Mao's hostility to the traditional family was provided a theoretical foundation, for the family was viewed by that theory as an institution for domestic domination created by class society. Mao came to echo that sentiment and consequently to believe that the family and male domination of women would cease to be problems as a result of the eventual victory of struggles on the political and economic fronts. [33] The policy towards the family and marriage in areas under the control of the CCP thus sought reforms to the family rather than its complete abolition. This is clearly reflected in the 'Provisional Marriage Regulation' of the Jiangxi Soviet signed by Mao in 1931:

Under feudal domination, marriage is a barbaric and inhuman institution. The oppression and suffering by woman is far greater than that of man. Only the victory of the workers' and peasants' revolution, followed by the first step toward the economic emancipation of men and women, brings with it a change in the marriage relationship and makes it free. In the soviet districts, marriages now are contracted on a free basis. Free choice must be the basic principle of every marriage. The whole feudal system of marriages for their children, to exercise compulsion, and all purchase and sale in marriage contracts shall henceforth be abolished. [34]

It is also clear that Mao was prepared to utilise the family as one of the social organisations whose task was the prosecution of the anti-Japanese war during the early 1940s. [35] Nevertheless, he believed that the importance of the family as an economic unit would decline with the spread of cooperative forces of production characteristic of socialist society; moreover, that this decline in the influence of the family was necessary because of the negative role it played in frustrating social change. [36]

In his approach to the role of culture in the revolutionary struggle, Mao echoed the orthodox Marxist position in insisting that culture was not autonomous but produced by and intimately linked to certain class structures within society. However, in his 'Talks at the Yan'an Forum on Literature and Art' of May 1942, Mao also insisted that revolutionary culture (literature and art) could play an important part in accelerating changes which had been created by developments within the material 'basis' of society. [37] To achieve this goal, revolutionary literature and art had to observe certain criteria. Firstly, Mao insisted that there was no such thing as a non-class form of art and literature; all art and literature served certain class positions. Consequently, artists and writers had to be conscious of the class position which they occupied in creating works of art, for many unconsciously adopted a 'petty bourgeois' position which emphasised individualism and 'love', and which ignored the needs of the masses. Secondly, Mao stressed that the question of 'audience' was critical in the production of literature and art which was genuinely revolutionary and would have the effect of inspiring the masses to 'propel history forward'. Too often, artists and writers produced works of art for a select few; such an approach to culture was elitist and had to be replaced by a form of art and literature which took 'popularisation' as the key criterion. 'Popularisation' necessitated that a 'simpler and plainer' style be adopted which could be readily comprehended and appreciated by the peasants and workers, many of whom were illiterate. Thirdly, Mao argued that the raw material for works of art and literature should be the 'life of the people'. This provided an endless source of inspiration for artists and writers, and it was their task to select and portray those experiences which would motivate the masses to 'unite and struggle to transform their environment'. In insisting that the 'life of the people' constituted the raw material for artistic and literary creations, Mao criticised the tendency to uncritically transplant or copy ancient or foreign styles; this lead to 'the most sterile and harmful dogmatism in literature and art'.[38]

Mao's criticism of 'dogmatism' in the field of art and literature was related to his rejection of a dogmatic adherence to a brand of Marxism unsuited to the particular needs and characteristics of Chinese society and the Chinese revolution. Marxism could only be of relevance and a 'guide to action' for Chinese revolutionaries if it disclosed the specific characteristics of Chinese society and led to the formulation of a strategy tailored to the possibilities and limitations of that concrete historical situation. However, while Mao insisted that Marxism had to be 'Sinified' to fulfil that function, he continued to insist that Marxism was a universal theory of history which contained a corpus of immutable universal laws. How did Mao harmonise this emphasis on the universality of Marxism while simultaneously insisting on its 'Sinification'? Let us turn to a brief reconstruction of the logic which underpinned Mao's 'Sinification of Marxism'.

The Form of Mao Zedong's 'Sinification of Marxism'

In his report to the Sixth Plenum of the Sixth Central Committee in October 1938, Mao called for the Sinification of Marxism in the following terms:

> A communist is a Marxist internationalist, but Marxism must take on a national form before it can be applied. There is no such thing as abstract Marxism, but only concrete Marxism. What we call Marxism is Marxism that has taken on a national form, that is, Marxism applied to the concrete struggle in the concrete conditions prevailing in China, and not Marxism abstractly used. If a Chinese communist, who is a part of the great Chinese people, bound to

his people by his very flesh and blood, talks of Marxism apart from Chinese peculiarities, this Marxism is merely an empty abstraction. Consequently, the Sinification of Marxism—that is to say, making certain that in all of its manifestations it is imbued with Chinese peculiarities, using it according to these peculiarities—becomes a problem that must be understood and solved by the whole party without delay. [39]

How is this Sinification of Marxism to be interpreted? Western critiques have tended to cluster around two lines of explication. The first suggests that the Sinification of Marxism entailed the elevation of Chinese tradition and realities at the expense of Marxism's universal truths. Stuart Schram, for example, has argued that Mao denied altogether the existence of 'a universally valid form of Marxism,' and that his 'preoccupation with the glory of China' led to a Sinification of Marxism which was 'hermetic'. [40] The second argues that the Sinification of Marxism was a ploy used by Mao to enhance his own position in the power struggle with the Moscow-oriented Returned Students' Faction which had favoured a more orthodox European and Soviet reading of Marxism. According to Robert North, Mao was 'adapting Russian communist political theory to meet peculiar Chinese requirements and the convenience of his own climb to power.' [41] However, a third explanation is possible: that Mao was attempting to establish a formula by which a universal theory such as Marxism could be utilised in a particular national context and culture *without abandoning the universality of that theory.* [42]

How can such an interpretation be justified? It is important to point out that Mao believed it possible to discover particular 'laws' (of nature, society, history, war) which unlike the universal laws of Marxism, have no universal applicability. This belief in the existence of particular 'laws' describing the regularities present in particular or localised contexts comes across clearly in the following interesting passage from 'Problems of Strategy in China's Revolutionary War', written by Mao in 1936:

...the different laws for directing wars are determined by the different circumstances of those wars—differences in their time, place and nature (*xingzhi*). As regards the time factor, both war and its laws develop; each historical stage has its special characteristics, and hence the laws in each historical stage have their special characteristics and cannot be mechanically applied in another stage. As for the nature of war, since revolutionary war and counter-revolutionary war both have their special characteristics, the laws governing them also have their own characteristics, and those applying to one cannot be mechanically transferred to the other. As for the factor of place, since each country or nation, especially a large country or nation, has its own characteristics, the laws of war for each country or nation also have their own characteristics, and here, too, those applying to one cannot be mechanically transferred to the other. In studying the laws for directing wars that occur at different historical stages, that differ in nature and that are waged in different places and by different nations, we must fix our attention on the characteristics and development of each, and must oppose a mechanical approach to the problem of war. [43]

It is evident from this passage that Mao rejected the notion that there can only be laws of war in general. On the contrary, he argues that it is possible and desirable to seek out 'laws' describing the characteristics of specific theatres of war.

But what is the relationship between universal laws of history and society and the particular 'laws' of Chinese society and the Chinese revolution which Mao was so eager to discover? In the first place, it would seem that universal laws are derived from the many particular 'laws' which describe the behaviour of the same phenomenon in different situations. For example, if different forms of class struggle are observed in many different social contexts, the particular 'laws' describing those specific instances of class struggle constitute the foundation of a universal law which asserts the existence of class struggle in *all* societies. In the second place, a universal law has a predictive value which asserts the certain existence of the phenomenon described by that law in instances as yet unobserved; the universal law thus draws attention to, and guides analysis of this phenomenon. The function of such a universal law was not, as far as Mao was concerned, to dictate the manner in which that phenomenon would assume concrete form; that could only be disclosed through an empirical investigation whose purpose was to arrive at an understanding of the characteristics of that phenomenon in its specific context. In other words, the particular 'law' would be revealed by an empirical investigation informed by knowledge of the relevant universal law. To pursue our example, the universal law of class struggle represented an abstract assertion of the existence of class struggle in all societies (save perhaps the most primitive); knowledge of that universal law had to be mobilised to discover the particular 'law' which described the nature of class struggle within Chinese society.

Mao believed that the abstract universal laws of Marxism performed an important function in directing attention to those aspects of society requiring analysis and study. However, such universal laws did *not* by themselves represent Marxism in its entirety. To become a complete ideology, the universal laws of Marxism had to be mobilised and applied to disclose a society's particular 'laws'. It was this union of the universal (abstract) laws and the particular (concrete) 'laws' which constitute Marxism in its totality. And obviously, such a union of universal and particular could occur only within a specific historical and social context such as the Chinese society during the period of the anti-Japanese war. Consequently, Marxism in the Chinese context consisted of Marxism's universal laws utilised to disclose the particular 'laws' describing the nature of Chinese society and the Chinese revolution. Once disclosed, those particular 'laws' became for Mao an integral element of Marxism within that historically defined situation. It is in this sense that Mao could call for the Sinification of Marxism.

From this perspective, the Sinification of Marxism was not a question of the elevation of Chinese realities at the expense of Marxism's universality, but the completion of Marxism as an ideological system. Inherent in Mao's Sinification of Marxism is the notion that Marxism as a complete ideological system (rather than just a body of abstract universal laws) is definable only within a concrete historical situation. Thus, although the Sinification of Marxism is, as Wylie claims, a 'culturally charged term', [44] it does not claim any cultural privilege over Marxism. Within a different cultural or historical context, the universal laws of Marxism would have to be joined with the particular 'laws' of that specific situation. Because these particular 'laws' would be different from those describing Chinese society, that particular Marxism would differ accordingly. Both, nevertheless, would share a common stock of universal laws.

This view of Marxism led logically to an insistence on the need to pay close attention to the particular characteristics of Chinese society and history. Mao was to return to this point again and again in subsequent writings of the Yan'an period, and he made no attempt to conceal his impatience with those Marxists who were preoccupied with foreign models and history to the exclusion of Chinese history and conditions. He perceived this preoccupation as largely a manifestation of an incorrect interpretation of Marxism, one which regarded the particular 'laws' of a largely European form of Marxism as having relevance within the Chinese context. In 'Reform our Study' (1941), Mao isolated three conditions having deleterious effect within the CCP: the study of current conditions was being neglected, as were the study of history and the application of Marxism-Leninism. For Mao, these failings were a manifestation of an incorrect interpretation of Marxism. His critique of them was inspired by his own view of Marxism which insisted on the integration of Marxism's universal laws with the particular 'laws' describing the regularities characteristic of Chinese society; and that integration was only possible through a detailed investigation and close knowledge of current conditions and Chinese history. Mao believed that Marxists labouring under a dogmatic misinterpretation of Marxism were guilty of 'subjectivism', an epithet intended to indicate divorce from reality and a preoccupation with theory for its own sake:

> With this attitude, a person does not make a systematic and thorough study of the environment, but works by sheer subjective enthusiasm and has a blurred picture of the face of China today. With this attitude, he chops up history, knows only ancient Greece but not China and is in a fog about the China of yesterday and the day before yesterday. With this attitude, a person studies Marxist-Leninist theory in the abstract and without any aim. He goes to Marx, Engels, Lenin and Stalin not to seek the stand, viewpoints and methods with which to solve the theoretical and tactical problems of the Chinese revolution but to study theory purely for theory's sake. [45]

During the *zhengfeng* (rectification) movement of 1942-4 there was a heavy emphasis on eradicating this 'subjectivism', and the *zhengfeng* documents indicate a general preoccupation with disclosing the distinguishing characteristics (the particular 'laws') of the Chinese revolution and Chinese society and the necessity for formulating policies in line with those characteristics. *Zhengfeng* must consequently be seen, in large part, as a move to gain partywide acceptance of the Sinification of Marxism (as Mao perceived it), a formulation which had found acceptance amongst an important section of party leaders and intellectuals since 1938 but had not found wide audience or comprehension amongst rank-and-file cadres.

In 'On the New Stage' (1938), Mao had asserted that Marxism had to be regarded as a guide to action. [46] He returned to this theme frequently in the *zhengfeng* documents, and it represented the major theme of his keynote speech originally entitled 'Reform in Learning, the Party and Literature'(1942):

> Our comrades must understand that we do not study Marxism-Leninism because it is pleasing to the eye, or because it has some mystical value...It is only extremely useful.... Marx, Lenin, and Stalin have repeatedly said, 'Our doctrine is not dogma; it is a guide to action.' ... Theory and practice can be combined only if men of the Chinese Communist Party take the standpoints, concepts, and methods of Marxism-Leninism, apply them to China, and create a theory from conscientious research on the realities of the Chinese revolution and Chinese history'. [47]

For Mao, Sinified Marxism represented the union of Marxism's universal laws and the particular 'laws' of Chinese society. How did he perceive this ideology as a 'guide to action'? It must be stressed that this ideological system did not contain within it the formulae for automatic and necessarily correct responses to the various political, economic or military contingencies which might arise in the course of revolution. The function of the ideology was to facilitate as accurate an interpretation of the historical context as was possible. This information would allow the revolutionary to take judicious action commensurate with the objective limitations of the situation as outlined by the ideology. The action could only be regarded as appropriate in its conception (rather than as necessarily correct), for there could be no formula for 'correct' action implicit in the information provided. Having a clear and, it could be hoped, accurate picture of the historical situation would act as a guide to action by ruling out inappropriate responses and presenting certain actions as preferable, or perhaps obvious.

It is in this context that Mao's theory of practice finds relevance. Ideology could only serve as a guide to action by presenting an accurate assessment of the historical situation or process. It was up to the political actor to take full cognizance of the particular 'laws' of the situation, to draw the necessary inferences and formulate an appropriate response accordingly. Such a response could not be regarded as 'correct' in advance of its implementation, only as appropriate. The only method of ascertaining whether the seemingly appropriate action was correct was by performing the action and evaluating its results. If there was an equivalence between intention and result, then the action and the interpretation upon which it was based were indeed correct; otherwise the disparity between intention and result served to indicate either faulty analysis of the situation, or formulation of seemingly appropriate but incorrect response. Only by thus engaging reality could experience be gained and action refined so that the gap between the seemingly appropriate and the correct response could be minimised.

In conclusion, it appears that for Mao, Marxism was a complex ideological system constituted of various elements and only capable of finding complete definition within an historically specific setting. From this perspective, the Sinification of Marxism was a function of Mao's perception that the universal laws of Marxism did not represent Marxism as a complete ideological system, and that for this completion, such universal laws had necessarily to be united with the particular 'laws' which described Chinese society. Mao believed that this union of the universal and the particular allowed the completion of the Marxist system, and created a genuinely Chinese Marxism which nevertheless did not detract from the universal status of Marxism as a theory of history and society.

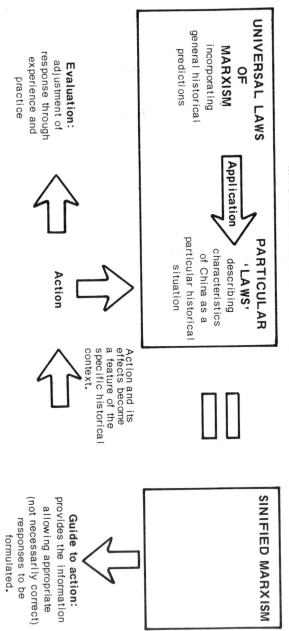

NOTES

1. Martin Bernal, 'The Triumph of Anarchism over Marxism, 1906-1907', in Mary Wright (ed.), *China in Revolution: The First Phase, 1900-1913* (Yale University Press, New Haven, 1968), pp. 140-2.

2. Li Dazhao, 'The Victory of Bolshevism', in Ssu-yu Teng and John K. Fairbank, *China's Response to the West: A Documentary Survey 1839-1923* (Atheneum, New York, 1963), pp. 246-9.

3. Maurice Meisner, *Li Ta-chao and the Origins of Chinese Marxism* (Atheneum, New York, 1973), pp. 67-70.

4. See Edgar Snow, *Red Star Over China* (Penguin, Harmondsworth, 1972, revised ed.), p. 176; also, Stuart Schram, *Mao Tse-tung* (Penguin, Harmondsworth, 1966), p. 54.

5. Meisner, *Li Ta-chao,* pp. 80-9.

6. Ibid., pp. 149-54.

7. *Selected Works of Mao Tse-tung* (4 vols. Foreign Languages Press, Peking, 1967), vol. 1, p. 341.

8. Stuart Schram, *Mao Tse-tung Unrehearsed* (Penguin, Harmondsworth, 1974), p. 83.

9. Meisner, *Li Ta-chao,* pp. 112-14.

10. Yu-ju Chih, 'Chen Tu-hsiu: His Career and Political Ideas', in Chun-tu Hsueh (ed.), *Revolutionary Leaders of Modern China* (Oxford University Press, New York, 1971), p. 357.

11. Meisner, *Li Ta-chao,* pp. 241-6; also, see Mao's estimation of Chen Duxiu in Snow, *Red Star Over China,* pp. 188, 190-1.

12. Stuart R. Schram, 'Mao Zedong and the Role of the Various Classes in the Chinese Revolution, 1923-1927', in *The Polity and Economy of China: The Late Professor Yuji Muramatsu Commemoration Volume* (Toyo Keizai Shinposha, Tokyo, 1975), p. 231.

13. See 'A Single Spark can Start a Prairie Fire', *Selected Works,* vol. 1, pp. 117-28.

14. 'Analysis of the Classes in Chinese Society', *Selected Works,* vol. 1, pp. 13-21; see also Snow, *Red Star Over China,* pp. 185-7.

15. *Selected Works,* vol. 1, pp. 23-4.

16. Schram, 'Mao Zedong and the Role of the Various Classes,' p. 235.

17. *Selected Works,* vol. 3, p. 11.

18. *Selected Works,* vol. 1, pp. 105-16.

19. It is not exactly certain what position Mao achieved at this Conference, but it is probable that he became Chairman of the Party's Military Council and Chairman of the Politburo (or perhaps Politburo Standing Committee). See Jerome Ch'en, 'Resolutions of the Tsunyi Conference', *China Quarterly* 40 (October 1969), pp. 1-38; also Dieter Heinzig, 'Otto Braun and the Tsunyi Conference', *China Quarterly* 42 (April 1970), pp. 131-5; also Warren Kuo, *Analytical History of the Chinese Communist Party* (3 vols. Institute of International Relations, Taipei, 1970), vol. 3, pp. 23-4.

20. The official text of *On Contradiction* can be found in *Selected Works,* vol. 1, pp. 311-47. For a translation of the unofficial text of *On Contradiction,* see Nick Knight, *Mao Zedong's On Contradiction: An Annotated Translation of the pre-Liberation Text* (Griffith Asian Papers, No. 3, School of Modern Asian Studies, Griffith University, Nathan, 1981); see also Nick Knight, 'Mao Zedong's *On Contradiction* and *On Practice* : Pre-Liberation Texts', *China Quarterly* 84 (December 1980), pp. 641-68.

21. *Selected Works,* vol. 1, pp. 295-309.

22. See for example, 'The Tasks of the Chinese Communist Party in the Period of Resistance to Japan', *Selected Works,* vol. 1, pp. 263-83.

23. See V.I. Lenin, 'Left-Wing Communism - An Infantile Disorder', *Selected Works* (3 vols., Progress Publishers, Moscow, 1975), vol. 3, pp. 291-370.

24. See in particular, 'On New Democracy', *Selected Works,* vol. 2, pp. 339-84.

25. Ibid.

26. *Selected Works,* vol. 2, p. 309; see also Stuart R. Schram, *The Political Thought of Mao Tse-tung* (Penguin, Harmondsworth, 1969, revised ed.), p. 114.

27. *Selected Works,* vol. 2, p. 196.

28. *Selected Works,* vol. 3, p. 119.

29. *Selected Works,* vol. 2, pp. 350-2.

30. *Selected Works,* vol. 3, p. 229.

31. *Selected Works,* vol. 4, pp. 417-8.

32. See Roxane Witke, 'Mao Tse-tung, Women and Suicide in the May Fourth Era', *China Quarterly* 31 (July-September 1967), pp. 128-47.

33. *Selected Works,* vol. 1, p. 46.

34. Schram, *Political Thought of Mao Tse-tung,* p. 337.

35. *Beijing Review,* vol. 26, no. 52 (December 26, 1983), pp. 15-16.

36. Schram, *Political Thought of Mao Tse-tung,* p. 331.

37. For a discussion of the relationship between the 'basis' of society and its culture in Mao's thought, see Nicholas James Knight, *Mao and History: An Interpretive Essay on Some Problems in Mao Zedong's Philosophy of History* (unpublished Ph.D. thesis, University of London, 1983), pp. 124-61.

38. *Selected Works,* vol. 3, pp. 69-98.

39. Schram, *Political Thought of Mao Tse-tung,* p. 172.

40. Ibid., pp. 112-16.

41. Robert C. North, *Moscow and Chinese Communists* (Stanford University Press, Stanford, 1953 & 1963), p. 193.

42. The following analysis is a truncated version of my 'The Form of Mao Zedong's "Sinification of Marxism"', *The Australian Journal of Chinese Affairs* no. 9 (January 1983), pp. 17-33.

43. *Selected Works,* vol. 1, pp. 181-2.

44. Raymond Wylie, *The Emergence of Maoism: Mao Tse-tung, Ch'en Po-ta, and the Search for Chinese Theory 1935-1945* (Stanford University Press, Stanford, 1980), p. 52.

45. *Selected Works,* vol. 3, p. 21.

46. Schram, *Political Thought of Mao Tse-tung,* p. 171.

47. Boyd Compton (trans.), *Mao's China: Party Reform Documents, 1942-44* (University of Washington Press, Seattle and London, 1952), pp. 21-2.

SELECT BIBLIOGRAPHY

Compton, Boyd (trans.), *Mao's China: Party Reform Documents, 1942-44* (University of Washington Press, Seattle and London, 1952). A useful compilation and translation of the major documents from the rectification campaign by Mao and other important leaders of the CCP.

Meisner, Maurice, *Li Ta-Chao and the Origins of Chinese Marxism* (Atheneum, New York, 1973). An excellent intellectual biography of Li Dazhao which also provides many interesting insights into the theories and ideas of other members of the early Chinese Communist Movement.

Schram, Stuart R., *The Political Thought of Mao Tse-tung* (Penguin, Harmondsworth, 1969, revised ed.). A very useful anthology of the most important of the Mao texts. Schram's Introduction presents an interpretation of Mao's 'Sinification of Marxism' very different to the one contained in this chapter.

Selected Works of Mao Tse-tung (4 vols., Foreign Languages Press, Peking,

1967). Contains the official version of many of the pre-1949 Mao documents. Essential reading for the student of Chinese Marxism.

Womack, Brantley, *The Foundations of Mao Zedong's Political Thought 1917-1935* (University Press of Hawaii, Honolulu, 1982). An excellent analysis of the emergence of Mao's political paradigm during the pre-Yan'an period. Womack pays particular attention to the political context within which Mao formulated key political concepts.

Wylie, Raymond, *The Emergence of Maoism: Mao Tse-tung, Ch'en Po-ta, and the Search for Chinese Theory 1935-1945* (Stanford University Press, Stanford, 1980). The most detailed study available of the development of Mao Zedong Thought during the Yan'an period.

4

MAO ZEDONG AND THE CHINESE ROAD TO SOCIALISM
Nick Knight

For many interpreters of Chinese Marxism, the Yan'an period (1936-47) constituted the highpoint of Mao Zedong's career as a Marxist intellectual. It was during this period that Mao penned some of his most important theoretical works; and it was during this period that Mao grappled with the problem of producing a Sinified Marxism. [1] While it is true that Mao did make a considerable contribution to the theory and practice of Marxism during the Yan'an period, this contribution was equalled, if not surpassed, by Mao's attempt to formulate an alternative economic strategy – the Chinese road to socialism – during the 1950s and 1960s. In this endeavour, Mao was navigating in largely uncharted waters, for he was seeking a developmental strategy very different from the Soviet model on which the Chinese had relied during the early 1950s. Mao had come to regard the Soviet model as largely unsuited to Chinese conditions, and it was his growing disenchantment with it that prompted him to seek a strategy for development in harmony with the particular characteristics and needs of the Chinese society and economy. Mao's attempt to formulate a Chinese road to socialism (whatever the contemporary Chinese evaluation of it) must be regarded as a most significant contribution to the theory and practice of Marxism, for it broke new ground in suggesting a strategy for development during the socialist transition well removed from the strictures of the Soviet model.

This chapter will analyse various theoretical elements of Mao's Marxism during the 1950s and 1960s, paying special attention to the Chinese road to socialism and the Cultural Revolution of the late 1960s.

The Events of 1956

It is clear in retrospect that 1956 represented something of a watershed in modern Chinese history in general, and in the development of Mao's thought in particular. What were the factors which constituted this watershed?

The first was the successful outcome of the campaign to cooperativise China's agriculture. The Chinese peasants appeared to Mao to be responding positively to the call for cooperativisation, and the success of this campaign was one of the factors which allowed Mao the political manoeuvrability necessary to seek an alternative economic strategy. [2] The positive response by the Chinese peasantry to the call for cooperativisation was in itself in marked contrast to the Soviet experience of agricultural collectivisation in which the peasants had had to be coerced (often with great violence) into joining cooperatives. It appeared to Mao that this positive response could function as the premise for a new initiative in the area of socialist construction, an initiative which combined a different strategy to that used by the Soviet Union with a more rapid pace of development.

The second was the deStalinisation speech made by Khrushchev at the XXth Congress of the Communist Party of the Soviet Union (CPSU) in February 1956. In his 'secret speech' to the XXth Congress, Khrushchev launched a bitter attack on Stalin and his methods of leadership. Stalin had 'acted not through persuasion, explanation, and patient cooperation with people', Khrushchev declared, 'but by imposing his concepts and demanding absolute submission to his opinion'. [3] As well as launching a bitter attack on Stalin's personality cult, Khrushchev attacked important aspects of the Marxism which Stalin had established as orthodoxy for the international communist movement. In his report to the XXth Congress, Khrushchev backpedalled on the mechanical Stalinist view of historical development, a view which indicated a fixed and undeviating path to socialism which all societies must tread. Khrushchev argued that although a transition to socialism was still inevitable for all nations, each nation might make that transition in a different manner. Khrushchev's position therefore emphasised not uniformity, but the diversity of forms which the transition to socialism might take:

With the fundamental changes that have taken place on the world scene, new prospects have also opened up for countries and nations to make the transition to socialism.... It is very probable that forms of transition to socialism will become more and more varied. And it is not necessarily true that pursuit of these forms involves civil war in all cases. [4]

There can be no doubt that Khrushchev and other Soviet leaders took (in the words of Benjamin Schwartz) an 'extremely nonchalant attitude towards the possible repercussions of their own ideological pronouncements'. [5] For in criticising Stalin and conceding that there could be varying roads to socialism, Khrushchev was in effect calling into question the ideological supremacy of the Soviet Union within the international communist movement. It is clear that this weakening of the ideological leadership of the Soviet Union was a significant factor in Mao's own decision to move away from a policy of 'leaning to one side', a policy of reliance on the Soviet Union and emulation of the Soviet model for economic development.

However, while Mao may have seized the opportunity created by Khrushchev to formulate a Chinese road to socialism, he perceived more clearly than did Khrushchev the ramifications of the Soviet leader's maladroit handling of the Stalin issue. In 1958, Mao was to recall his reaction to the revelations of the XXth Congress, and his recollection indicates this ambivalent attitude towards deStalinisation:

When Stalin was criticized in 1956, we were on the one hand happy, but on the other hand apprehensive. It was completely necessary to remove the lid, to break down blind faith, to release the pressure, and to emancipate thought. But we did not agree with demolishing him at one blow. [6]

Contradictions in Socialist Society

DeStalinisation prompted Mao to formulate more clearly the theoretical premises for his belief that contradictions would remain an important characteristic of socialist society. Stalin had asserted in 1936 that the achievement of socialism in the Soviet Union had witnessed the 'obliteration' of contradictions amongst the Russian people. [7] Mao could not agree with such an analysis. In *On Contradiction* (1937), Mao had objected to Stalin's thesis of the 'obliteration' of contradictions in a socialist society. 'Even under the social conditions existing in the Soviet Union', Mao had declared, 'there is a difference between workers and peasants and this difference is a contradiction, although unlike the contradiction between labour and capital, it will not become intensified into antagonism or assume the form of class struggle'. [8] Mao's divergence from Stalin's position was made quite explicit when he declared:

> The question is one of different kinds of contradiction, not of the presence or absence of contradiction. Contradiction is universal and absolute, it is present in the process of development of all things and permeates every process from beginning to end. [9]

Following Khrushchev's 'secret speech', Mao set forth an analysis of the contradictions characterising Chinese society. In *On the Ten Great Relationships* (25 April, 1956), Mao argued that if contradictions were analysed and handled correctly, it could prevent mistakes in policy formulation and implementation, the implication being that it had been Stalin's failure to perceive and correctly analyse the contradictions within Russian society which had led to serious negative consequences. [10] Mao then proceeded to detail several contradictions within the Chinese economy, and in each instance proposed solutions to those contradictions by means of a paradox. In solving the contradictory relationship between heavy industry on the one hand and light industry and agriculture on the other, it was necessary to increase investment in light industry and agriculture in order to develop heavy industry. This in itself constituted a significant departure from Soviet practice which had consistently and one-sidedly stressed the role of heavy industry at the expense of light industry and agriculture. In a similar vein, Mao challenged those who wanted greater industrial development in China's hinterland to concentrate on making use of and further develop industry in coastal regions. For those who wanted an expansion of China's military capability, the correct method was to decrease the level

of military expenditure and increase investment in economic construction. On the relationship between the state, the units of production and the individual producers, Mao argued that an increase in the rewards to the individual producers, and greater
autonomy for local units of production would be of benefit to
the industrialisation of the entire country. Similarly, on the question of the relationship between the centre and the regions, Mao
started from the premise of putting the interests of the whole
state first; in order to do this, greater autonomy and initiative
had to be given to the regions.

Mao then turned his attention to other contradictions characterising Chinese society. Of these, the relationship between
China and other countries is perhaps the most significant. Mao
stressed that China had to learn from the good points of other
countries (not just the Soviet Union), and not adopt an arrogant
attitude which might prevent a genuine appreciation of China's
weaknesses. Such weaknesses could, however, constitute virtues,
for being 'poor and blank', China's attitude had to remain
'modest and cautious'. Moreover, poorness and blankness implied a subjective advantage, poorness being the starting point on
the road to development, and blankness signifying a receptivity
to cultural change. As Mao pointed out, 'Those who are poor
want change; only they want to have a revolution, want to burst
their bonds, and seek to become strong. A blank sheet of paper
is good for writing on.' [11] Mao was therefore suggesting that
China's development might be predicated on her backwardness
and poverty, for these provided her population with an urgent
desire for change and improvement. In the light of the political
context in which this speech was written, how should *On the Ten
Great Relationships* be interpreted? Firstly, by enumerating and
analysing the major contradictions within the Chinese society
and economy, Mao was laying the foundations for future policy
formulation which would be geared, not to a foreign model, but
to China's specific characteristics. Secondly, Mao hoped by such
analysis to prevent the abuses of power which had resulted from
Stalin's incorrect analysis of the 'obliteration' of contradictions
within the Soviet Union and his subsequent presumption that
there would be unanimity on all policy questions. As contradictions would, in Mao's opinion, remain a persistent and important feature of socialist society, unanimity and uniformity imposed by dictatorial methods would lead to a pattern of

development with serious defects and negative consequences. Thirdly, Mao's paradoxical solutions to the contradictions within China's economy suggest an attempt to persuade China's economic planners that their goals would still be realised through the change in economic direction that he envisaged; that a departure from the Soviet emphasis on heavy industry would have the effect of improving heavy industry's performance.

Mao was therefore predicating any formulation of a specifically Chinese road to socialism on a close analysis of the contradictions which characterised Chinese society. It was faulty reasoning to presume that a socialist society was not marked by contradictions, and the fact that contradictions did exist was a positive factor; for it was contradictions (their ceaseless emergence, development and resolution) which pushed society forward. Without contradictions, change and development would not be possible, and without change and development, socialism and communism would be impossible goals.

This emphasis on the persistence of contradictions within Chinese society is an important feature of Mao's thinking during the late 1950s. If contradictions existed, they had to be recognised, brought out into the open and resolved; ignoring or repressing contradictions could lead to those contradictions developing into antagonisms which would damage the socialist cause. This is the central theme of Mao's important speech of 27 February 1957 'On the Correct Handling of Contradictions Amongst the People'. [12] Building on a distinction which he had made in *On Contradiction* between antagonism and contradiction, Mao argued that it was possible to differentiate between two different categories of contradiction—antagonistic and non-antagonistic. Contradictions vary in type according to whether they exist among the people, or between the enemy and the people; the former are non-antagonistic, the latter are antagonistic. Non-antagonistic contradictions could be handled and resolved by peaceful means whereas antagonistic contradictions could only be resolved by recourse to violence and repression. While contradictions among the people were non-antagonistic, they had to be handled correctly or there was the danger that they could be transformed into an antagonistic form. The experience of Hungary had indicated that this danger always faced a socialist government.

It is important to note that, in this speech, Mao conceded

that there could exist contradictions between the government and the people even in a socialist society. These included the contradictions 'among the interests of the State, the interests of the collective and the interests of the individual; between democracy and centralism; between leadership and led; and the contradiction arising from the bureaucratic style of work of certain government workers in their relations with the masses.' [13] Such contradictions were, however, amongst the people and as such were non-antagonistic. Efforts had to be made, nevertheless, to correctly handle such contradictions to avoid their transformation into an antagonistic form.

Much of Mao's speech was devoted to an analysis of the contradictions amongst the people (that is, non-antagonistic contradictions).In order to avoid contradictions developing to the point of antagonism, Mao deemed it necessary to allow a more open atmosphere in which differing opinions could emerge and contend. This would have the effect of bringing the contradictions out into the open so that they could be evaluated and resolved without damage being done to the cause of socialist construction. This, in part, was the reasoning behind Mao's decision to allow an 'open-door' rectification of the Chinese Communist Party (CCP); by 'open-door' is meant that non-party persons would be allowed to raise criticisms of the party. The slogan 'let a hundred flowers bloom, let a hundred schools of thought contend' had been put forward in 1956, but it was not until May of 1957 that the 'open-door' rectification campaign got underway which allowed this 'blooming and contending'. It is evident that Mao had expected that this campaign would be conducted in an atmosphere of 'gentle breezes and mild rain'. [14] What emerged was, however, a latter-day May Fourth Movement characterised by an intense and indignant outpouring of criticism of the party. Moreover, this criticism was also accompanied by fairly widespread student unrest, and it was this which prompted Mao to move against opponents who had voiced their opinions and criticisms. By the first week of June, the campaign had been thrown into reverse gear, and was transformed into an anti-rightist campaign, the target of which was those who had accepted the invitation to 'bloom and contend'. One result of the 'hundred flowers' campaign was that it bore out Mao's belief that contradictions were very much in evidence within Chinese society, although in the event it turned out that some of these contradictions were of an antagonistic character and required the machinery of the people's dictatorship for their resolution.

The importance of the 'hundred flowers' episode lies in the fact that Mao did *not* presume the CCP, despite its status as the vanguard party of the working class, to be above criticism or reproach. On the contrary, it was necessary for the party to undergo periodic rectifications in order to prevent a deterioration of its revolutionary workstyle and a degeneration of its revolutionary goals. The 'hundred flowers' episode is also of importance for it signalled Mao's willingness to go *outside* the party for support if it appeared that the party was failing in its duty. Both of these features of the 'hundred flowers' campaign were to reappear with a vengeance in Mao's thought and actions during the Cultural Revolution of the late 1960s when he set out deliberately to demolish the party for its failure to maintain a correct revolutionary line. The 'hundred flowers' campaign was therefore an early indication of Mao's willingness to diverge from important elements of Leninism; for Leninism stressed the vanguard character of the communist party, and its leading role in the revolutionary struggle; a concomitant of this emphasis on the party in Lenin's thought was his distrust of the sort of mass spontaneity which Mao so frequently encouraged to resolve political problems or to achieve economic goals.

'Permanent Revolution'

Mao's belief that contradictions would persist within socialist society and beyond was an important premise for the formulation of his theory of 'permanent revolution' (*buduan geming*). The concept of 'permanent revolution' suggested that the victory of 1949 had not signalled the end of the Chinese revolution. Rather, new contradictions (demands, problems, tasks) would emerge as China strove to modernise and to build a powerful socialist economy. These continually emerging contradictions would necessitate a maintenance of revolutionary zeal; for the seizure of power on its own did not terminate the revolutionary struggle, and the tasks of socialist construction had to be perceived as a phase of a revolution which would continue well into the future. In a speech to the Supreme State Conference in January 1958 Mao referred to the concept of 'permanent revolution' as follows:

I stand for the theory of permanent revolution. Do not

mistake this for Trotsky's theory of permanent revolution. In making revolution one must strike while the iron is hot—one revolution must follow another, the revolution must continually advance. The Hunanese often say, 'Straw sandals have no pattern—they shape themselves in the making.' Trotsky believed that the socialist revolution should be launched even before the democratic revolution is complete. We are not like that. For example after the Liberation of 1949 came the Land Reform; as this was completed there followed the mutual aid teams, then the low-level cooperatives, then the high-level cooperatives. After seven years the cooperativization was completed and productive relationships were transformed; then came Rectification. After Rectification was finished, before things had cooled down, then came the Technical Revolution... [15]

Mao was to end this particular speech with a quote from Sun Yat-sen, the father of the Chinese revolution; 'The revolution has not yet been completed. Comrades must still bend every effort.' [16] Mao was to repeat this formulation of the concept of 'permanent revolution' in the important document of January 1958 entitled 'Sixty Articles on Work Methods':

> Our revolutions come one after another. Starting from the seizure of power in the whole country in 1949, there followed in quick succession the anti-feudal land reform, the agricultural cooperativization, and the socialist reconstruction of private industries, commerce, and handicrafts...Our revolutions are like battles. After a victory, we must at once put forward a new task. In this way, cadres and the masses will forever be filled with revolutionary fervour, instead of conceit. [17]

It is clear from these references that Mao could foresee no cessation of the revolutionary struggles within China. As soon as one revolutionary task had been completed, another would emerge to occupy the attention and energies of the revolutionaries. This would continue without cessation, and hence the state of revolution would be 'permanent'. It is clear, however, that such a view bears implications for Mao's view of the future and the nature of historical development (an important aspect of

Marxism). Does the concept of 'permanent revolution' suggest that Mao saw the revolution continuing even after the attainment of communism? Would contradictions continue to exist, necessitating revolutionary responses? The logic of Mao's theory of the ubiquity and universality of contradictions led inevitably to a perception of communist society in which contradictions would still emerge, and in which revolutionary struggles (although not class struggles) would persist:

> Will there be revolutions in the future when all the imperialists in the world are overthrown and classes are eliminated? What do you think? In my view, there will still be the need for revolution. The social system will still need to be changed and the term 'revolution' will still be in use. Of course, revolutions then will not be of the same nature as those in the era of class struggle. But there will still be contradictions between the relations of production and the productive forces, between the superstructure and the economic base. When the relations of production become unsuitable, they will have to be overthrown. If the superstructure (ideology and public opinion included) protects the kind of relations of production the people dislike, they will transform it. [18]

Elsewhere, Mao asserted that a future communist society would be subject to ceaseless 'struggles between advanced and backward techniques', [19] and would still be subject to 'uninterrupted development'. [20] Thus, while communism still represented for Mao the 'ideal' society and mankind's 'bright destiny', [21] the image of communism raised was significantly different from that contemplated during the Yan'an period; for after 1955 the notion of communism as a settled society of perpetual peace and harmony (the Yan'an perception) is replaced by the anticipation of a society in which development would continue, which would still be characterised by struggle and contradiction, and which would have to pass through 'many stages and many revolutions' on its relentless progression through time. [22]

The Great Leap Forward

The theory of 'permanent revolution' emerged at the beginning of 1958, at the moment China was about to embark on the Great Leap Forward. For Mao, the Great Leap Forward represented another of the 'revolutions' which constituted the permanent revolution. Through the Great Leap Forward, Mao hoped to propel China from its state of underdevelopment to a state of modernisation and industrial development in which the establishment of communism would be a feasibility; and this was to be accomplished in the space of a few short years.

Why did Mao believe the Great Leap Forward could achieve this ambitious goal? Firstly, Mao believed that a 'leap forward' in the forces of production came only after fundamental changes within the relations of production and the superstructure, and that only small-scale changes within the forces of production were sufficient to trigger this process. The success of the revolution in China had indicated to Mao that large-scale transformations of China's 'material base' came only after changes elsewhere in society (and especially in changes in the relations of production and the superstructure). By radically restructuring China's relations of production and superstructure, it would consequently be possible to generate a 'leap forward' of the productive forces. Moreover, changes within the relations of production and the superstructure could be pursued with relatively little in the way of capital investment, and basically involved changes in the relationships between people at a productive and ideological level. Mao, therefore, perceived the changes required for a 'leap forward' in China's productive forces in human and ideological, rather than technological, terms. China might not have the capital to pursue the Soviet pattern of development, in which huge amounts of capital were pumped into creating an industrial base; China had, however, large numbers of people and through a reorganisation of China's millions, and a transformation in their ideology, the conditions could still be created for a transition to communism.

In this resides a basic difference between Mao's Marxism and that of the Soviet Union. Under Stalin, the assumption had been made that a transition to communism required first and foremost the development of Russia's productive forces; the creation of modern institutions, an industrialised base to the economy, and a sophisticated technological infrastructure. Through this development of the productive forces, changes would result in other areas of society (and particularly within the relations of production) which would lead to communism. In the attainment of communism, the productive forces (from the Stalinist perspective) were principal. Mao, on the other hand, saw the process of development in a rather different light. In Mao's opinion, it was necessary (after small-scale advances in the forces of production) to drastically alter the productive relationships and ideology within society—that is, man and his relationships and ideas—before communism could be achieved. From changes in relationships and ideology would flow developments in the productive forces which would permit a transition to communism. Mao's emphasis was thus on the human aspects of social development, rather than on its purely technological dimensions. This is illustrated by Mao's succinct criticism of Stalin; 'he saw only things, not man'. [23] It is also illustrated by his criticism of the *Soviet Manual of Political Economy,* a Soviet text which argued that the development of the productive forces was primary:

> It is not enough to assert that the development of large industry is the foundation for the socialist transformation of the economy. All revolutionary history shows that the full development of new productive forces is *not* the prerequisite for the transformation of backward production relations. Our revolution began with Marxist-Leninist propaganda, which served to create new public opinion in favour of revolution. After the old production relations had been destroyed new ones were created, and these cleared the way for the development of new social productive forces. With that behind us we were able to set in motion the technological revolution to develop social productive forces on a large scale. [24]

Therefore, an overemphasis on the forces of production ignored the fact (established by historical experience) that it was transformations in the relations of production and superstructure which gave rise to rapid and large-scale development of the productive forces. The Great Leap Forward was premised on this view of social and economic development. Through the organisation of the people's communes, relations of production would be altered; and through ideological campaigns, attitudes and values inconsistent with communism would be transformed.

Secondly, Mao perceived the Great Leap Forward as achieving its goals through the deployment of an alternative approach to economic and industrial development and management. The over-reliance of the Soviet model on very large industrial enterprises had to be discarded in favour of a more balanced use of medium and small-scale enterprises. This would have several benefits. Firstly, it would allow a more rational utilisation of human resources, enterprises being decentralised and located in areas where there was abundant labour. Secondly, such a policy would serve to educate a broader range of China's workforce in the technical skills associated with modern industry. Thirdly, through decentralisation of industry, the subjective enthusiasm of the Chinese people (so evident to Mao in the success of cooperativisation in 1955) could be more readily harnessed. Fourthly, the establishment of small and medium sized enterprises was a less capital intensive operation than the establishment of large enterprises. This policy initiative was described as 'walking on two legs', for it rejected an excessive reliance on large industrial complexes at the expense of smaller, but still economically viable, enterprises. [25]

Thirdly, Mao's alternative economic strategy emphasised self-reliance, which meant getting along with low or medium technology instead of high technology requiring large capital outlay. China just did not have the economic capacity to use high technology in all areas of production. It was therefore necessary to employ a strategy which combined low technology with high labour inputs, and through the optimal deployment of the resource which China had in abundance (human labour), rapid economic growth could be achieved.

The success of the Great Leap Forward was therefore predicated on Mao's theoretical belief that changes in the relations of production and the superstructure, combined with an alternative strategy for economic development, would bring about a rapid advance of the Chinese economy. However, Mao did not believe that it was possible to maintain a high and constant rate of development through such measures. Rather, he believed the development of society proceeded through a wave-like form of advance, in which periods of rapid development alternated with periods of consolidation in which gains made during periods of rapid advance would be strengthened and broadened. The Great Leap Forward thus represented a period of rapid advance, which would of necessity be followed by a period of consolidation. At the Chengdu Conference of 1958, Mao referred to this wave-like form of advance as follows:

> Under the general line of going all out and aiming high to achieve greater, faster, better and more economical results, a wave-like form of progress is the unity of opposites, deliberation and haste, the unity of opposites, toil and dreams. If we have only haste and toil, that is one-sided. To be concerned only with the intensity of labour—that won't do, will it? In all of our work, we must use both deliberation and haste...This means also the unity of hard fighting with rest and consolidation. [26]

Mao's Views on the Family

At the time of the Great Leap Forward, Mao reiterated his belief that the importance of the family would decline as the organisation of production altered with the increasing socialisation of society:

> Under socialism private property still exists, the small group still exits, the family still exists. The family, which emerged in the last period of primitive communism, will in future be abolished...Historically, the family was a production unit, a consumption unit, a unit for the procreation of the labour force of the next generation, and a unit for the education of children. Nowadays the workers do not regard the family as a unit of production; the peasants in the cooperatives have also largely changed, and peasant families are generally not units of production...In short, the family may in future become something which is unfavourable to the development of production... After maybe a few thousand years, or at the very least several hundred years, the family will disappear. [27]

Indeed, several policies of the Great Leap Forward had the explicit intention of accelerating the disappearance of the family and increasing the social importance of larger cooperative units. These included the establishment of communal mess halls, nurseries, kindergartens and boarding schools in order to free women from domestic duties to allow their participation in production. It was hoped that this would aid in 'obliterating the role of family head and the bourgeois authoritarian ideology in respect to family relations'. [28] These policies, were, however, quickly abandoned as the Great Leap Forward ran into difficulties, and according to one authority, the renewed radicalism of the Cultural Revolution did not witness a further attempt to reform or change family organisation and functions. [29] Thus, while Mao may have echoed the Marxist antipathy towards the family, there was little serious attempt during the 1950s and 1960s to eradicate it. The family would disappear, Mao believed, but its disappearance would involve a lengthy process, one which might occupy 'thousands of years' and involve the total elimination of the class-based organisation of production which had necessitated the original emergence of the family as an economic and social unit.

Mao on Marxism

It is evident from Mao's writings of the late 1950s and early 1960s that he remained convinced that Marxism's universal truths had to be united with Chinese realities in order for Marxism to have any utility in the Chinese context. In April 1956, Mao reaffirmed that the 'study of universal truth must be combined with Chinese reality. Our theory is made up of the universal truth of Marxism-Leninism combined with the concrete reality of China.' [30]

In 'A Talk to Music Workers' (August 1956), Mao returned to the point made in 'On the New Stage' (1938), that China, as a particular instance of historical development, manifested universal laws of development in its own specific way. He likened this variation in the particular manifestation of universal laws to the leaves of a tree; 'at first sight they all look much the same, but when you examine them closely, each one is different; to find two absolutely identical leaves is impossible.' [31] In a speech to the Ninth Plenum of the Eighth Central Committee (1961), Mao was to apply this 'tree' analogy directly to Marxism, and once again his purpose was to indicate that Marxism's universal laws did not and could not presume how such laws might assume concrete form in a particular historical context:

Marxism-Leninism is basically one (*genben yiyang*) with

different twigs and leaves, like a single tree that has many twigs and leaves. Circumstances vary in different countries. In the past we suffered from having paid attention to universal truths without paying attention to investigation and study. [32]

In asserting the Chinese example to be a particular manifestation of universally valid laws, Mao was once again insisting that Chinese Marxism (despite its success within China) could *not* be assumed to have any necessary relevance in other historical contexts. While Chinese Marxism incorporated experience which Marxists in other countries might find useful, it could not be automatically transplanted into a foreign context as though it constituted a body of universal truths unconstrained by national particularities. In a discussion with representatives of Latin American Communist Parties in September 1956, Mao emphasised that they should utilise Chinese experience selectively and only where it clearly corresponded to the characteristics of their own countries:

> The experience of the Chinese revolution, that is, building rural base areas, encircling the cities from the countryside and finally seizing the cities, may not be wholly applicable to many of your countries, though it can serve for your reference. I beg to advise you not to transplant Chinese experience mechanically. The experience of any foreign country can serve only for reference and must not be regarded as dogma. The universal truth of Marxism-Leninism and the concrete conditions of your own countries—the two must be integrated. [33]

Mao therefore continued to believe that Marxism, as a complete ideological system, was constituted of a body of universal laws plus particular 'laws' specific to each historical situation. The particular 'laws' would alter as the context altered. The universal laws of Marxism, however, could not be changed.

Mao's differences with Khrushchev grew out of a complex matrix of historical factors, one of which was a disagreement over what constituted the universal and unalterable laws of Marxism. At the XXth Congress of the CPSU, Khrushchev had suggested that the transition from capitalism to socialism could now, because of a change in world conditions, come about through nonviolent means; violent revolution no longer constituted the indispensable medium through which the transition had to be achieved. There could now be a peaceful transition to socialism, this peaceful transition coming about through the gaining of a parliamentary majority by socialist and communist parties in capitalist and ex-colonial countries. [34]

Khrushchev's notion of a peaceful transition to socialism via the parliamentary road offended Mao's Marxism in several ways. Firstly, Khrushchev's heavy reliance on the parliamentary assemblies within capitalist social systems was an abrogation of the universal law of Marxism which declared that the state was a class state functioning to protect the economic interests of the dominant economic class. It also suggested a misunderstanding of the historical significance of such parliamentary assemblies; for the parliament was not the locus of power within capitalist systems, nor did it necessarily comprise the dominant feature of the state apparatus. Mao believed that should a socialist or communist party eventually secure a majority in parliament, the rules of the game would be redrawn by the ruling class to ensure a hollow victory for the forces of reform. In a talk to a delegation from the Japan Socialist Party in 1964, Mao insisted that they would never achieve power through parliamentary means; and should it look as though they would, the ruling class would redraw electoral boundaries, alter the constitution, declare their party illegal—whatever it took to prevent them from taking power. It was therefore useless to talk about 'reform' of the capitalist system or its state, for the state (which was for Mao an institution of class violence) had to be smashed through violence and recreated by the forces of progress to serve their own interests. For this reason, all talk of 'structural reformism' was useless and based on a complete misunderstanding of the nature of the state. The fact that the state had at its disposal the armed forces with which to crush any possible threat made any such reformism impossible:

> The first aspect of the superstructure, the basic and principal thing, is the armed forces. If you want to reform them, how do you go about it? An Italian[Togliatti?] put forward this theory, and said that the structures must be reformed. Italy has an army and police force of several

hundred thousand; what method can be used for their reform?...You and I are of one mind on this, we don't believe in structural reformism. [35]

Secondly, Khrushchev's accent on the peaceful nature of
this transition was for Mao a clear departure from the Marxist
view that the ruling class in any society would never relinquish
power without an intense struggle; 'the bourgeoisie', Mao declared, 'will never hand over state power of their own accord,
but will resort to violence'. [36] Consequently, those who would
seize state power had to employ the violence of revolution. For
Mao, it was almost inconceivable that a peaceful transferral of
power could be achieved, and it is because of this that the relationship between revolution and the seizure of state power
persisted in his thinking. Khrushchev's belief that the eventual
world-wide victory of socialism could come about via 'peaceful
competition' between the socialist and capitalist blocs was thus
regarded by Mao as a clear revision of Marxism.

Mao was therefore constrained to reject the notion of a
peaceful transition to socialism via the parliamentary road for it
represented a departure from several of the universal laws of
Marxism. Khrushchev was guilty of 'revisionism' for he had tam-
pered with laws which, because of their universal status, could
not be altered. Needless to say, the laws of Marxism 'revised' by
Khrushchev were those designated as universal by Mao himself;
that Khrushchev did not perceive such laws as universal and beyond revision was beside the point. By the same token, Khrushchev regarded Mao as an unbending 'dogmatist' unwilling to
alter features of Marxism which history had demonstrated as no
longer of utility. The disagreement was therefore over what constituted the universal laws of Marxism, and it is clear that Mao
perceived himself as having a correct appreciation of such essential truths. With Khrushchev's 'revision' of laws deemed universal, it must have appeared to Mao that he was now the only
Communist leader faithfully safeguarding the purity of the
Marxist ideological heritage.

Mao's Marxism and the Cultural Revolution

We have already noted that the concept of contradictions
comprised a most important element of the manner in which
Mao interpreted Chinese society. The contradictions which em-

erged could be of two types—antagonistic and non-antagonistic—and it was possible for the latter to develop into the former if not handled correctly. There was, therefore, given the multi-class character of the Chinese 'people', a constant potential for non-antagonistic contradictions to turn into antagonisms requiring a violent struggle for their resolution. That Mao perceived such a potential for antagonism within Chinese society is indicated by his response to the failure of the Hundred Flowers Movement; because the contradiction between the CCP and the intellectuals had not been handled correctly, it had become antagonistic and had resulted in a struggle which necessitated recourse to repression and coercion.

The concept of 'permanent revolution', which was constructed on the basis of the theory of contradictions, also suggested a perception of historical development which incorporated a belief in continued upheavals and periods of struggle within society as it advanced towards communism.

Mao's perception of the nature of society and social development thus predisposed him to accept the possibility that there could be large-scale struggles during the socialist transition as new challenges and contradictions emerged. In addition, several specific elements of Mao's analysis of Chinese society led to a conviction that a struggle of revolutionary dimensions was unavoidable if the goals of the Chinese revolution were not to be vitiated. Let us look briefly at these specific elements.

Firstly, Mao held a rather distinctive view of the function of the superstructure within society. By 'superstructure', Mao meant the political, ideological and cultural aspects of society. These were by and large a reflection of the economic base; feudal class relations, for example, giving rise to feudal ideology and political institutions. Developments within the economic base were reflected eventually within the superstructure. Mao did not believe, however, that such reflection was necessarily immediate or entirely automatic. By the end of the 1950s, much of the ownership system of the Chinese economy (the principal aspect of the economic base) had been transformed into socialist or semi-socialist types. In terms of orthodox Marxist theory, one might expect that the superstructure of Chinese society would consequently alter to reflect this fundamental transformation of the economic base. Mao recognised that this process of superstructural reflection had not been satisfactorily accomplished. By way of explanation, Mao suggested that there tended to be a time lag between the transformation of the economic base and consequent modifications to the superstructure. Ideas and attitudes of some sections of the population clung stubbornly to the past; political institutions became bureaucratically conservative and less than responsive to developments within the economy. The superstructure could thus come to constitute a log-jam which impeded the further development of the economic base through ideological conservatism and institutional inertia.

Mao did not, however, perceive the superstructure as an undifferentiated social category. There were those whose ideology faithfully reflected developments within the economic base, and it was their mission to challenge the conservative ideology of others. Changes within the economic base were therefore reflected unevenly throughout the superstructure, and it consequently became an arena for struggle. Only through a satisfactory resolution of that struggle could the superstructure be brought into line with its economic base. This process of ensuring faithful superstructural reflection of developments within the economic base would continue without cessation as economic advances necessitated renewed assaults on conservative aspects of the superstructure.

Mao thus perceived the superstructure as an important and at times vital arena in the struggle to realise a socialist society. During the early 1960s, Mao came to the realisation that negative ideological and cultural features of China's feudal society stubbornly persisted amongst sections of the population. This would require an extensive campaign of ideological struggle to weaken the hold of the force of habit within Chinese society. Such a campaign would differ from the struggles of the past in which the clash of classes at an economic level had been the dominant form. As Mao was to point out:

> ...the form of the struggle is different as the era is different. As to the present, the social and economic systems have changed, but the legacy of the old era remains as reactionary ideology in the minds of a relatively large number of people. The ideology of the bourgeoisie and the upper stratum of the petty bourgeoisie will not change at a stroke. Change may take time, and a long period of time at that. [37]

Secondly, Mao's belief that a struggle of revolutionary dimensions might be needed was also fostered by his perception that a 'new bourgeoisie' was emerging within Chinese society. Mao's preoccupation with the emergence of a 'new bourgeoisie' developed during the early 1960s. In his important January 1962 speech, Mao asserted that 'in socialist society new bourgeois elements continue to emerge', [38] and in *The First Ten Points* (1963), Mao complained that 'in addition to the old bourgeoisie who continue to engage in speculation and profiteering activities, there also emerge in today's society new bourgeois elements who have become rich by speculation'. [39]

Moreover, Mao declared to an Algerian Cultural Delegation in April 1964 that there were many such 'new bourgeois elements' within the CCP itself. [40] Mao's belief that a 'new bourgeoisie' could emerge within socialist society raises important implications for Marxist theory; for if the ownership system had been basically transformed into a socialist type, how was it possible for such a class to emerge? Mao's answer was that the emergence of a 'new bourgeoisie' was largely a product of the relations of production and ownership system itself. China's ownership system was still not yet completely socialist, and was characterised by three different property types; ownership by the state, ownership by the collective, and individual ownership. This differentiation in the ownership system was regarded by Mao as an important factor facilitating the emergence of a 'new bourgeoisie'. [41] However, to fully understand Mao's position on this issue, it is necessary to refer to his views on the 'dual nature' of China's peasantry. The peasants were, Mao believed, by virtue of their economic position and class outlook, petit-bourgeois in character. [42] As small producers, they retained a certain ambivalence (or 'dual nature') towards the socialisation of property, and this ambivalence would persist until the realisation of a system of ownership by the whole people (that is, by the state) in the rural areas. [43] Until that time, the peasants would, Mao remarked drily, 'remain peasants'. [44] In the communique of the Tenth Plenum of September 1962, some of these small producers were attributed with producing a 'spontaneous tendency toward capitalism', [45] and in Mao's actual speech at the Tenth Plenum, it is made clear that the persistence of the petit-bourgeoisie (which itself was made possible by a continued differentiation in the ownership system), [46] was a significant factor in the production of a 'new bourgeoisie':

> We can now affirm that classes do exist in socialist countries and that class struggle undoubtedly exists. Lenin said: After the victory of the revolution, because of the existence of the bourgeoisie internationally, because of the existence of bourgeois remnants internally, because the petit bourgeoisie exists and continually generates a bourgeoisie, therefore the classes which have been overthrown within the country will continue to exist for a long time to come and may even attempt restoration. [47]

Mao's perception of the emergence of a 'new bourgeoisie' was, therefore, largely a function of his belief that while there continued a differentiated ownership system which maintained both the peasantry as a class and its 'dual nature', the socioeconomic factors existed for the generation of individuals who gravitated towards a form of economic activity characteristic of an incipient bourgeoisie; profiteering and speculation, the exploitation of hired hands, engaging in usury, and the buying and selling of land. [48]

Mao's views on the emergence of a 'new bourgeoisie' were closely allied to his belief that classes and class struggle would continue to exist throughout the socialist transition. The struggle between the classes would be fought out on various fronts, either within the economic base, or the superstructure of society. The important point is that the ingredients existed within Chinese society for a revolutionary struggle; class formations whose relationships might become antagonistic, and a superstructure, large sections of which were out of step with developments in the economic base. These elements of Mao's thought, plus his views on 'permanent revolution', underpinned his belief that it was necessary to continue the revolution under the dictatorship of the proletariat. The theory of 'continuing the revolution' (*jixu geming*) was never developed by Mao, but was elaborated by some of his radical supporters (branded the 'gang of four' after Mao's death) and served as a theoretical justification for the radical policies pursued during the Cultural Revolution and the early 1970s. [49] Zhang Chunqiao in particular argued that it was necessary during the socialist transition to restrict 'bourgeois right' (a concept explained in Chapter 1). Without the restriction of 'bourgeois right' social inequalities, rather than diminishing, would grow, and without a continuous revolution under the dictatorship of the proletariat, the bourgeoisie would reemerge to vitiate the goals of the revolution and take China along the road to capitalism. Only through continual suppression of capitalist tendencies and emerging inequalities, and the purging of 'capitalist roaders', could a capitalist restoration be prevented and socialism achieved. And this state of 'continuous revolution' would have to be maintained until the economic base had been transformed into a fully socialist form. [50]

As the 1960s progressed, Mao became increasingly convinced that the contradictions characterising Chinese society were becoming antagonistic, and that only through a violent struggle could they be satisfactorily resolved. Moreover, Mao was convinced that these contradictions within the wider context of Chinese society were reflected within the CCP itself, and that the party would consequently become one of the arenas for struggle.

The struggle which eventually broke out in 1966 in the form of the Cultural Revolution is of significance in the context of a discussion of Mao's Marxism for several reasons. Firstly (and as with the theory and practice of the Hundred Flowers movement), Mao indicated his willingness to depart from an essential feature of Leninism by not only launching an attack on the party, but by mobilising non-party elements as the spearhead of that attack. For Lenin, the party represented the vanguard of the working class, its most advanced and politically conscious section. In the Leninist conception, there is no suggestion that the vanguard party might itself become an agency for retrogressive ideas, policies or actions which might threaten the attainment of the revolutionary goals of the working class. Mao, however, appears to have made no presumption that the party was above and beyond the struggles taking place elsewhere in society. Contradictions and class struggles occurring in society were reflected within the party, leading to the possibility that the party could be characterised by negative and counter-revolutionary elements. Such elements had to be struggled against, and if their position within the party was so powerful that they could not be dislodged by an intra-party struggle, then it was necessary to mobilise progressive forces from the wider community to dislodge them. During the years of the Cultural Revolution, Mao led a coalition of non-party elements (students, youth, the military) in his attack on those within the party who 'had taken the capitalist road'.

However, although Mao demonstrated a rather different appreciation of the vanguard status of the party than had Lenin, it remains true that Mao would not permit the final destruction of the party. In 1967, radicals proposed a reorganisation of China into communes modelled after the Paris Commune. Mao refused to allow such a reorganisation, for it was not clear to him what the role of the party would be in such a federation of communes. [51] Moreover, following the Ninth Party Congress in April 1969, Mao set about rebuilding the party along orthodox Leninist lines.

Secondly, Mao argued (in the context of the Cultural Revolution and his polemic with the Soviet Union) that it was possible for a socialist system to degenerate into a capitalist form; this degeneration occurring through a process of 'peaceful evolution'.[52] The notion of a 'peaceful evolution' from a socialist (or basically socialist) society into capitalism bears serious implications for Marxist theory. It suggests that Mao no longer viewed the development of society through socialism to communism as inevitable. Indeed, if we examine Mao's speeches and writings of the Cultural Revolution period, it appears evident that there is a considerable lessening in the degree of historical optimism which had formerly marked his perception of society's progression through time. The future is now perceived as a series of gargantuan struggles, the outcome of which cannot be certain; and the concept of a communist society of peace and harmony is now no longer present in Mao's thought:

> The victory or defeat of the revolution can be determined only over a long period. If it is badly handled there is always the danger of a capitalist restoration. All members of the party and all the people of our country must not think that after one, two, three or four great cultural revolutions there will be peace and quiet. They must always be on the alert and must never relax their vigilance. [53]

It would appear that the Cultural Revolution so influenced Mao that he was no longer optimistic about the possibility of achieving a communist society; there was always the danger of a 'capitalist restoration'.

In addition to this decline in historical optimism, the notion of a 'peaceful evolution' to capitalism is difficult to accommodate within Mao's theory of contradictions. The fact that Mao indicated that such a 'peaceful evolution' could lead to a restoration of capitalism suggests that such a major qualitative transformation could come about through merely quantitative means, and without the struggle which Mao had perceived as characterising the relationship between aspects of a contradiction. There would thus appear something of a theoretical gap between this concept and the notion of overt struggle that would need accompany the 'conspicuous change' between aspects of the principal contradiction leading to a qualitative transformation of society. One gathers the impression that the concept of 'peaceful evolution' represented something of an improvised formula devised by Mao to explain a contingency not readily incorporated within the framework of his conception of historical causation or his theory of contradictions. This is especially the case when we remember that Mao had refused to entertain the notion that there might be a peaceful transition from capitalism to socialism, and had accused Khrushchev of revisionism for suggesting such a possibility; yet here was Mao suggesting a possibility seemingly equally incompatible with the Marxist conception of historical development.

Thirdly, the documents of the Cultural Revolution raise the question whether Mao continued to believe his contributions to Marxism to have been only in the area of analysing the particular 'laws' of Chinese society. Prior to the Cultural Revolution, Mao himself had laid no claim to having added to the universal laws of Marxism; he had admonished visiting revolutionaries not to mechanically apply the experience of the Chinese revolution in their own countries, for even though it had been successful, the specific nature of Chinese society and the Chinese revolution precluded its exact replication in another context. Mao's own analysis of the particular 'laws' of the Chinese revolution was not, therefore, of universal status, and could be employed in other countries only with discretion and with a sensitivity to their specific features. In the documents of the Cultural Revolution, however, the impression is given that Mao's contribution to Marxism had transcended its specific relevance to Chinese society and the Chinese revolution, and that it had assumed a universal stature describing laws of universal relevance. [54] There can be no doubt that this was an integral feature of the continuing polemic with Soviet leaders; by claiming a universal status for Mao Zedong Thought, the Chinese were laying claim to a prerogative over Marxism. Before 1956, that prerogative had been Moscow's; with Khruschev's 'revisionism' and the open split between the two parties, the Marxist apostolic succession had been diverted (so the Chinese liked to think) to those who had safeguarded its universal truths. The deepening hostility between the CPSU and the CCP led the Chinese to elevate Mao's thought to universal status in order to enhance their claims to be the genuine defenders of Marxism.

This elevation of Mao Zedong Thought to a universal status was a clear departure from Mao's long-standing practice of claiming only to have unravelled the specific 'laws' of Chinese society and the Chinese revolution. Whether Mao really believed his thought to be of universal status is a moot point; it may be of course that this was merely a clever tactical ploy in the feud with the Soviet leaders. At the very least, this claim to universality, being such a departure from Mao's previous practice, adds reinforcement to the argument that the Mao of the Cultural Revolution does not represent, as some interpretations would have us believe, the 'essential' Mao. Rather, certain elements of his thinking during this period clearly appear as aberrations when compared with his previous record.

Fourthly, during the Cultural Revolution Mao became the centre of an intense and widespread cult of personality. As with Stalin in the Soviet Union, Mao was projected to the Chinese masses as having god-like qualities, an infallible leader embodying the cause of the Chinese revolution and the aspirations of the Chinese people. Throughout China, statues and portraits of Mao proliferated; Mao's 'little red book' of quotations became a symbol of revolutionary purity with almost mystical powers; and Mao Zedong Thought was depicted as the solution to every problem. However, Mao's cult of personality was not as prolonged as that of Stalin, and it declined in intensity after the Ninth Party Congress of April 1969.

At the Sixth Plenum of the Eleventh Central Committee of the CCP in June 1981 (some five years after Mao's death), Mao's thought and actions during the Cultural Revolution were roundly condemned. Mao had ignored his own injunction 'to seek truth from facts', had overemphasised the acuteness of class struggle within socialist society, and had consequently led China into ten years of turmoil and chaos. A similar harsh judgement was made of Mao's attempt to forge a Chinese road to socialism during the late 1950s; Mao was guilty of overlooking 'objective economic laws' and had become 'impatient for quick results and overestimated the role of man's subjective will and efforts'. [55] Only Mao's contributions to the Chinese revolution up to 1949 and to socialist construction in the early 1950s are accorded unqualified praise.

Whether one agrees or disagrees with the judgement of the Sixth Plenum, there can be no doubt that Mao Zedong was one of the most imposing Marxist figures of the twentieth century. His attempt to solve the theoretical problem of Sinifying Marxism without detracting from its universality, and his formulation of an alternative strategy for development during the socialist transition, are clearly of great significance for Marxism in general, and in particular for the history of Marxism in Asia.

NOTES

1. Stuart Schram, for example, has referred to Mao's 'Sinification of Marxism' as his 'greatest theoretical and practical achievement'; see *Mao Tse-tung* (Penguin, Harmondsworth, 1966), p. 68.

2. See Mao's 'Preface' to *Socialist Upsurge in China's Countryside* (Foreign Languages Press, Peking, 1957), pp. 7-10.

3. For the text of the 'Secret Speech', see Dan N. Jacobs (ed.),*From Marx to Mao and Marchais* (Longman, New York and London, 1979), pp. 160-230.

4. H. Carrère d'Encausse and Stuart R. Schram, *Marxism and Asia: An Introduction with Readings* (Allen Lane, London, 1969), p. 283.

5. Benjamin I. Schwartz, *Communism and China: Ideology in Flux* (Atheneum, New York, 1970), p. 96.

6. Stuart Schram (ed.), *Mao Tse-tung Unrehearsed* (Penguin, Harmondsworth, 1974), p. 101.

7. J.V. Stalin, *Problems of Leninism* (Foreign Languages Press, Peking, 1976), p. 803.

8. Mao Tse-tung, *Selected Works* (4 vols., Foreign Languages Press, Peking, 1967), vol. 1, p. 318.

9. Ibid.

10. The original text of this speech can be found in Schram, *Mao Tse-tung Unrehearsed,* pp. 61-83. The official revised text is in Mao Tse-tung, *Selected Works* (Foreign Languages Press, Peking, 1977), vol. 5, pp. 284-307.

11. Schram, *Mao Tse-tung Unrehearsed,* p. 83.

12. *Selected Works,* vol. 5, pp. 384-421.

13. Ibid., pp. 385-6.

14. For Mao's views on the 'Hundred Flowers' campaign, see Ibid, pp. 366-71, 408-14.

15. Schram, *Mao Tse-tung Unrehearsed,* p. 94.

16. Ibid., p. 95.

17. Jerome Ch'en (ed.), *Mao Papers: Anthology and Bibliography* (Oxford University Press, London, 1970), pp. 62-3.

18. *Selected Works,* vol. 5, p. 338.

19. Ch'en, *Mao Papers,* p. 65.

20. Mao Tse-tung, *A Critique of Soviet Economics* (Monthly Review Press, New York and London, 1977), pp. 57-8.

21. *New China News Agency,* 1717 (31 December 1956), Suppt. 250, p. 23.

22. Mao Tse-tung, *A Critique of Soviet Economics,* p. 71.

23. *Mao Zedong sixiang wansui (Long live Mao Zedong Thought)* (n.p., Taiwan, 1967), p. 156.

24. Mao Tse-tung, *A Critique of Soviet Economics,* p. 51. Emphasis added.

25. See *Peking Review* no. 48 (November 27, 1970), pp. 14-17.

26. Schram, *Mao Tse-tung Unrehearsed,* p. 106.

27. Ibid., p. 116.

28. T'ien Sheng, 'The Outlook of Communism as seen from the People's Communes', *Political Study,* No. 10 (October 13, 1958), quoted in Richard Solomon, *Mao's Revolution and the Chinese Political Culture* (University of California Press, Berkeley, 1971), p. 341.

29. Andrew J. Watson, 'A Revolution to Touch Men's Souls: The Family, Interpersonal Relations and Daily Life', in Stuart R. Schram (ed.), *Authority, Participation and Cultural Change in China* (Cambridge University Press, Cambridge, 1973), p. 321.

30. Schram, *Mao Tse-tung Unrehearsed,* p. 82.

31. Ibid., p. 84.

32. *Mao Zedong sixiang wansui,* p. 262.

33. *Selected Works,* vol.5, p. 326.

34. See Carrère d'Encausse and Schram, *Marxism and Asia,* pp. 282-7.

35. *Mao Zedong sixiang wansui (Long live Mao Zedong Thought)* (n.p., Taiwan, 1969), p. 544.

36. *Selected Works,* vol. 5, p. 495.

37. Ch'en, *Mao Papers,* pp. 144-5.

38. Schram, *Mao Tse-tung Unrehearsed,* p. 168.

39. Richard Baum and Frederick C. Teiwes, *Ssu-ch'ing: The Socialist Education Movement of 1962-66* (Chinese Research Monographs, University of California, Berkeley, 1968), p. 61.

40. *Mao Zedong sixiang wansui* (1969), p. 488; see also p. 424, where Mao declared 'the bourgeoisie can reemerge (*xinsheng de*), and this is what happened in the Soviet Union'.

41. 'If there are three types of ownership there will be contradiction and [class] struggle.' *Critique of Soviet Economics,* p. 107.

42. *Selected Works,* vol. 5, p. 474.

43. *Mao Zedong sixiang wansui* (1969), p. 247.

44. Ibid.

45. Baum and Teiwes, *Ssu-ch'ing,* p.60. See also *Selected Works,* vol. 5, pp. 260-1.

46. *Peking Review,* no. 25 (21 June, 1963), p. 17.

47. Schram, *Mao Tse-tung Unrehearsed,* p. 189.

48. Baum and Teiwes, *Ssu-ch'ing,* p.61. For an alternative interpretation of Mao's views on the 'new bourgeoisie', see Joseph Esherick, 'On the "Restoration of Capitalism": Mao and Marxist Theory', *Modern China,* vol. 5, no. 1 (January 1979), pp. 41-78.

49. Chang Chun-chiao, 'On Exercising All-Round Dictatorship Over the Bourgeoisie', *Peking Review,* no. 14 (April 4, 1975), pp. 5-11.

50. For a detailed discussion of this theme, see John Bryan Starr, 'Conceptual Foundations of Mao Tse-tung's Theory of Continuous Revolution', *Asian Survey* vol. 11, no. 6, (June 1971) pp. 610-28. See also John Bryan Starr, *Continuing the Revolution: The Political Thought of Mao* (Princeton University Press,Princeton 1979), pp. 300-7.

51. See *Mao Zedong sixiang wansui* (1969), pp. 671-2; also Schram, *Mao Tse-tung Unrehearsed,* p. 278. See also Stuart R. Schram, 'The Marxist', in Dick Wilson (ed.), *Mao Tse-tung in the Scales of History* (Cambridge University Press, Cambridge, 1977), pp. 47-8.

52. Baum and Teiwes, *Ssu-Ch'ing,* p. 119.

53. Ch'en, *Mao Papers,* p. 139.

54. See particularly the references to Mao Zedong Thought in the Draft Party Constitution circulating towards the end of 1968; the text of this constitution is in *China Quarterly,* no. 37 (January-March 1969), pp. 169-73.

55. *Beijing Review,* no. 27 (6 July 1981), pp. 10-39.

SELECT BIBLIOGRAPHY

Ch'en, Jerome (ed.), *Mao Papers: Anthology and Bibliography* (Oxford University Press, London,1970). A useful compilation of Mao's letters, talks and instructions. Contains the important 'Sixty Articles on Work Methods' of January 1958.

Mao Tse-tung, *Critique of Soviet Economics* (Monthly Review Press, New York and London, 1977). A useful translation of Mao's criticisms of the *Soviet Manual of Political Economy.* This source sheds much light on Mao's disenchantment with the Soviet model of socialist construction.

Schram, Stuart (ed.), *Mao Tse-tung Unrehearsed* (Penguin, Harmondsworth, 1974). Contains translations of the unoffical versions of some of Mao's most important talks and letters from the late 1950's and 1960's.

Selected Works of Mao Tse-tung (Foreign Languages Press, Peking, 1977), vol.5. Incorporates the official version of many of the important Mao texts from the period September 1949 to November 1957.

Starr, John Bryan, *Continuing the Revolution: The Political Thought of Mao* (Princeton University Press, Princeton, 1979). A carefully documented analysis of nine major themes in Mao's thought which form the foundation of his theory of continuing the revolution under the dictatorship of the proletariat.

Wilson, Dick(ed.), *Mao Tse-tung in the Scales of History*(Cambridge University Press, Cambridge, 1977). A collection of ten essays on different aspects of Mao's political and intellectual career.

5

CHINESE MARXISM SINCE MAO
Colin Mackerras

The death of Mao Zedong on 9 September 1976 and the over-throw in the following month of the faction which had strongly supported the ideas of his later years have led to enormous changes in Chinese political, economic and social life. There has been a major attempt to reexamine Marxism to suit the new cir-cumstances. De-Maoification in the political economy has gone hand in hand with a changed interpretation of Mao Zedong Thought. No longer the system of philosophy attributed to the individual Mao, Mao Zedong Thought is now officially defined as 'Marxism-Leninism applied and developed in China', a sum-mary of experience which 'represents the crystallized, collective wisdom' of the CCP. [1] This formula greatly broadens the possi-bilities for the development of Marxist thinking in China, ac-knowledging a wide range of philosophers who have contributed to it and who may do so in the future. In contrast to the situation in the Democratic People's Republic of Korea (see Chapter 6), the issue of determining the basic theme of philoso-phy is not generally regarded as an overriding one. Most Marxist thinkers still accept that it lies in the dichotomy between matter and consciousness. [2]

Analyses of Historical Development

All Chinese Marxists of all periods claim to uphold historical materialism. However, this has not solved the debate over wheth-er the motive forces of history lie in class struggle or in the pro-ductive forces. The view supported by Mao's followers between 1966 and 1976 was that class struggle was decisive, that it would produce revolution which would in turn liberate the productive forces. The slogan was 'grasp revolution, promote production'. It was necessary to continue the revolution in the superstructure, even after the revolutionary classes had taken over ownership of the means of production; thus for a time the productive forces might not correspond with the relations of production.

Mao's supporters were not denying the role of the productive forces or rapid economic growth, but they did give primacy to class struggle which they believed would result in a flowering of the productive forces. After all, Marx and Engels had begun the first major section of *The Communist Manifesto* with the ringing statement that 'the history of all hitherto existing society is the history of class struggles'. [3]

With the fall of Mao, therefore, class struggle was in effect demoted in favour of economic progress as the 'key link' in Chinese politics. The communique of the Eleventh Central Committee's Third Plenum of December 1978, stated that 'the large-scale turbulent class struggles of a mass character have in the main come to an end' and decreed that the Party and people should shift their prime attention to socialist modernisation. It also observed that the implementation of the four modernisations 'requires great growth in the productive forces' and that 'those aspects of the relations of production and the superstructure not in harmony with the growth of the productive forces' would need to undergo major changes, [4] and was thus a major departure from the ideas current during the Cultural Revolution. This appeared to make class struggle an obstacle to the productive forces rather than their liberator.

Like their predecessors, however, the current CCP leadership also ties their analysis closely to the words of Marx. They cite, for instance, Marx's statement that 'at a certain stage of their development, the material productive forces of society come in conflict with the existing relations of production' and 'then begins an epoch of social revolution'. [5] This indeed appears to support the new emphasis for it implies that the productive forces and relations of production will again harmonise *after* the period of revolution.

From this perspective, class struggle under socialism does not disappear, but it does cease to be the primary issue. The view of the present leadership, expressed by the senior Marxist theorist Liu Danian holds that 'the advance of human society is, in the last analysis, determined by the development of productive forces'. As for class struggle, Liu contends that its status as the primary motive force for historical development 'refers mainly to the turbulent transformation from the old society, the old social system to a new society, a new social system'. [6] Class struggle thus becomes something which was vital in past eras, but is less relevant now. Moreover, the targets of the class struggle are no longer the exploiting classes themselves, but enemy agents, new exploiters who embezzle, steal, speculate and profiteer, or gang of four remnants, the chief ones being 'serious economic criminals'. [7]

Another argument used to reinforce the deemphasis on class struggle is the one which holds that the material needs and economic interests of human beings are the fundamental motive force of history. Two Chinese Marxists note that the real reason why the CCP made revolution was to improve the livelihood of the masses. It is in these terms that they discredit the Cultural Revolution:

> One of its results was that, despite their industrious labour..., the material and cultural life of the labourers underwent no corresponding improvement. Their reasonable needs did not reach minimum satisfaction. The productive forces made no advances, and even went backwards. In contrast to this, since the Third Plenum of the Party's Eleventh Central Committee, the Party Centre has corrected left errors in economic work, and clarified that the aims of socialist production are to the utmost extent to satisfy the constantly expanding material and cultural life needs of the whole of society. [8]

So the failure of the gang of four can be explained by an appeal to the theory of productive forces which is held to constitute the essence of Marxism. Class struggle becomes, in this view, 'merely a means for a class to realize its material or economic interests'. It is 'only a direct motive force of history, not the basic motive force'. [9]

Chinese Marxists, then, have come up with various interpretations of what constitutes the ultimate motive force or forces in history, and there are others which I have not considered here. But all can be interpreted as attempting justification for the general direction of Chinese politics since the Third Plenum. They tend to downgrade the class struggle and they directly or indirectly attack the Cultural Revolution. They also justify the transfer of full Party and governmental emphasis to socialist modernisation.

Up to this point consideration has been given only to those problems of a theory of history which have asked the question 'what?' But Marx also wrote in a famous passage that 'men make their own history', suggesting that 'who?' is a legitimate question. Marx went on to argue that people make history under circumstances transmitted from the past. [10] Both this statement and the whole concept of productive forces and class struggle and so on in the determination of history suggest that people must be seen as groups, not individuals.

No Chinese Marxist of the pre-1976 period formally denied that it is the masses, not individuals or leaders, who make history. But the constant and almost exclusive credit for the revolution which was given to Mao Zedong during the Cultural Revolution left the impression that his followers regarded him as a moulder of history in and by himself and not simply as the embodiment of the will of the proletariat.

From a theoretical point of view, the leaders of the Cultural Revolution made a big mistake in allowing the cult of Mao Zedong to reach the proportions familiar in the late 1960s and early 1970s. This has given the Marxists of the post-Mao years a golden chance to attack Maoism. On the academic plane, Pang Zhuoheng, among others, presents cogent reasons for arguing that it is 'the people' from whom the motive forces of history derive. [11] On a more popular level, an (unnamed) commentator in *People's Daily* (4 July 1980) acknowledges that in Marxist theory great characters may play a major role in history, but he attacks any exaggeration of the role of the individual. He points out that China's own Communist Party fell into the error of allowing one person to dictate the Party line.

Other writers have appealed directly to Marx's authority to justify their opposition to the cult of the individual. One author reminds his readers that when the first volume of *Capital* was published in 1867 'the bourgeois press tried silently to smother it', but 'the proletariat saw it as a strong ideological weapon for its own emancipation', so that many friends sent Marx congratulations. One correspondent passed on a view he had heard from a Berlin economics professor that 'its appearance was the greatest event of the century etc. etc.' Marx reacted strongly against such adulation. [12]

The developments just described in Chinese Marxism are obviously inspired by the political needs of de-Maoification. During the meetings leading up to the Third Plenum, conflict erupted between the 'whatever' (*fanshi*) and the 'practice' (*shijian*) factions over the evaluation of Mao Zedong. The 'whateverists' held that 'we firmly uphold whatever policy decisions Chairman Mao made, and we unswervingly adhere to whatever instructions Chairman Mao gave'. [13] The slogans of the other group were 'practice is the only standard for evaluating truth' and 'seek truth from facts'. The victory of the 'practice' faction led to the progressive discrediting of Mao's last years and the Cultural Revolution, and ultimately to formal attacks on Hua Guofeng, Mao's successor as Party Chairman, as a 'whateverist' at the Sixth Plenum of the Eleventh Central Committee in late June 1981.

While it is arguable that the major ideological documents of the Cultural Revolution placed far too much emphasis on Mao's role in the modern Chinese revolution, its followers appear generally to have applied a materialist view in their study of the centuries before the twentieth. Mao Zedong, above all, gave a very high evaluation to the role of peasant rebellions as progressive forces in Chinese history and true examples of class struggle.

The new post-Mao historiography takes a broader and more varied view which generally gives less importance to the peasant rebellions, and assesses them less positively. The fundamental reason is that 'in the old society, the peasants were scattered small-scale producers, they were not representatives of advanced modes of production'. [14] Even basically negative evaluations of peasant rebellions have appeared, arguing that such rebellions were unable to bring about production relations higher than those of feudal society; that they constituted no motive force because they obstructed the struggle for production; and that their thinking was too egalitarian. One historian has gone so far as to describe them as 'historical tragedies'.

Not surprisingly, such views have provoked response. As one scholar points out, the view that they were not a motive force negates the idea that class struggle was a motive force even in the history of feudal times. Egalitarianism in contemporary society may be attacked, but to deny its progressive role in the feudal period would be wrong because of the vastly more unequal conditions of those times. Far from being historical tragedies, he considers that 'peasant revolutions were inevitable and necessary', just as 'feudal production relations were inevitable and necessary'. He thus sees a necessary historical role both for feudalism and the forces producing the class struggle which seeks to bring feudal society forward into one with more advanced production relations. [15]

Continuing the Revolution

One of the most fundamental doctrines and justifications of the Cultural Revolution was the need for continuing the revolution (*jixu geming*). This doctrine, explained in detail in Chapter 4, held that the revolution was anything but complete with the accession of the CCP to power; it was necessary to continue the struggle against class enemies and the bourgeoisie within society more or less indefinitely. The Party itself, the vanguard of the proletariat, was not without bourgeois elements, hence the need to dismiss so many leading members. Mao also came to think that a new bourgeoisie was actually engendered after the victory of the Communist Party. His ardent follower Zhang Chunqiao, one of the 'gang of four', wrote of his anxiety because 'our economic base is still not firm'. More serious still was the situation in 'the various spheres of the superstructure' in some of which the bourgeoisie was still actually in control, so that old ideas and habits continued to obstruct the growth of socialism, even after the Cultural Revolution itself. [16]

In the early days after the fall of the 'gang of four' the theory of continuing the revolution and the prevention of bourgeois restoration remained intact. In his political report to the Eleventh National Congress of the CCP given on 12 August 1977, Hua Guofeng even described the 'theory of continuing the revolution under the dictatorship of the proletariat' as 'the most important achievement of Marxism in our time'. He also accepted, as Zhang had done, that there may be need for revolution in the realm of the superstructure so that it 'will correspond better with the socialist economic base'. [17] Above all he retained the notion of newly engendered bourgeois elements and of their presence within the Party. However, he attacked the 'gang of four' and others for wildly exaggerating the scope of the problem.

They had carried out their worst distortion by 'equating veteran cadres with "democrats" and "democrats" with "capitalist-roaders"', whereas Mao had 'explicitly pointed out that there were only a handful among the cadres in our Party'. [18] A few representatives could not be described as a bourgeois class within the Party.

By the beginning of 1978 the distinction drawn between the situations in the economic base and the superstructure had come under attack. 'It is inconceivable', wrote one Marxist ideologue, 'that shortly after building its own economic base, our socialist superstructure should ... be in disharmony with its base'. [19] The other main arms of the theory of continuing the revolution were unchanged.

It was the attack on the Cultural Revolution that led to the negation of the capitalist restoration concept. Statements opposing anything remotely in defence of the Cultural Revolution became more strident from the Third Plenum on, reaching a climax in its decisive official rejection at the Sixth Plenum of late June 1981.

Naturally, the Central Committee majority at the Sixth Plenum also formally discarded the theory which underpinned the Cultural Revolution. It attacked the thesis that bourgeois elements had found their way into the Party, government, army, and cultural circles and asserted that there 'were no grounds at all' for defining the Cultural Revolution as a struggle against the capitalist road. [20] It denied that small-scale production would continue to engender a bourgeoisie after the basic completion of socialist transformation. [21] Above all, it declared that 'class struggle no longer constitutes the principal contradiction after the exploiters have been eliminated as classes', [22] a happy state in which China found itself both at the time of the Cultural Revolution and of the Plenum. The idea that political revolutions in which one class overthrows another would recur in the future was also rejected. [23]

The Central Committee denounced the theory of 'continuing the revolution under the dictatorship of the proletariat' as Mao and his followers had understood it at the time of the Cultural Revolution. However, the members of the Central Committee upheld the theory as such. They reinterpreted it, however, to signify that revolutionary goals would be reached through a lengthy and orderly process without 'fierce class confrontation and conflict'. The aims of China's revolution were now set out to include the expansion of the productive forces, presumably both a by-product and a result of a successful modernisation programme, but also the elimination of 'all class differences and all major social distinctions and inequalities'. [24] When Party Secretary-General Hu Yaobang gave a long speech on 13 March 1983 commemorating the centenary of Karl Marx's death, he listed the abandonment of the theory of 'continued revolution under the dictatorship of the proletariat' as the CCP's major political achievement of recent years. [25] Clearly Hu Yaobang had in mind the Cultural Revolution's interpretation of this theory, not the Sixth Plenum's.

The long-range objectives of continuing the revolution remain basically unchanged, but the methods by which the followers of Mao and the new leadership of Deng Xiaoping expect to reach them are fundamentally different. A contemporary follower of the ideas of Mao in his last years would certainly have argued that current policies are exacerbating social distinctions and inequalities, not tending to eliminate them, but neither the Plenum nor Mao, nor indeed Marx, predicted when the society without major inequalities would arrive.

A precursor to the concept of 'continuing the revolution', which is similar but not identical to it, is that of uninterrupted revolution (*buduan geming*), explained in Chapter 4. One Western scholar argues that the link between the earlier 'uninterrupted revolution' and the later 'continuing the revolution' is 'the idea of intentional destabilization of the society as a means for realising revolutionary goals'. [26] So both these Maoist concepts are alike in being totally at variance with the theory proposed at the Sixth Plenum. Only one arm of Mao's thought on this subject has been praised and emphasised since the Third Plenum: that which calls for the technological revolution. [27]

Mao and his followers may well have worked out a more carefully formulated theory of uninterrupted revolution or 'continuing the revolution' than that achieved by his Marxist predecessors. It was a theory based upon the actual conditions he saw around him. Nevertheless, there are references to uninterrupted revolution in the works of Marx himself, and they have drawn comment from Marxists in China today.

The most famous passage occurs in *The Class Struggles in France 1848 to 1850*, written in 1850, and is worth quoting:

While this *utopia, doctrinaire Socialism*, which subordinates the total movement to one of its moments, which puts in place of common, social production the brainwork of individual pedants and, above all, in fantasy does away with the revolutionary struggle of the classes and its requirements by small conjurers' tricks or great sentimentality; ... wants to achieve its ideal athwart the realities of present society; ... the *proletariat* rallies more and more round *revolutionary Socialism,* round *Communism* ... This Socialism is the *declaration of the permanence of the revolution*, the *class dictatorship* of the proletariat as the necessary transit point to the *abolition of class distinctions generally*, to the abolition of all the relations of production on which they rest, to the abolition of all the social relations that correspond to these relations of production, to the revolutionising of all the ideas that result from these social relations. [28]

The Chinese use the term *buduan geming* for 'the permanence of the revolution', so this phrase and 'uninterrupted revolution' both translate into Chinese through the same characters.

The passage quoted above makes no reference to whether the bourgeoisie continues either to operate or to be engendered within the vanguard party after its victory, since Marx did not live to see a consolidated socialist state. But Marx scoffed at the type of socialism which aspired to avoid class struggle, although he did not make it clear how important he expected class struggle to be *after* the establishment of the dictatorship of the proletariat. Moreover, the phrase 'declaration of the permanence of the revolution' has a ring about it which accords nicely with either of Mao's two concepts.

Contemporary Chinese Marxists have not skirted the apparent problems in reconciling Marx with current viewpoints. Several explanations have emerged. One, put forward by Xin Zhongqin and Xue Hanwei, argues that the idea of uninterrupted revolution characterised only one phase of Marx's career. The object of the passage quoted from *The Class Struggles* was 'not specially to expound and prove uninterrupted revolution, but to explain the essential differences between revolutionary socialism and empty socialism'. [29] This is true, but hardly comes to grips with why Marx listed the declaration of the permanent revolution as the first hallmark of genuine proletarian socialism.

Another line of argument has been to ask what precisely Marx meant by the 'genuine socialism' which declares the permanent revolution. True, he listed four of its characteristics, but he did not state at which stage of social development it would fall. Xin Zhongqin and Xue Hanwei claim that he was talking about the period *before* the victory of the socialist revolution. [30] Applied to China this would mean that uninterrupted revolution became irrelevant with the establishment of the People's Republic of China. One scholar, Xu Jingze, has challenged this view directly, arguing that Marx's phraseology shows that 'the uninterrupted revolution does not stop with the time when the proletarian dictatorship is established, but permeates the whole period of the proletarian dictatorship'. Marx, he believes, was referring to the period 'right down to when all classes are thoroughly eliminated in the economic, political, ideological and social spheres'. [31] Applied to China, this includes not only the democratic revolution but also the socialist period, up to and beyond the present. Xu Jingze does not define the concept of uninterrupted revolution, but presumably would understand by it a vision much closer to the Sixth Plenum's than to Mao's, either of the late 1950s or the Cultural Revolution.

Social Inequalities - Bourgeois Right

The Sixth Plenum removed from the theory of uninterrupted revolution one of the principal features which Mao had included in it during the Cultural Revolution. This was that continuous campaigns would be necessary to maintain the purity of the revolution and to prevent backsliding. One key concept of the last years of Mao's leadership revolved around Marx's theme of 'bourgeois right', a term explained in Chapter 1. The movement to limit bourgeois right took place principally in 1975, and raised a number of issues which continued to arouse great interest in the years after the fall of the 'gang of four'. As in so many other areas, *formal* adherence to Marxism has remained while the political line on the specific issues has changed fundamentally. Mao is charged with having misunderstood Marx's exposition on bourgeois right, while Zhang Chunqiao and the 'gang of four' are accused of having wilfully distorted it. [32]

In 1975 the 'gang of four' argued clearly that inequalities

would grow unless the Party attempted to restrict bourgeois right. This was indeed one of the factors which they believed would engender a new bourgeoisie. The only way to prevent the exacerbation of the inequalities was to strengthen the dictatorship of the proletariat.

The central issue was not the existence of inequalities; all Chinese Marxists accepted that inequalities could lawfully exist. What mattered was whether they grew or shrank. Restricting bourgeois right meant pressing for the latter tendency. Certain forms of material incentive were denounced as leading to the former.

It was not long after the fall of the 'gang of four' that these ideas came under attack. As early as the Eleventh Party Congress in August 1977, when the general theory of the Cultural Revolution was still intact, Hua Guofeng had already denounced the 'gang of four' for 'waving the revolutionary banner of "restricting bourgeois right"' in order to describe the 'differences in distribution' between the leading Party, army and government cadres on the one hand and the masses on the other as tantamount to class exploitation. [33]

As from 1 October 1977 half the workers of China were given a wage rise for the first time since before the Cultural Revolution. In later months the trend towards material incentives accelerated and bonuses, overtime, piecework and so on were reintroduced. A theory to justify these changes began to crystallise in 1978. The Constitution adopted by the First Session of the Fifth National People's Congress on 5 March 1978 stipulated that 'the state applies the socialist principles: "He who does not work, neither shall he eat" and "from each according to his ability, to each according to his work"'. [34] Meanwhile a press campaign emphasised the correctness of these principles according to Marxist criteria.

Rather than arguing that bourgeois right, if unrestricted, would widen, the new ideologues stressed that it was not only acceptable but could exist *only* in a socialist society because no exploitation survived there. 'The prerequisite for the enforcement of the principle "to each according to his work" is the public ownership of the means of production'. It follows from this reasoning that bourgeois right is desirable at the present stage of development. It cannot possibly engender capitalism or a new bourgeoisie. Eventually the communist principle enunciated by

Marx, 'from each according to his ability, to each according to his needs', will be implemented, but not for many generations. [35]

Another arm of the new argument was to defend the whole idea of material interests through an appeal to the works of Marx, Engels, Lenin and Mao. I have already noted that economic material interests were seen by some Chinese Marxists as the main motive force of history, but the aim in combating the 'gang of four's' attitude towards bourgeois right was to show that the classical Marxists advocated material interests as desirable. If workers do not receive material benefits, their labour enthusiasm will suffer. [36]

Another element was added to the discussion when Hua Guofeng declared at the Second Session of the Fifth National People's Congress on 18 June 1979 that the exploiting classes had ceased to exist in China. He said:

Owing to the adoption of correct and reasonable measures, supported by the vast majority of the people, the feudal and capitalist systems of exploitation have already been abolished, the system of small-scale production has been transformed, and the socialist system has been through rigorous tests and established its own firm rule. The landlords and rich peasant classes have been eliminated as classes. Under the historical conditions of our country, the capitalists are a part of the People's Republic of China. Our government adopted a correct policy towards them of buying them out and has successfully transformed capitalist industry and commerce. The capitalists no longer exist as a class. [37]

So all the claims of the 'gang of four' that small-scale production would help engender a new bourgeoisie were said to be groundless because of its elimination through popular means. Unlike the 'gang of four', Hua was confident that the socialist system was firmly established. Since there are no Chinese exploiting classes, the argument for struggle against them loses force. There is no reason to strive for equality if the forces preventing it have mainly vanished.

At about the time of the Twelfth Party Congress of September 1982 a new emphasis on class struggle developed as part of a political movement against 'the corrosive influence of bourgeois ideology' and other backward systems of thought. However, it is most important to note that the trend quite explicitly maintained the notion that exploiting classes such as the national bourgeoisie, let alone the landlords, no longer existed. Class struggle was to be directed against hostile elements in society, and should be as peaceful as possible. 'Compared with the past class struggle, the disruptive activities of these hostile elements are a mere remnant of class struggle'. [38] In other words, there is absolutely no question of further cultural revolutions or of any turbulence which could impede modernisation.

Chinese ideologues now argue that Marx's description of the distribution of the product of labour is essentially what prevails in China, and Marx's defence of bourgeois right justifies the analogous situation. But what of the question of trend? The official response is that 'the differences will gradually be narrowed with the development of the productive forces and labourers' skills, as well as with the general enhancement of their scientific and cultural levels', [39] though no evidence of this is offered. It is arguable that measures such as the increase of sideline production raises the living standards of the peasantry and hence relieves social inequalities. However, developments in other countries would appear to suggest that the elimination of classes is not likely to be the end result of current Chinese policy.

What the Chinese have done is to give up systematically seeking social equality by redistribution of class and regional income. They have devised a theory based on Marx to justify present inequalities and to convince the masses that equality must come eventually.

Even more striking is the fact that Chinese Marxists have come to talk about a timetable, albeit still a vague one. In a speech of December 1982, no less a person than the Head of the Party Central Committee's Propaganda Department, Deng Liqun, stated:

> Recently, we criticized the theory that 'communism is dim and remote'. Some comrades have argued that what they meant was that the higher stage of communism was dim and remote. True, it will require the efforts of several generations to reach the higher stage of communism. But we must acknowledge that we have entered the initial stage of communism. [40]

Deng Liqun goes on to argue that already Chinese society contains elements of Marx's 'higher stage of communism', one example being that there are many Party members who regard labour as life's prime want. In the light of history 'several generations' is hardly remote if what is predicted is the higher stage of communism. It is far more optimistic and specific than the statements of Mao or his Cultural Revolutionary followers.

The Paris Commune, the Masses and Peasantry

Marx had raised the problem of social equality not only in his doctrine of bourgeois right, but also in his discussion of the Paris Commune (see Chapter 1). Marx drew attention to some aspects of its administration he believed should be followed.

On 29 February 1980 the Fifth Plenum of the Eleventh Central Committee adopted a communique which declared that the members had discussed the draft of the revised CCP Constitution. Among a number of new provisions on the party's cadre system was one putting 'an end to the practice of being a lifelong cadre'. [41] Article 37 of The Constitution adopted by the Twelfth Party Congress in September 1982, incorporating the provision, stated that leading Party cadres at all levels are 'not entitled to lifelong tenure, and they can be transferred from or relieved of their posts'. Cadres who are old or in bad health should retire, the Article declared. [42]

Part of the ideological justification for this policy comes from the Paris Commune. One writer summarises the history of revolutionary attitudes towards administrators. He notes with approval that the officials of the Commune had been subject to recall and received the same wages as workers; as well as Engels' dictum, which he wrongly ascribes to Marx, that these policies prevented the 'servants of society' from turning into the 'masters of society'. After quoting Lenin to the same effect he concludes: 'from this we can see that to abolish the life-long tenure system which actually exists in cadre posts is in total accordance with what Marxism-Leninism teaches on the cadre problem'. [43] The writer cites no evidence that the Paris Commune developed a policy on lifelong tenure. Moreover, he does not use its example to suggest that Chinese cadres should receive the same wages as workers or be subject to recall. Nevertheless, he is surely right to stress that cadres 'must make up their minds, no matter under what circumstances, to serve the people to the end'; and to suggest that Marx and Engels saw and supported such an attitude in the Paris Commune.

'Serving the people' was also a Maoist slogan and implied the mass line. Despite its departure from so many of Mao's ideas favoured during the Cultural Revolution, the Sixth Plenum came out with a strong and unequivocal restatement of the mass line. 'Isolation from the people', it declared, 'will render all the Party's struggles and ideals devoid of content as well as impossible of success'. The Party must rely on the masses and serve them wholeheartedly. [44]

But this does not mean that all mass movements are desirable. The historian Li Yuanming took the opportunity of the 110th anniversary of the Paris Commune to consider the attitudes of Marx and Engels towards it and other mass movements. Although he retains a generally positive evaluation of the Commune as a mass movement, he is also at pains to point out that Marx was not wholly supportive of its aims and behaviour and was quite prepared to 'undertake a calm analysis' of it, in other words criticise its failings. Marx and Engels were very discriminating in their attitude towards mass movements in general, and Li Yuanming cites specific cases which they strongly opposed.

The lesson for the present is as follows:

> Mass movements of differing natures exist in the same way under conditions of socialism. Therefore we should likewise make specific analyses of them. We should fully support those which in general push forward the development of the history of society and the productive forces. But we should also make a clear-headed analysis of certain defects and abuses which the movements manifest, and point them out warmly so that the mass movements can develop healthily along a correct road. As to those mass movements which impede the development of the history of society and the productive forces and even play a retrogressive role, no matter whether they are spontaneous, or launched from above or below, we should not only 'shake our finger' at them, but also ... take up a clear stand against them. This alone is the Marxist attitude. [45]

Although Li does not say so in so many words, the most obvious example of his last category is the Cultural Revolution, so the weight of Marx and Engels is being indirectly enlisted against it.

Where does all this leave the role of the masses? It is still affirmed as positive both as a historical force and as a current one. But in history it is hemmed around with reservations which cannot but detract from it. Despite the positive statement of the Sixth Plenum, the power of the masses is more explicitly subjected to directors, executives, technicians and experts now than was the case at least in theory in Mao's later years. 'We do not need, nor should we launch tempestuous mass movements as those in the past', wrote one ideologue just before the Twelfth Party Congress. He ruled out any mass movement 'in the present struggle against economic criminals', adding that 'instead, we will rely on legal procedures'. [46] In fact, the mass line may survive, but with quite clearly reduced emphasis, priority and status.

In China, the largest part of the masses is the peasantry. The high evaluation which Mao gave to their role in society and the revolution is discussed in earlier chapters. In his last years his view was symbolised in the praise lavished upon the Dazhai Brigade in Shanxi Province.

After the Third Plenum a study group was sent to Dazhai to investigate it. As a result, in mid-1980 the model was discredited and the provincial Party committee even accused of corruption in promoting it. An official opinion emerged as to the lessons to be learned from the Dazhai fiasco. One of them, that 'the scope of class struggle must not be arbitrarily enlarged', repeats a point that has come forward several times already in this chapter. Another bears on the whole question of the status of the peasantry in society: although their political consciousness has risen greatly since liberation, 'the peasants have a long tradition as small producers and this must not be overlooked'. It is wrong not to heed their material rewards and compensations, or to take away their private plots. A serious way of violating their interests is arbitrarily to switch 'the system of ownership without regard to the degree of development of the forces of production'. [47]

The differing function of the idea of small-scale production in works by the Maoist radicals of the mid-1970s and thinkers since 1976 is worth noting. The former followed Lenin in seeing petty-commodity production as the source which engenders capitalism and the bourgeoisie. The dictatorship of the proletariat must act against it to preserve the revolution, [48] which otherwise small-scale production may destroy. The new official theoreticians have changed the thrust completely. While agreeing that small-scale production is a force for conservatism they single out the peasants as particularly susceptible to its influence. This becomes a reason for allowing a partial return to private production and family farming in the countryside. In other words one concept is used by one group to implement the very policies which the other, appealing to the same notion, wished to prevent.

The new theories downgrade the peasantry as a revolutionary force. They attack the commune system, because they imply that the forces of production in rural China were not ready for the change in the system of ownership when the communes were set up. The production responsibility system in the countryside formalises and implements the new ideas on the peasantry and reverses the commune policy. In his speech commemorating the centenary of Marx's death Hu Yaobang listed the changes in the countryside as one of the main improvements in China in the past few years and an implementation of the Marxist principle of 'to each according to his work'. Socialism, he said, had been consolidated and 'is taking big strides forward in our rural areas'. He also attacked any adherents to an alternative view as 'half-baked critics'. [49]

Humanitarianism, The Family

The change in attitudes towards the peasantry is part of the general retreat from the Cultural Revolution. Another very important aspect is the discussions on the relationship between humanitarianism (*rendaozhuyi*) and Marxism. These began just after the Third Plenum took the lid off official criticism of the Cultural Revolution as such, as distinct from just the role of the 'gang of four' in it.

There are basically two approaches to the subject of humanitarianism. One is that humanitarianism is a fundamentally different stream of thought from Marxism, because Marx emphasised not human nature or humanity but human social relations and classes. Humanitarianism derived from the European Renaissance and arose at almost exactly the same time as capitalism. In the light of these arguments it can be characterised as a bourgeois system of thought. [50] This view of humanitarianism has declined in influence among Chinese Marxists in recent years. It is redolent of the sort of view on humanitarianism which prevailed during the Cultural Revolution. The major reason why the adherents of the Cultural Revolution opposed humanitarianism as anti-Marxist was because they perceived it as ignoring, and hence attacking, the key link of class struggle.

It is the demotion of class struggle from its position as 'key link' that allows for the dominant attitude, namely that Marxism, far from being opposed to it, is essentially and tightly linked to philosophical humanitarianism.

This line begins by looking at humanitarianism as a broad phenomenon. The term refers not to the specific humanism (renbenzhuyi) so closely associated with the European Renaissance, but to the general idea that one should regard human beings according to the dignity of their species and treat them in a way appropriate to their value.

The dominant view emphasises that Marx gave humankind an extremely central place in his philosophy. An important article by Xue Dezhen in *People's Daily* (25 April 1981), entitled 'The status of "man" in Marxist philosophy', demonstrated how high and valuable it was by reference to such passages as that in Marx's 'Introduction' to his *Contribution to the Critique of Hegel's Philosophy of Law* where he applauds the 'theory which proclaims man to be the highest being for man'. [51] '"Man" is the starting point of Marxist philosophy', states Xue, 'and also its objective'. Other authors, [52] leading to a similar conclusion, cite the almost identical wording elsewhere in the same work that ' *man is the highest being for man*' and Marx's consequent call ' *to overthrow all relations* in which man is a debased, enslaved, forsaken, despicable being' (italics in original). [53]

One writer claimed early in 1983 that, in the past three years, there had been over 400 academic papers written in China on Man, 'of which a great many had explored Marxist humanitarianism', thus emphasising the importance of the subject. He attaches great political significance to the new philosophic development for several reasons. Humanitarianism will help socialist modernisation because it opposes such excesses as the 'overall dictatorship' found in the Cultural Revolution, 'and maintains the equality of all people before truth and the law'. Moreover, it 'acknowledges that man is the end not only of socialist production, but of all work'. It also opposes privilege and the worship

of material wealth; and 'places weight on education, the fostering of talent and the overall development of man'. [54] He is saying that not only is humanitarianism indeed Marxist, but it is an
essential arm of the philosophy which will tie Chinese society
together in the interests of modernisation, so that Chinese people
will not only grow richer together, but also treat each other better. In this view social equality derives not from class struggle
but from humanitarianism.

Marx was at pains to point out the difference between the
idealist notion of the abstract man, as espoused by philosophers
like Hegel, [55] and his own of the material, real man who lives
within a society and belongs to a class. Chinese Marxists have
generally followed him in denying the existence of 'the ordinary
man' (*yibande ren*) or of a 'human nature' existing beyond
classes. [56]

One feature of Marx's approach to humanitarianism was
his theory of alienation, which received very little attention in
China during the Cultural Revolution and succeeding years. [57] It
was not until August 1980 that public discussion began with an
important and full-page article in *People's Daily* (15 August
1980) by a Marxist writing under the pen-name Ru Xin. The author recapitulates Marx's ideas on the dehumanisation of labour
in capitalist countries and refutes any suggestion that humanitarianism might be revisionist. He warns that to ignore this aspect of
Marxism could bring about a new form of alienation. 'Have
there not been lessons of this kind in the history of the international communist movement?' he asks, in a fairly clear reference
to the Cultural Revolution. Indeed partly because of that movement's effects, alienation is perceived in China still to exist in
China today. Society stands at the socialist stage, not the communist, and thus the influences of feudalism and capitalism
persist. [58] The theory of socialist alienation, however, has not
been unreservedly accepted. In particular, it was officially criticised in the second half of 1983 because of its implication that
exploitation still existed in China today.

During the Cultural Revolution, of course, Mao regarded
the family as an important feudal institution to be abolished. In
September 1980, however, a new Marriage Law was adopted. It
reaffirmed the family revolution of the 1950s in the sense of
abolishing the feudal family system and maintaining the illegality
of such feudal practices as arranged marriages and concubinage.

The law also made divorce somewhat easier than it had been. [59] The new Marriage Law, however, made it clear that the Chinese government had no intention of moving towards the abolition of the family as such. This was supported as usual by reference to Mao's own work. On 26 December 1983, in commemoration of the ninetieth anniversary of Mao's birth, a number of his letters were published for the first time. One of these letters dealt with the family, advocating a transformation of the feudal family in conjunction with social mass movements without, however, envisaging the eventual disappearance of the family. [60] In the countryside the basis of the attempt to enrich the peasantry is the production responsibility system by which groups or individuals reach contracts with the commune management for specific tasks; in fact, many of these groups are family based. In 1981 the All-China Women's Federation sponsored a movement to select 'happy families', the criteria being such 'fine traditions of the Chinese family' as harmonious family relations and reverence for the old. [61] What all this means is that the family has strengthened in China recently, both as a social and even economic unit, both in policy or theory and in practice.

Equality between the sexes is still laid down by law. The 1982 Chinese Constitution stipulates that women 'enjoy equal rights with men in all spheres of life, political, economic, cultural and social, including family life'. [62] In the urban regions women have made some headway, with government approval, in entering the professions and power-holding positions on a par with men. In the countryside, however, the competitiveness associated with the production responsibility system and the importance of people as 'labour units' have increased the economic and social gap between men and women, partly because peasants perceive the former as muscularly stronger and hence more productive. The consequent downgrading of females has been serious enough to lead to the recurrence of some iniquitous practices eliminated after 1949, even including female infanticide and the abuse of mothers who give birth to daughters. [63]

Conclusion

Whatever the social results, there has clearly been a substantial broadening in the Chinese approach to Marxism since the Third Plenum. To judge from what they write, Chinese Marxists show greater familiarity with the works of Marx and Engels now than was ever the case during the decade 1966 to 1976. Far more scholars have written theoretical articles in a much wider range of journals and newspapers. Their publications not only quote far more from Marx and Engels but from a broader range of their works. Whole new areas of thought, such as alienation and Marx's humanitarianism, have come up for discussion. There are still limitations: support for the Cultural Revolution is impermissable; and also contemporary Chinese Marxists rarely cite the works of their European contemporaries, but then neither did the Chinese Marxists of the 1966 to 1976 era. Mao Zedong, on the other hand, is quoted with dramatically reduced frequency.

Together with this broadening has come a greater emphasis on formal attempts to encourage research into Marxism. For example, in mid-1981 a symposium specifically devoted to research on volume II of *Capital* took place in Fuzhou, capital of Fujian Province, with over 100 people attending. It had a particular political-economic purpose, and 'emphasised discussing Marx's theories on reproduction and their significance as guides to our country's socialist construction'. [64] To coincide with the centenary of Marx's death in March 1883, Beijing University held a conference on 'Marxism and Man', in which some 100 theoreticians and scholars from 65 institutions took part. [65] Academic conferences on such topics were notable for their absence during the Cultural Revolution, and their convention shows greater activity in research on Marxism in China today.

The rise in status of intellectuals has facilitated the broadening of Marxist thinking, and is indeed itself an aspect of Marxist ideology. Hu Yaobang gave them considerable emphasis in his speech commemorating the centenary of Marx's death, declaring it to be 'imperative that we oppose the erroneous tendency of separating intellectuals from the working class'. Not a special class by themselves, they have definitely become members of the working class, despite the differences in their forms of labour from those of workers and peasants. Hu called for intellectuals to receive greater material remuneration than 'those who do manual labour or whose scientific and educational level is relatively low'. [66]

One feature of the Cultural Revolution decade under particular attack is its dogmatism. The discussions on approaches to the motive forces of history, the continuing revolution and humanitarianism indicate that a range of views on particular topics is not only possible but encouraged, provided it does not overstep the mark of support for the Cultural Revolution.

The political negation of the Cultural Revolution is part and parcel of the ideological criticism of Mao in his last years. The CCP still adheres formally to Mao's thought, as the Sixth Plenum made clear. But it insisted on making a 'distinction between Mao Zedong Thought... and the mistakes Comrade Mao Zedong made in his later years'. [67] This separates the Mao Zedong of the Cultural Revolution and later from Mao Zedong Thought. What has happened in fact is that Chinese Marxists have renounced virtually all that Mao advocated in his late years. The discussions on the continuing revolution and bourgeois right bear out this assertion. The major exception is Mao's doctrine on the mass line, but the reservations expressed on mass movements in history and on the Paris Commune suggest that, even here, contemporary understanding differs somewhat from Mao's. Such is the extent of the negation of his last years that Chinese ideological circles no longer regard the Cultural Revolutionary Mao as a genuine Marxist. Mao 'imagined that his theory and practice were Marxist', states the communique of the Sixth Plenum; 'herein lies his tragedy'. [68] Chinese Marxists appeal to Marx himself to discredit the personality cult which Mao once unwisely allowed to develop around him.

The most important single idea which has changed with the demotion of the late Mao is in the evaluation and reinterpretation of class struggle. No longer the 'key link' from the time of the Third Plenum, it has changed meaning and come to rank lower in the minds of Chinese Marxists than it once did. The Constitution adopted by the Twelfth Party Congress declared as follows:

> After the elimination of the exploiting classes as such, most of the contradictions in Chinese society do not have the nature of class struggle, and class struggle is no longer the principal contradiction. However, owing to domestic circumstances and foreign influences, class struggle will continue to exist within certain limits for a long time, and may even sharpen under certain conditions. [69]

Although the Party Congress foresees the possibility that class struggle may sharpen in the future, the whole tenor of this

statement is to downgrade its significance. The domestic circumstances and foreign influences which maintain class struggle do
not mean the survival of exploiting classes but corruption in society, especially economic criminals as well as 'newborn counter-
revolutionaries and enemy agents sent in from outside'. [70] In
virtually all ideological areas discussed in this chapter, the current line has been influenced by the demotion and reinterpretation of class struggle. In considering the motive forces of history
much weight can be transferred to the role of the productive
forces or elsewhere. The significance of mass rebellions or mass
movements declines, whether it be of the peasants in China or
the workers in the Paris Commune. It is no longer necessary or
even desirable to restrict bourgeois right. 'Continuing the revolution' becomes a question of modernisation and expanding technology. Humanitarianism becomes an important component of
Marxism, not one to arouse suspicion and distrust.

The reevaluation of the status of class struggle accords well
with the renewed emphasis on stability which followed immediately upon the fall of the 'gang of four'. In fact, the ideological
change succeeded and resulted from the political, not the other
way around. The same conclusion follows in virtually all other
areas of Marxist thought. The political line demanded more
freedom to apply material incentives, so the ideological justification came to back it up; arguments were found in Marx himself
why it was good and useful to care for the people's material interests. Economic pressures required promoting directors and experts, so the new ideologues found reasons, again from Marx
himself, why social inequalities need not be prevented from
growing, at least for the time being. The same line of thought
could be recapitulated from any section of this chapter.

In any event, the Chinese still claim to be Marxists. Indeed
they argue they are more so than ever, because primary authority
in Marxist ideology has been transferred from Mao Zedong to
Marx, where surely it rightfully belongs. Few would wish to take
issue with that. But it is ironical to find Marxism used to justify
two such different political ideologies as that of the Cultural
Revolution on the one hand and, on the other, that of the period
since the Third Plenum of December 1978.

NOTES

1. 'Constitution of the Communist Party of China', *Beijing Review* (hereafter *BR*), vol. 25, no. 38 (20 September 1982), p. 8.

2. For example, see Wang Pengling, 'Three Issues Concerning Dialectical Materialism', *BR*, vol. 26, no. 21 (23 May 1983), p. 17.

3. *Karl Marx and Frederick Engels Selected Works* (3 vols., Progress, Moscow, 1969-70), vol. 1, p. 108.

4. 'Communique of the Third Plenary Session of the 11th Central Committee of the Communist Party of China', *BR*, vol. 21, no. 52 (29 December 1978), p. 11.

5. 'Preface' to 'A Contribution to the Critique of Political Economy', *Selected Works*, vol. 1, pp. 503-4.

6. Liu Danian, 'Class Struggle is the Motive Force in Private Ownership Society', *BR*, vol. 23, no. 35 (1 September 1980), pp. 14-15.

7. Zhou Yan, 'On China's Current Class Struggle', *BR*, vol. 25, no. 33 (16 August 1982), p. 19.

8. Yin Jizuo and Yao Bomao, in *Guangming ribao (Guangming Daily)*, 11 June 1981.

9. Yan Zhongkui, 'Material or Economic Interests of Mankind', *BR*, vol. 23, no. 35 (1 September 1980), p. 17.

10. 'The Eighteenth Brumaire of Louis Bonaparte', *Selected Works*, vol. 1, p. 398.

11. 'The Marxist Theory of the Motive Force of History and its Significance Today', *Social Sciences in China, A Quarterly Journal*, vol. 1, no. 4 (December 1980), p. 169.

12. *Renmin ribao* (hereafter *RMRB*), 4 September 1980.

13. 'On Questions of Party History - Resolution on Certain Questions in the History of Our Party since the Founding of the People's Republic of China', *BR*, vol. 24, no. 27 (6 July 1981), p. 26.

14. Chen Mingkang and Zheng Zemin, in *Guangming ribao*, 27 July 1981.

15. Yang Bing, 'Zhongguo fengjian shehui nongmin zhanzheng de lishi zuoyong' ('The Historical Role of the Peasant Wars of Chinese Feudal Society'), *Shehui kexue yanjiu (Social Science Research)*, no. 4 (1982), reprinted in *Xinhua wenzhai (New China Digest)*, no. 10 (25 October 1982), pp. 65-7.

16. 'Lun dui zichanjieji de quanmian zhuanzheng' ('On Exercising All-Round Dictatorship over the Bourgeoisie'), *Hongqi* (*Red Flag*), no. 4 (1 April 1975), p. 8.

17. *Peking Review* (hereafter *PR*), vol. 20, no. 35 (26 August 1977), p. 31.

18. Ibid., pp. 32, 33.

19. Wu Chiang, 'The Tasks of Continuing the Revolution Under the Dictatorship of the Proletariat', *PR*, vol. 21, no. 3 (20 Janurary 1978), p. 7.

20. 'On Questions of Party History', pp. 20, 21.

21. Ibid., p. 25.

22. Ibid., p. 37.

23. 'Continuing the Revolution', *BR*, vol. 24, no. 34 (24 August 1981), p. 3.

24. 'On Questions of Party History', p. 39.

25. *China Daily, Karl Marx Commemorative Supplement*, 14 March 1983.

26. John Bryan Starr, *Continuing the Revolution, The Political Thought of Mao* (Princeton University Press, Princeton, 1979), p. 303.

27. See Mao's article, dated January 1958, on 'Uninterrupted Revolution', *BR* , vol. 22, no. 1 (5 Jan. 1979), p. 11. The article is actually the twenty-first of

Mao's 'Sixty Points on Working Methods'. See Jerome Ch'en (ed.), *Mao Papers, Anthology and Bibliography* (Oxford University Press, London, 1970), pp. 62-4.

28. *Selected Works*, vol. 1, pp. 281-2. Italics in original.

29. 'Zai tan Makesi de buduan geming lun' ('More on Marx's Theory of Uninterrupted Revolution'), *Wen shi zhe (Literature, History, Philosophy)*, no. 3 (1981), reprinted in *Xinhua wenzhai*, no. 8 (25 August 1981), p. 34.

30. *RMRB*, 19 June 1980.

31. 'Ye tan "shehuizhuyi jiushi xuanbu buduan geming" - yu Xin Zhongqin, Xue Hanwei er tongzhi shangque' ('More on "Socialism is the Declaration of the Uninterrupted Revolution" - Consultations with Comrades Xin Zhongqin and Xue Hanwei'), *Wen shi zhe*, no. 1 (1981), reprinted in *Xinhua wenzhai*, no. 8 (25 August 1981), p. 32.

32. For example, see Shi Zhongquan, 'What is Meant by "Bourgeois Right"?', *BR*, vol. 24, no. 52 (28 December 1981), pp. 11, 20.

33. 'Political Report to the 11th National Congress of the Communist Party of China', *PR*, vol. 20, no. 35 (26 August 1977), pp. 35-6.

34. *PR*, vol. 21, no. 11 (17 March 1978), p. 7.

35. Li Hung-lin, 'To each According to His Work: Socialist Principle in Distribution', *PR*, vol. 21, no. 7 (17 Feburary 1978), p. 7.

36. See *RMRB*, 12 September 1978, and abridged translation in 'How Marxists Look at Material Interests', *PR*, vol. 21, no. 41 (13 October 1978), pp. 5-10.

37. *RMRB*, 26 June 1979. See also 'Report on the Work of the Government', *BR*, vol. 22, no. 27 (6 July 1979), p. 9, where an alternative translation is given.

38. *Jiefang jun bao (Liberation Army Daily)*, 9 Oct. 1982, as translated in 'Scientifically Understand and Handle Class Struggle in China', *BR*, vol. 25, no. 49 (6 December 1982), p. 19.

39. Shi Zhongquan, 'What is Meant by Bourgeois Right?', p. 11.

40. 'The Initial Stage of Communism', *BR*, vol. 26, no. 5 (31 January 1983), p. 21.

41. *BR*, vol. 23, no. 10 (10 March 1980), p. 8.

42. *RMRB*, 9 September 1982, as translated in *BR*, vol. 25, no. 38 (20 September 1982), p. 19.

43. Wu Liping, 'Ganbu zhidu shang yixiang zhongda de gaige' ('A Major Reform in the Cadre System'), *Hongqi*, no. 11 (1 June 1980), pp. 6-7.

44. 'On Questions of Party History', p. 34.

45. 'Zhengque renshi Bali gongshe de lishi jingyan' ('Correctly Understanding the Historical Experience of the Paris Commune'), *Hongqi*, no. 6 (17 March 1981), pp. 24-5.

46. Zhou Yan, 'On China's Current Class Struggle', p. 19.

47. Zhou Jinhua, 'Appraising the Dazhai Brigade', *BR*, vol. 24, no. 16 (20 April 1981), p. 28.

48. For instance, see Zhang Chunqiao, 'Lun dui zichanjieji de quanmian zhuanzheng', p. 4.

49. *China Daily, Karl Marx Commemorative Supplement*, 14 March 1983.

50. See Cui Wenyu in *RMRB*, 19 October 1981. See a summary of Cui's article in 'Discussion on Humanism', *Ta Kung Pao*, no. 799 (29 October 1981), p. 10.

51. Karl Marx and Frederick Engels, *Collected Works, Volume 3* (Lawrence and Wishart, London, 1975), p. 187.

52. Zhang Kuiliang, Bi Zhiguo and Wang Yalin, 'Lun shehuizhuyi shehui ren de jiazhi wenti' ('On the Problem of the Value of Man in Socialist Society'), *Xuexi yu tansuo (Studies and Explorations)*, no. 1 (1981), reprinted in *Xinhua wenzhai*, no. 4 (25 April 1981), p. 24.

53. *Collected Works, Volume 3*, p. 182.

54. Ruoshui, in *Wenhui bao*, 17 Janurary 1983. See also an English summary of the article in *China Daily*, 23 Feburary 1983.

55. For example, see his attack on Hegel on this point in *The Holy Family*, in Karl Marx and Frederick Engels, *Collected Works, Volume 4* (Lawrence and Wishart, London, 1975), p. 192.

56. See Cui Wenyu, in *RMRB*, 19 October 1981.

57. See Donald J. Munro, 'The Chinese View of "Alienation"', *The China Quarterly*, no. 59 (July/September 1974), pp. 580-2.

58. Zhang Kuiliang, Bi Zhiguo and Wang Yalin, 'Lun shehuizhuyi shehui ren de jiazhi wenti', p. 26.

59. 'Quarterly Chronicle and Documentation', *The China Quarterly*, no. 84 (December 1980), p. 803.

60. See the letter to Qin Bangxian, dated 31 August 1944, in *Mao Zedong shuxin xuanji (The Selected Letters of Mao Zedong)* (People's Press, Beijing, 1983), pp. 237-9.

61. *BR*, vol. 24, no. 22 (1 June 1981), pp. 7-8.

62. 'Constitution of the People's Republic of China', *BR*, vol. 25, no. 52 (27 December 1982), p. 17. The Constitution was adopted on 4 December 1982.

63. See the summary of the report to the Fifth National Women's Congress in September 1983 by Kang Keqing, Chairwoman of the Executive Committee of the All-China Women's Federation, in *BR*, vol. 26, no. 38 (19 September 1983), p. 6.

64. *RMRB*, 6 July 1981.

65. *Ta Kung Pao*, no. 874 (21 April 1983), p. 3.

66. *China Daily, Karl Marx Commemorative Supplement*, 14 March 1983.

67. 'On Questions of Party History', p. 35.

68. Ibid., p. 23.

69. *BR*, vol. 25, no. 38 (20 September 1982), p. 9.

70. 'Scientifically Understand and Handle Class Struggle', p. 18.

SELECT BIBLIOGRAPHY

Beijing Review. A weekly official view of China in English. It contains numerous documents and articles, including some on current Marxist ideological debates.

China Daily. The PRC's first English-language daily which began publication on 1 June 1981. It sometimes includes articles on Marxism.

Mackerras, Colin, 'Chinese Marxism Since 1978', *Journal of Contemporary Asia*, vol. 12, no. 4 (1982), pp.387-414. The present chapter is an updated and abbreviated version of this earlier article.

Makesizhuyi zhexue yuanli (Principles of Marxist Philosophy) (People's Press, Tianjin, 1981). A textbook of Marxism published recently in the PRC and a good example of contemporary understanding of Marxism there.

Marx, Karl, *Capital, A Critique of Political Economy Volume One* (Vintage Books, New York, 1977). A standard English-language edition of Marx's most carefully worked out book.

'On Questions of Party History—Resolution on Certain Questions in the History of Our Party Since the Founding of the People's Republic of China', *Beijing Review*, vol. 24, no. 27 (6 July 1981), pp.10-39. The official view adopted by the Sixth Plenum of the 11th CCP Central Committee on 27 June 1981. This enormously long communique contains extremely valuable material on official Chinese Marxism in the last few years.

Social Sciences in China. The English version of the journal of the Chinese

Academy of Social Sciences. It began publication in March 1980 and appears quarterly. Among those articles of relevance to Marxist thinking since 1976 are Pang Zhuoheng, 'The Marxist Theory of the Motive Force of History and its Significance Today', vol. 1, no. 4.

Xinhua wenzhai (New China Digest). A monthly digest of Chinese-language material drawn from an amazing variety of PRC periodic literature. It always includes ideological articles, especially on Marxist thought.

6

THE *JUCHE* IDEA AND THE THOUGHT OF KIM IL SUNG
Colin Mackerras

The earliest Korean Marxist group, the Korean People's Socialist Party, was formed in 1918, ironically not in Korea itself but in Khabarovsk in the far eastern region of Siberia. In January 1921 it was renamed the Communist Party of Koryo, and grew rapidly with branches, not necessarily united, in Siberia, Shanghai, Korea and Manchuria. In the Democratic People's Republic of Korea (DPRK) of the 1980s, the Marxists of the early 1920s are branded as 'pseudo-communists who indulged in empty talk and failed to strike roots among the masses'. [1]

Marxism was given an impetus by the famous March 1st Independence Movement, so called because on 1 March 1919 a declaration of independence was read seeking to free Korea from its status as a Japanese colony, which it had held since 1910. The March 1st declaration was followed by demonstrations which attracted thousands of citizens and students in Seoul and many other centres throughout the country. The movement was brutally suppressed but, like its May 4th counterpart in China, contributed to the deep roots of nationalist sentiment among the Koreans.

Although the Marxist movements were extremely factionalised in the 1920s this was a period of growing consciousness among the workers as well as students and peasants. Between 1920 and 1925 there were over 330 workers' strikes, a particularly important one being the general (workers') strike by over 5,000 transportation workers in Pusan in September 1921 in demand for better working conditions. The Comintern took some interest in the Korean revolution; Korean delegates took part in its Second and Third Congresses in 1920 and 1921 as well as in the First Congress of the Toilers of the Far East the following year. However, the role of the Comintern through the rest of the 1920s was not significant. [2]

Just as in other parts of Asia, the emergence of peasant guerrillas against the Japanese was a very important aspect of the growth of Marxism-Leninism in Korea. The communists found great support among the masses by fanning and exploiting an anti-Japanese feeling. The most important of the guerrillas, although not the only one, was Kim Il Sung, himself of peasant background and with revolutionary antecedents. With brief exceptions Kim lived in Manchuria from 1925 to 1945, but did build a major reputation as a focus of hostility to Japanese colonialism in Korea.

Kim himself wrote in 1965 that the armed struggle against the Japanese had caused Marxism-Leninism to become 'intertwined with the realities of our country and the communist movement with the revolutionary struggle of our people for national and social emancipation'. [3] This is really another way of saying that he saw himself as produced by the nationalism of the Koreans against Japan. Some Western scholars have taken a more cynical view. Gregory Henderson, for instance, writes that 'the Soviets picked Kim, for reasons still obscure, to receive a hero's welcome' in Pyongyang on 10 October 1945, and goes on to describe Kim's provisional administration founded at the end of the war as 'obviously a puppet government' of the Soviet Union.[4] The Soviet troops which entered the northern part of Korea at the end of the war are nowadays ignored in the DPRK museums, which wish to emphasise a history of independence; but they were nevertheless of great value to Kim. Likewise, the Henderson view overlooks the immense popular support Kim had gained through his guerrilla activities against the Japanese, whether carried out in Manchuria or Korea itself.

Meanwhile, United States troops entered south Korea on 8 September 1945. The Soviet forces in the north tolerated the neutralist People's Republic of Korea, which had been established in August with its capital in Seoul, as well as the spontaneous people's committees which answered to it. The US troops, on the other hand, forcefully suppressed both government and committees in the south. Kim's return to Pyongyang and the establishment of the Korean Workers' Party, which still rules the

DPRK, both occurred in October and followed the US suppression of the unified government. [5]

In the founding of rival governments it was the south which took the lead, at least in chronological terms. In June 1948, the Republic of Korea was set up in the south, but it was not until 9 September that it was followed by Kim Il Sung's DPRK.

Since this chapter is not about Korean history, there is no need to recapitulate the development of the DPRK beyond saying that Kim Il Sung has encountered some fairly stiff opposition in the Workers' Party of Korea. He has repressed it savagely and appears to dominate the Korean state and party like a colossus. By his seventieth birthday, in April 1982, he had already begun taking very active steps to ensure a smooth succession after his passing from the political scene. His chosen successor is his son Kim Jong Il.

The DPRK state is based upon the philosophy of the *juche* idea. Kim Jong Il claims that it was in 1930 that his father 'put forward a Juche-oriented line for the Korean revolution' and that this 'historical event....heralded the creation of the Juche idea'. [6] Kim Il Sung's first clear enunciation of it came in a 'speech to Party propagandists and agitators' on 28 December 1955, [7] not very long after the Korean war (1950-3) had resulted in the virtually total destruction of the country. The move reflected the dominance of Kim Il Sung and did not come without severe opposition. One DPRK historian writes that 'the anti-Party factionalists, flunkeys and dogmatists, swallowing foreign things whole and copying them mechanically, opposed overtly and covertly our Party's independent lines and creative policies which embodied the Juche idea'. [8] So the official view was that opposition to *juche*, undoubtedly real, stemmed from unnecessarily heavy support on foreign ideas as opposed to the notion of independence which is inherent in *juche*. It was not until after a conference of the party's representatives in October 1966, that the DPRK 'began to assert the concept of *chuch'e* [*juche*] as the single ideological system'. [9]

Although in the DPRK, Kim Il Sung is universally given credit for authorship of the *juche* idea, he is on record as saying: 'We are not the author of this idea. Every Marxist-Leninist has this idea. I have just laid a special emphasis on this idea'. [10]

The *juche* idea is nevertheless equated in the DPRK with

Kimilsungism and Kim's stamp upon it is unquestioned. It is a body of thought on which much material is available and its importance in one half of Korea today entitles it to fairly detailed treatment here. It is the only accessible form of Marxist thought in Korea.

As explained to me during a personal interview with an offically sanctioned social scientist, Kim Chi Gun, in September 1982, the *juche* idea goes beyond Marxism in that it shifts the basic problem of philosophy from whether matter or idea is primary to the relationship of humankind to the world. It answers the question by asserting the total primacy of people. It is they who play the decisive role in changing nature and society. *Juche* holds people, matter and spirit to be interlinked, but humans are always in the leading position. 'Man alone is capable of transforming the world. It is man and none other that requires its transformation and performs this work'. [11] Humans are social beings with three essential characteristics: independence, creativity and consciousness.

Independence (*chajusong*) is both individual and collective. It involves the individuals' awareness of themselves and their ability, and the way in which they are integrated into society as a whole. However, in practice Koreans very rarely stress the *chajusong* of a single person but almost always that of groups, especially large ones.

Independence means that the masses must oppose submission to great powers and that humankind must assert its superiority over nature as an ability to control it. Humans must control their own destiny. It also means that the masses must give play to their enthusiasm for labour to create a better world for themselves. This cannot be done by force. Enthusiasm thus plays a vital role in the revolution. Of course it must suit actual conditions which differ from place to place and time to time; but the idea is that the will of people can accomplish an enormous amount.

Creativity enables humankind to render the transformation of nature and society 'more useful... by changing the old and creating the new'. Whereas *chajusong* 'finds expression mainly in man's position as master of the world; creativity is expressed mainly in man's role as transformer of the world'. As for the third attribute, consciousness, it guarantees that humankind 'understands the world and the laws of its motion and development'. It hence buttresses the other two basic characteristics of humankind 'and ensures his purposeful cognition and practice'.[12]

Among other elements of the *juche* idea Kim Jong Il points to one that stands out as critically important. To acquire genuine independence, creativity and consciousness humankind requires wise leadership. The former are not natural but social attributes of man; consequently, wise leadership is indispensable to their development. Kim Chi Gun further expanded on the idea of leadership when he talked about the creative ability of the masses as not being spontaneous in itself but nevertheless a force which given the proper impetus and guidance by enlightened leadership could be harnessed to accomplish greater deeds. He elaborated even further by the use of an historical event, namely the Japanese occupation, which stifled Korean creativity until 1945 when wise government emerged to lead the masses onto a new historical plane.

Kim Jong Il wrote on the occasion of the centenary of Marx's death:

> In a revolutionary movement of the working class, the leader plays the decisive role. As early as the initial period in the history of the international communist movement this valuable truth was proved by the activities of Marx. If Marx, the first leader of the working class, had not founded Marxism for the international working class, they would have groped in darkness, not knowing their historic mission, nor could they have triumphed in their revolutionary struggles. [13]

Thus, Kim Jong Il uses Marx to present his case. However, he does not cite Marx's authority; Marx certainly did not claim that the liberation of the working class from darkness would be achieved by founding Marxism.

The force which leads society is the party which itself needs to be led. It cannot otherwise fulfil its role effectively. The individual leader determines the role of the party, which thus becomes a weapon to materialise leadership. The leader thus creates the party, not the other way around. Professor Kim Sang Ryol, a member of the Central Committee of the Korean Social Scientists Association, told me in July 1981 that under *juche* there could be no party without a wise leader to embody the will of the party so that the party and leader become one; the leader the party, the party the leader.

What happens when such a leader dies? A successor must be found who fulfils four characteristics. He must, firstly, be boundlessly loyal to the leader; he must, secondly, believe in the *juche* idea and the ideology of the leader; he must, thirdly, hold fast to the leader's leadership art; and must, finally, love the people as strongly as does the leader.

It is quite obvious that there is a strong political implication in these aspects of the *juche* idea. They are the ideological justification for a personality cult around 'the great leader' Kim Il Sung, which in extent goes beyond any other in modern history. The cult allows the argument that although the masses create history they do so only with the right leader. Professor Kim and other Koreans with whom I have discussed this matter come very close to arguing that it is Kim who has created the modern history of Korea, rather than that he is the embodiment of material forces which created that history.

There is politics also in the solution offered for the problem of the succession to the leadership. It can be argued that only Kim Jong Il fulfils the four criteria laid down, only he embodies his father's love for the people, so leadership should devolve upon him. In preparation for this event a subsidiary but strong cult has arisen around the person of Kim Jong Il, who in the DPRK is usually called 'the dear leader', [14] even though opposition to his succession remains, especially within the army.

We now turn to look more closely at what Kim Il Sung himself has said on particular problems of general concern to Asian Marxism. This change does not ignore the tight link between the *juche* idea and the thought of Kim Il Sung, for the two are more or less synonymous.

Despite their voluminosity, Kim's works lack variety in terms of form and substance. [15] Most are long addresses given to various bodies such as congresses of the party or women's groups, or reports on important occasions such as the twentieth anniversary of the founding of the Workers' Party. There is nothing corresponding to Ho Chi Minh's passionate indictment of French colonialism or to Mao Zedong's theoretical works *On Practice* and *On Contradiction*.

Although *juche* is said to shift the central philosophical

problems away from the relationship between matter and idea, this dichotomy remains of interest to Kim Il Sung:

> If we are to build socialism and communism with success, we must occupy two fortresses, that is, the material and ideological fortresses. Certain persons consider that communism will have been built when strong material foundations of society are laid and the people live in abundance. That is wrong. Even if a society attains material wealth and the people are well-off, communism cannot be built successfully so long as outdated ideas survive in the minds of people. Nor can the people who retain these ideas be regarded as Communists. [16]

Here ideology appears to be almost synonymous with what Marx described as the superstructure. Kim places no hierarchy between the material and ideological fortresses but he does clearly depart from Marx's notion that a change in the material base automatically leads to the transformation of the superstructure. In the paragraph immediately following the extract he berates countries with developed material foundations of society which have ignored the ideological revolution. These countries he believes will never succeed in building communism. Although he does not say so specifically, he is presumably referring to socialist countries.

Kim's stress on ideology becomes clearer in a discussion of education: 'Thinking determines the value and quality of a person and regulates all his activities'. This means that remoulding people is essentially equivalent to remoulding their thinking, 'and what is basic to the upbringing of a communist man is to arm him with communist ideas'. [17]

The important role of ideological remoulding comes through with crystal clarity. The person who rejects the party's or leader's line should in theory receive not punishment but education, but in any case should definitely not be allowed to persist in false thinking. Despite the central place of independence in *juche*, overt challenges to party ideology are notable by their absence in the DPRK.

There is an inherent value judgement in Kim's verdict on ideas and the knowledge which flows from them. 'Learning that is not based on revolutionary, communist ideas is of no use at all', [18] he states. This makes no reference to neutral ideas, but certainly does attach enormous significance to the social context of concepts as a prerequisite for determining their value.

One reason why correct thought is so essential is because of the mass line. The popular masses, properly led, make history [19] and exercise immense power; they must do so on behalf of socialism.

> It is important to closely unite the masses around the Party, strengthening the Party as the General Staff of the revolution. Without uniting the masses, we can neither strengthen the Party nor make the revolution.

> Our Party's consistent mass line is to unite the masses with the Party by re-educating them and to carry out revolutionary tasks by enlisting their energy and wisdom.

> The mass line is the fundamental principle of our Party's activities based on the Juche idea that the working masses are the masters of everything and decide everything.[20]

The mass line which was here spelt out so forcefully in 1974 was among the earliest doctrines to become explicit after the founding of the Workers' Party in 1945. [21] It was essential to the Chollima movement which was part of the economic and social programme decided at the Party Central Committee Plenum held in December 1956 and was a factor in the cooperativisation of agriculture as well as the socialist transformation of private trade and industry, both being completed by 1959. [22] *Chollima* is the flying horse, a symbol one sees frequently in the DPRK, and it symbolises extremely rapid economic development. The Chollima movement remains official policy in the DPRK and its emphasis on the enthusiasm of the masses is believed to be an important factor in the country's extremely impressive economic progress.

The other point to emerge from the 1974 passage cited above concerns the role of the party. Here Kim calls it 'the General Staff of the revolution', and the phrase is found continually throughout his works, beginning with the earliest of them all, dated 30 June 1930. [23] He emphasises not only the mass line but also the Party's role in educating and uniting the masses. Kim appears here to be taking a line very close to Lenin but also with links to Mao. What is clear in practice, however, is that Kim has never led any movement comparable to the Cultural Revolution in China which sought temporarily to destroy the party and pass even more power to the masses. The Koreans have always thought the Cultural Revolution disruptive and a catastrophic mistake. The theme of the work from which the 1974 cited passage comes is a call for unity and cohesion in the party.

The party leads the masses, not the other way round, yet it also implements the mass line. It is interesting to notice in this context that the Korean Workers' Party is a very large party, and can in that sense claim a basis in the masses. Some figures illustrate the point. [24]

Date	Workers' Party Members	Percentage of DPRK Population
August 1946	366,000	4
March 1948	750,000	8
April 1956	1,164,945	10
September 1961	1,311,563	12.2
November 1970	1,600,000	11.4
July 1981	2,000,000	12
1983	3,000,000	16

Not only is the absolute number continuing to expand but the proportion in relation to the population has gone up greatly although not consistently. The last figure of 16 per cent is by far the highest for any socialist party in Asia and higher even than the socialist states of Eastern Europe. [25] A political grouping containing so high a proportion of the population can legitimately be called a mass party, but it needs to be added that figures tell us nothing about the locus of power within the party itself.

The class nature and structure of the Korean society which the Workers' Party leads must be an important theoretical problem for a leader such as Kim Il Sung. The state constitution of 1972 approaches it as follows:

Article 6. In the Democratic People's Republic of Korea class antagonisms and all forms of exploitation and oppression of man by man have been eliminated for ever.

The State defends and protects the interests of the workers, peasants, soldiers and working intellectuals freed from exploitation and oppression.

Article 7. The sovereignty of the Democratic People's Republic of Korea rests with the workers, peasants, soldiers and working intellectuals...

Article 10. The Democratic People's Republic of Korea exercises the dictatorship of the proletariat and pursues class and mass lines.

Article 11. The State defends the socialist system against the subversive activities of hostile elements at home and abroad and revolutionizes and working-classizes the whole of society by intensifying the ideological revolution.[26]

A number of significant points emerge from these articles and require expansion.

The first is that the DPRK indeed considers itself as an example of the dictatorship of the proletariat. This is a structure in which four classes or parts of classes are positive contributors to the revolution: the workers, peasants, soldiers and working intellectuals. The Constitution lists the workers first and Kim is elsewhere quite explicit that they are the vanguard of society. In his report to the Fourth Congress of the Workers' Party in 1961 he asserted that 'the working class has strongly maintained its position as the leading force in our society' and went on to claim that factory and office workers, the working class, made up 52 per cent of the population. He called the peasantry 'a reliable ally of the working class' and spoke highly of its role in socialist construction and patriotism.

In the report Kim did not mention the soldiers as a class, but did praise the intellectuals, including those who had been remoulded from the old society and the 'large army of new intellectuals from the working people'. [27] He did not say directly, but implied, that the intellectuals are an ally of the working class. In the DPRK a prominent symbol shows the hammer and sickle on two sides with the writing brush between them, representing respectively the workers, peasants and intellectuals. So DPRK society is based on the worker-peasant-intellectual alliance. Education is compulsory for eleven years and free throughout the system from creches up to university. It is formal policy to 'intellectualise' the whole of society, at which stage both workers and peasants will be intellectuals. The notion that the intellectuals count as a separate class, not found in Marx himself but nonetheless not peculiar to the DPRK in Asia, will then become irrelevant.

Another very important point to come forward from the Constitution is the contention in Article 6 that class antagonisms and exploitation of all forms have disappeared completely. It is as confident a view of class harmony as can be found anywhere in the socialist world. As early as 1958 Kim had stated, in even more specific terms, that 'there are no landlords or capitalists any longer in our country'. [28] He thus went beyond the claim that these two groups had disappeared as classes to denying even that individual landlords or capitalists continued to operate.

And yet, only five articles after this extraordinarily optimistic statement on class harmony, the Constitution concedes in Article 11 that subversive activities and hostile elements indeed persist, not only abroad but even at home. As late as 1981 Kim declared that 'in our country a fierce struggle is going on uninterruptedly against the enemies of the revolution in many spheres of social life'. [29] This raises the question of who the enemies are if not landlords or capitalists. Possibly it could be interpreted in purely political terms as a reference to opposition to Kim Jong Il's succession, but in a Constitution which formally pronounces that class antagonism has disappeared this issue clearly requires explanation in theoretical terms.

One clue lies in the weaknesses which Kim Il Sung finds in the positive classes, and the constant exhortations to 'working-classise' habits and thinking. The term 'working-classise' means that the peasants and intellectuals as well as the working class should be influenced by and eventually become members of the working class itself. It means, moreover, that the working class must become more and more like an ideal revolutionary and cultured class, which is one totally committed to the *juche* idea. The working class must increasingly assert its leadership in society in order to cement political and ideological unity. [30] Naturally the DPRK leadership sees the members of particular classes as having made enormous progress; but not yet as having reached the ideal. The weakness of the working class is that it 'cannot be entirely free from the influence of bourgeois ideology', because some of its members 'have lived in capitalist society' and their families are newcomers to the proletariat. 'Moreover, many working-class people are former peasants, small and middle entrepreneurs and merchants'. The sons and daughters of such people, even though themselves members of the working class, 'were profoundly influenced by the class position of their parents'. [31]

It is very clear that Kim considers bourgeois ideology, which he acknowledges as persisting in the working class, to be due to the existence of bourgeois members within society. Bourgeois ideology is not the result of any regenerated bourgeoisie, but of the influence of remnants from the past. However progressive peasants or intellectuals in capitalist society may be, they will still be tainted with bourgeois thinking. The reference to the small-scale entrepreneurs and former peasants also shows that Kim Il Sung acknowledges Marx's view of the conservative influence of such elements within society. Kim is most certainly not conceding that they generate hostile classes under conditions of socialism. Like the workers, the peasants retain backward influences from the past. They suffer from 'egoistic and small-proprietorial hangovers', which are 'deep-rooted and bequeathed from generation to generation over many centuries'. The cure is 'unremitting struggle' in favour of collectivism and the slogan so widespread now in the DPRK 'one for all and all for one'. [32] He recognises problems, but at the same time there is an extremely optimistic stamp in everything he writes about his own country.

There is, however, one respect in which behaviour based on backward thinking must be tolerated for the time being. Kim Il Sung explains as follows:

> There is more good than bad in the continued existence of sideline production and the peasant market in socialist society. We are not yet in a position to supply everything necessary for the people's life in sufficient quantities, through state channels, especially miscellaneous goods for daily use like brooms and calabash-ladles, and subsidiary provisions like meat, eggs, sesame, both wild and cultivated. Under the circumstances, what is wrong with individuals producing these things on the side and selling them in the market? Even though it is a backward way, it should still be made

use of when the advanced ways are not sufficient to cover everything.

Some functionaries are afraid that sideline production, or the peasant market, could revive capitalism right away. But there is no basis for this fear. [33]

Kim goes on to declare that these sideline productions and peasant markets will disappear only when the state can provide all the goods required by the people and when cooperative ownership has become that of the entire people. In September 1982 I was informed in the DPRK that this time had not been reached and was not immediately visible.

What is under discussion is the phenomenon Marx described as 'bourgeois right'. Kim acknowledges that the peasant markets are indeed survivals from capitalism, at least in some of their features. He justifies the residue not because it is good, but because it is necessary, and will remain so until the productive forces are further developed. It is striking that he does not appear to find it necessary to restrict or combat this bourgeois right. Neither does he concede that these sidelines and markets will lead to greater social inequalities. As usual his is a very optimistic view.

Koreans nowadays take the theme of social equality extremely seriously. Income differentials between the city and countryside, and within units in each, are remarkably small. Perfect equality, however, has not been achieved nor claimed.

Two functional aspects of equality require treatment here. The first is the relationship between basic-level leaders and those under their guidance. Kim Il Sung pointed out problems in the reality of the early 1970s and made his ideal abundantly clear:

We have always stressed the need of doing away with the abuse of Party authority, bureaucracy and subjectivism among the functionaries. But some still resort to such practices; they regard themselves as special beings, pay no heed to the voices of the masses, and work bureaucratically, issuing commands to their subordinates. If functionaries do their work in such a bureaucratic manner, their subordinates will fear and flatter them, finding it hard to tell them the truth.

... Urged to discard the bureaucratic method of work and *go among the masses*, some functionaries *only go about like sightseers, and this is also wrong.* Because in this way, they cannot hear the real opinions of the masses. (Emphasis in original). [34]

Kim is here arguing that the functionary should be not the lord but the servant of the masses. He or she should stay always in close contact with the masses in order to discuss matters properly with them and understand fully what they are thinking on concrete problems. Bureaucratism and the seizure of privileges by grass-roots leaders are anathema to Kim.

Elsewhere, he applies similar strictures not only to party functionaries but to intellectuals. In a list of their shortcomings the first is their tendency 'to get swell-headed because they have a little knowledge'. He accuses 'some comrades' of looking down on others as 'ignoramuses'. 'The masses', he suggests, 'do not want to have anything to do with such persons'. [35] He is correspondingly very insistent that science and technology, which are so vitally important to development, are not the preserve of experts. He attacks the view that they are mysterious and demands that the creativity of the masses not only can but must be enlisted in technological renovation. [36]

One contemporary scholar has argued that, despite the democratic ideas which can be found in Kim's works, political practice in the DPRK has shown a tendency, from 1959 on, for the mass line to suffer competition from an approach which gives much more authority to the leaders of society; and for the top-down form to become predominant by the late 1960s. [37] Certainly Kim's ideology does not allow the distinction between leaders and led to disappear. The point can best be clarified by a brief explanation of 'the great Chongsan-ri spirit and Chongsan-ri method' laid down as exemplary in the state Constitution for all work.

Chongsan-ri is the name of a model co-operative farm just outside Pyongyang. It is highly mechanised with tractors, harvestors and trucks and the material standard of living of the peasants is extremely high. Not only are all health services and education entirely free, as in the rest of the DPRK, but all houses have television, wireless, kitchen and other useful items. Kim Il

Sung has defined the essence of the Chongsan-ri method as follows: 'the higher body helps the lower, and the superior assists those under him' by visiting the work place to gain a firm grasp of actual conditions. The good leader 'gives priority to political work, works with people in all undertakings and enlists the conscious enthusiasm and initiative of the masses'. [38] So the Chongsan-ri method includes the mass line, enthusiasm, high technology and intimate knowledge of the problems, an emphasis on politics and close personal relations. Above all it includes leadership, assistance from the higher to the lower, not the other way round.

Another aspect of the Chongsan-ri method has become very important in the DPRK: Kim Il Sung's 'on-the-spot guidance'. When I visited Chongsan-ri in July 1981 I learned that Kim Il Sung had given on-the-spot guidance there eighty times since liberation, including a talk to the peasants in October 1978. Kim himself states that the guidance he gave in February 1960 marked a turning point in the renovation of the work of state and economic institutions. [39] It appears that for him the visit to Chongsan-ri in 1960 was the beginning of an emphasis on personal visits to selected units. Certainly it has become a major feature of administration in the DPRK. In those factories, farms or other institutions I have visited there, the first item of information I received was when and how often Kim had come to give on-the-spot guidance. It is possible to see the practice as part of the cult of Kim Il Sung, but equally I believe it symbolises the very personal style of leadership favoured in the DPRK not only at the highest but also at other levels. It may well be reasonable to see it as a major link in a process which shifts power from the masses to the leaders of society. [40] It gives the masses the illusion of consultation, but probably not the substance of democratic power.

The other aspect of social equality is that between the sexes. In the Korean slogan male and female represent the two equal wheels of a cart which requires both to operate effectively. According to the Constitution, 'women hold equal social status and rights with men'. To this end the state gives women and children a variety of special facilities such as 'maternity leave, shortened working hours for mothers of large families', a wide network of maternity hospitals, creches and kindergartens. In addition, it 'frees women from the heavy burdens of household chores and provides every condition for them to participate in public life'. [41]

In practice the DPRK's efforts to allow women to reach this very important objective of participating in public life include an extremely impressive array of child-minding facilities, all of which are entirely free. Kim Chi Gun informed me in September 1982 that there were about 60,000 kindgartens and creches for 3,500,000 children, nearly one-fifth of the total DPRK population. Not only mothers of large families but all those in the labour force receive special benefits. By law, pregnant women must be given light suitable work and the state 'provides systematic medical service and midwifery to them free of charge and protects their health after childbirth'. It also allows mothers with babies necessary suckling time during working hours. [42]

Kim Il Sung stated in October 1980 that it was one of the major tasks of the technical revolution to free women from the burden of household chores, and thus mobilise them into the work force. Among the measures taken to this end he listed the building of nurseries and kindergartens. [43] Though much progress has been made, the ideal is not yet reality. In the DPRK one sees innumerable women with a baby strapped to the back, but I have never once seen a man thus burdened.

Equality between male and female means a diminution of sex roles but not their elimination. Women enter the professions readily and about 70 per cent of all doctors are female. Some senior functionaries are women, though far fewer than men.

On the other hand, Kim Il Sung clearly sees the main responsibilities of family life as falling on women. In a girls' school I visited in Pyongyang in July 1981 I was informed that Kim Il Sung had come to give on-the-spot guidance and told the school that girls ought to be able to cook, as a result of which the leadership laid some stress on the culinary arts.

In an article on women, Kim Il Sung emphasises their impact on society because of the influence they wield on men and children. This is a major reason why they must be revolutionised and working-classised. 'Some men, badly affected by their wives, committed errors and were demoted or dismissed', says Kim, laying at least part of the blame for male delinquency on women. For the behaviour of children too, women hold still greater responsibility. Kim cites an analysis by the Ministry of Social Security according to which the mothers of most delinquent children are women who are not revolutionised. [44] From an ideological point of view the important point here is that in Kim's thought women are expected not only to play a role equal with men in public life but to bear the brunt of that family burden and responsibility which is left over after the very generous assistance of the state. The cure for the problem of bad influences is less to share out family responsibility between father and mother than to revolutionise women. Equality between male and female in no way implies the elimination of sex roles.

The revolutionisation of women is a major prerequisite for building socialism and communism. We now come to Kim Il Sung's vision of what the future communist society will be like.

Our ideal is to build a society where everyone is well fed, well clothed and lives a long life, a society where there is no laggard nor idler and all are progressive and work devotedly, a society where all people live united in harmony as one big family. Such a society, we can say, is precisely a communist society.

In a communist society, there is such plenty that people work according to their abilities and receive according to their needs. In other words, people can have as much as they want and their life's demands are fully satisfied. Further, in a communist society people will have still closer relationships with each other and the principle of 'One for all and all for one' will be fully realized.

Can we build such a society? Certainly, we can. Our people can say so on the strength of the achievements they have made so far.

... We shall come closer to communism when we fulfil the Seven-Year Plan, reunify the country and conquer new peaks.

It is wrong, therefore, to regard communist society as something of a mystery which can only become a reality in the distant future. By working hard at it we can concretize our ideal of communist construction in the not-too-distant future. [45]

Kim here uses the slogan 'one for all and all for one', but refers to Marx for the higher stage of Communist society: 'to each according to his needs, from each according to his ability'. He lays great emphasis both on the material and social aspects of the communist society.

What is perhaps most interesting about Kim's comments is his confidence that the communist society can be achieved and 'in the not-too-distant future'. Of the three prerequisites listed, two are very specific. The Seven-Year Plan began in 1961, the same year Kim Il Sung made the above statement. It was due to end in 1967, but was in fact not completed until 1970. Reunification is unfortunately not yet realised and is unlikely in the near future. [46] So only one of the two prerequisites is now fulfilled. The third one, 'to conquer new peaks' is extremely vague and allows for the deferment of the claim that a communist society has been reached.

The northern Koreans do not currently believe themselves to be living in a communist society, even though they call the DPRK 'a paradise'. The state Constitution lays down not the communist slogan of distribution but the equivalent of the socialist: 'citizens work according to their ability and receive remuneration according to the quantity and quality of work done'.[47] In 1983 Kim Jong Il wrote that labour 'does not yet become a primary requirement of life' in socialist society. [48] He is citing Marx's famous dictum that in 'a higher phase of communist society' labour will be 'not only a means of life but life's prime want', [49] and is clearly implying that such a happy stage still belongs to the future. However, several senior people told me both in July 1981 and September 1982 that they still expected communist society reasonably soon. The major unfulfilled prerequisite is still reunification. As far as I know the view of Kim Il Sung and his followers on the nearness of the communist society is the most optimistic of any of the world's socialist countries.

Kim Il Sung sees the principal difficulty in the path of the communist society in the DPRK as ideological backwardness. 'Remodelling all people in communist fashion is far more difficult than supplying them with enough food and clothes', [50] he states. He insists here, as elsewhere, that no matter how revolutionised the material base of society, the ideological superstructure requires prodding to catch up, and will not automatically follow.

CONCLUSION

We are now in a position to ask a question which must be central to a book on Marxism in Asia: are the *juche* idea and the ideas of Kim Il Sung truly Marxist-Leninist?

My interview with Kim Chi Gun in September 1982 isolated several areas where *juche* was different from Marxism. The most important was that it posed the fundamental philosophical question differently, asking not 'is it matter or consciousness which is primary?', but 'what is the relationship between man and the world?' Another was the definition of a human; whereas Marx sees the human essence as 'the ensemble of the social relations',[51] *juche* defines man as 'a social being with independence, creativity and consciousness'. Kim Chi Gun was quite clear that *juche* is *not* the application of Marxism to Korea but much more than that. 'We cannot say that *juche* is Korean Marxism because there are innovations in *juche* ', he informed me. 'There are aspects of inheritance from Marxism-Leninism, but the innovations are more important than what is transmitted'. Koreans recognise that Marx correctly solved the problem he posed; matter indeed takes priority over consciousness. The *juche* idea 'raised a new problem concerning the position and role of man in the world' and answered not with 'abstract views on pure man', but by declaring humanity to be 'master of the world'. [52]

Foreign observers published in the DPRK, and thus expressing an official line, have suggested different interpretations on whether the *juche* idea is Marxist-Leninist. An unsigned article reprinted from a journal in Japan averred that 'Kimilsungism is not a mere inheritance and development of Marxism-Leninism. It has brought about a great revolutionary turn in the sphere of human ideology'. [53] In the same collection of 'essays and articles', another piece declared, in contrast, that 'The Juche idea is the Marxism-Leninism of the present day, that has highly developed Marxist-Leninist theory'. [54]

The perfectly reasonable suggestion that Marxism-Leninism is not a rigid set of formulae but must develop 'to suit the changes of the times and each country's conditions' [55] recurs throughout the DPRK literature. There is every reason to expect a country which stresses independence so heavily to vary any doctrine it embraces to suit its own needs.

As early as 1930, in the first of the entire published complete *Works*, Kim Il Sung called for the foundation of a Marx-ist-Leninist party. [56] His works bristle with comments like: 'Com-rades, as Marxism-Leninism teaches us, the masses of the people create history', [57] suggesting most strongly that he regards him-self as a Marxist-Leninist. The Constitution states in Article 4 that the *juche* idea 'is a creative application of Marxism-Leninism to our country's reality'. [58]

The principal argument against accepting the claim lies not in the *fact* of innovations in the *juche* idea but in their nature. [59] It can be argued that the emphasis on the leader as a person is such as to deny materialism. In the DPRK today, Koreans ritual-ly ascribe all achievements of the Korean people to 'the wise leadership of the great leader Comrade Kim Il Sung' sometimes adding 'the dear leader Comrade Kim Jong Il'. Everywhere Kim Il Sung is regarded as having personally created the Korean revo-lution and the Workers' Party. Rarely do the masses take pre-cedence, their role is always subsidiary to the leader's and lies largely in extolling him.

To declare humankind as 'master' of the world and inde-pendent can be reconciled with materialism only if the emphasis lies on the masses, on class struggle and production relations as determinants of social development. Kim Il Sung himself perhaps meets the criterion, but his followers appear to come very close to voluntarism, to saying that one person's will determines the movements of history and society.

Juche and the thought of Kim Il Sung play an intensely nationalistic role in the DPRK today. This is due partly to the emphasis on independence, but is much more than that. The re-fusal to acknowledge Soviet assistance in the establishment of the DPRK or Chinese against the Americans in the Korean war springs to some extent from *juche* and is part of a nationalism which amounts to a serious distortion of history. The function of *juche* as a bulwark of anti-Japanese nationalism is also impor-tant. [60]

On the other hand, both Kim Il Sung and his followers ap-pear to think in Marxist-Leninist terms in the stress they lay on the party, on the leadership of the working class, the composi-tion of society, and the type and scope of equality within it. The vision of the future is also strongly Marxist. There is a strong dialectic element in Kim Il Sung's thinking and that of his followers in the DPRK.

There are aspects of Kim's thought which are contrary to Marx, but not necessarily fundamentally so. One is the suggestion that the ideological revolution must be consciously pushed forward even after the material has gained victory. Kim's view may well be realistic in Korea, and one can quite logically see the change as a development of Marxism to suit a particular country's needs, rather than a departure from it.

Overall, it appears to me that *juche* and Kim Il Sung's thought are indeed a creative development of Marxism-Leninism. Its emphasis on leadership and its nationalism are unmarxist, but the general categories which it adopts are closer to Marxism-Leninism than to any other philosophy. The proposition that a Korean ought to follow foreign thinkers only critically and independently is a reasonable one. *Juche* and the passion for independence and creativity which is part of that idea have indeed contributed to the regrowth of the DPRK and the extent of prosperity and unity there, [61] achieved on the ashes of the Korean war. [62]

NOTES

1. Interview by the author with Kim Chi Gun on 12 September 1982 in Pyongyang. See also Kim Jong Il, *On the Juche Idea* (Foreign Languages Publishing House, Pyongyang, 1982), p. 5. For material on the very early Korean Marxists see Dae-Sook Suh, *Documents of Korean Communism 1918-1948* (Princeton University Press, Princeton, 1970) and for documents down to 1922 in particular pp. 21-105.

2. See Kim Han Gil, *Modern History of Korea* (Foreign Languages Publishing House, Pyongyang, 1979), p. 20; Suh, *Documents*, pp. 508, 507, 10-17, 227-30.

3. 'On the Occasion of the 20th Anniversary of the Workers' Party of Korea' (10 October 1965), *Kim Il Sung Selected Works*, vol. 4, p. 297. All seven volumes of Kim Il Sung's *Selected Works* (hereafter SW), are published by the Foreign Languages Publishing House in Pyongyang. The date of the first five is 1976, of the sixth 1975, and of the last 1979.

4. *Korea, The Politics of the Vortex* (Harvard University Press, Cambridge, Mass., 1968), p. 326.

5. The most detailed account in English of the immediate post-war period is Bruce Cumings, *The Origins of the Korean War, Liberation and the Emergence of Separate Regimes 1945-1947* (Princeton University Press, Princeton, 1981).

6. *On the Juche Idea*, p. 8. Kim Jong Il is referring to a report Kim Il Sung made to the 'meeting of leading personnel of the Young Communist League and the Anti-Imperialist Youth League held at Kalun', that is Jialun in Jilin Province, China, on 30 June 1930. See 'The Path of the Korean Revolution', *Works*, vol. 1 (Foreign Languages Publishing House, Pyongyang, 1980), pp. 1-10. According to Dae-Sook Suh, *Korean Communism 1945-1980, A Reference Guide to the Political System* (The University Press of Hawaii, Honolulu, 1981), p. 19, this report was not made public until July 1978. Kim there called for a specifically Korean revolution to gain independence from the Japanese. Only the

germ of the *juche* idea is present, and Kim Jong Il claims no more than that. In an interview with H.D. Malabya, Vice-Chairman of the National India-Korea Friendship Society, Kim Il Sung claimed, in Malabya's words, that 'even at that early stage [1926] he was definite that Koreans have to depend upon themselves to attain their objectives'. See 'President Kim Il Sung and the DPRK', in *Kim Il Sung, The Brilliant Banner of Juche* (Foreign Languages Publishing House, Pyongyang, 1981), p. 48.

7. 'On Eliminating Dogmatism and Formalism and Establishing *Juche* in Ideological Work', SW, vol. 1, pp. 582-606.

8. Kim Han Gil, *Modern History of Korea*, p. 417.

9. Ilpyong J. Kim, *Communist Politics in North Korea* (Praeger, New York, 1975), p. 55.

10. 'On Some Problems of Our Party's Juche Idea and the Government of the Republic's Internal and External Policies' (17 September 1972), SW, vol. 6, pp. 253-4.

11. Kim Jong Il, *On the Juche Idea*, p. 13. See another discussion on the role of humankind in *juche* in Tai Sung An, *North Korea in Transition From Dictatorship to Dynasty* (Greenwood Press, Westport, Connecticut, 1983), pp. 56-61.

12. Kim Jong Il, *On the Juche Idea*, p. 11.

13. Kim Jong Il, *Let Us Advance under the Banner of Marxism-Leninism and the Juche Idea* (Foreign Languages Publishing House, Pyongyang, 1983), p. 4.

14. See an extreme but nevertheless fairly typical example of this cult, by a foreigner, in Muhammad al Missuri, *Kimilsungist Cause Admirably Carried Forward* (Foreign Languages Publishing House, Pyongyang, 1982). The author describes Kim Jong Il as 'possessed with flawless personality of a great leader - unusual acumen, distinguished leadership, noble morality required to carry forward the cause of great Kimilsungism to consummation' (p. 26). For a very different view of Kim Jong Il's succession, see Chong-Sik Lee, 'Evolution of the Korean Workers' Party and the Rise of Kim Chŏng-Il', in Robert A. Scalapino and Jun-yop Kim (eds.), *North Korea Today, Strategic and Domestic Issues* (University of California Institute of East Asian Studies, Berkeley, 1983), pp. 65-80.

15. As of September 1982 the collected *Works* of Kim Il Sung covered nineteen volumes in the Korean language, but only ten had been translated into English. The *Selected Works* occupied seven volumes. All versions are arranged chronologically, the collected *Works* beginning in June 1930 and progressing to October 1965 for vol. 19 of the Korean and December 1956 for vol. 10 of the English edition. The first item of vol. 1 of the *Selected Works* is dated 13 October 1945, the last in vol. 7, 17 December 1977. For a description of the contents and some analysis of Kim's articles from 30 June 1930 to 10 October 1980 see Dae-Sook Suh, *Korean Communism*, pp. 19-229.

16. 'On Revolutionizing and Working-classizing Women' (7 October 1971), SW, vol. 6, p. 105.

17. 'Theses on Socialist Education' (5 September 1977), SW, vol. 7, p. 347.

18. Ibid.

19. See Kim Il Sung, 'Report on the Work of the Central Committee to the Fourth Congress of the Workers' Party of Korea' (11 September 1961), SW, vol. 3, p.94.

20. 'On Further Strengthening Party Work' (31 July 1974), SW, vol. 7. p. 80.

21. See Cumings, *The Origins of the Korean War*, p. 404.

22. See Ilpyong J. Kim, *Communist Politics*, pp. 79-84.

23. 'The Path of the Korean Revolution', *Works*, vol. 1, p. 9.

24. The sources for the figures are Ilpyong Kim, *Communist Politics*, p. 34, Richard F. Staar (ed.), *Yearbook on International Communist Affairs 1984*

Parties and Revolutionary Movements (Hoover Institution Press, Stanford, 1984), p. xviii, and personal sources in the DPRK.

25. See statistics of communist party memberships and mid-1983 populations in Richard F. Staar (ed.), *Yearbook on International Communist Affairs 1984*, pp. xvii-xx. Some of the most relevant comparative figures, showing the size of the party and in parentheses proportion of population are: USSR, 18,331,000 (6.7 per cent); Czechoslovakia, 1,600,000 (10.4 per cent); Romania, 3,300,000 (14.6 per cent); Vietnam, 1,727,784 (3.0 per cent); Mongolia, 76,240 (4.2 per cent); China, 40,000,000 (3.8 per cent).

26. 'Socialist Constitution of the Democratic People's Republic of Korea' (27 December 1972), SW, vol. 6, p. 355. See also *Socialist Constitution of the Democratic People's Republic of Korea* (Foreign Languages Publishing House, Pyongyang, 1975), pp. 2-3. According to Dae-Sook Suh (*Korean Communism*, p. 185), 'there is no reference to the fact that Kim authored this constitution'. He cannot understand why it is included in Kim's works. Whoever actually wrote it is not as important as its clear reflection of his ideas.

27. 'Report on the Work of the Central Committee to the Fourth Congress of the Workers' Party of Korea' (11 September 1961), SW, vol. 3, pp. 101-2.

28. 'Report at the Tenth Anniversary Celebration of the Founding of the Democratic People's Republic of Korea' (8 September 1958), SW, vol. 2, p. 207.

29. *The Youth Should be Dependable Heirs to the Revolutionary Cause of Juche* (Foreign Languages Publishing House, Pyongyang, 1981), p. 6.

30. See, for instance, Kim Il Sung, 'The Present Situation and the Tasks of Our Party' (5 October 1966), SW, vol. 4, pp. 384-5.

31. Kim Il Sung, 'On the Elimination of Formalism and Bureaucracy in Party Work and the Revolutionization of Functionaries' (18 October 1966), SW, vol. 4, p. 423.

32. Kim Il Sung, 'Theses on the Socialist Rural Question in Our Country' (25 February 1964), SW, vol. 4, pp. 56-7.

33. 'On some Theoretical Problems of the Socialist Economy' (1 March 1969), SW, vol. 5, pp. 315-16.

34. 'On Improving and Strengthening the Training of Party Cadres' (2 December 1971), SW, vol. 6, p. 141.

35. 'On Correctly Implementing Our Party's Policy Towards Intellectuals' (14 June 1968), SW, vol. 5, p. 99.

36. 'On the Successful Accomplishment of the Technical Revolution' (11 August 1960), SW, vol. 2, p. 560.

37. David Kho, 'The Political Economy of the DPRK in the Post-1958 Period', *Journal of Contemporary Asia*, vol. 12, no. 3 (1982), pp. 304-19.

38. 'On the Occasion of the 20th Anniversary of the Workers' Party of Korea' (10 October 1965), SW, vol. 4, p. 312.

39. 'The Democratic People's Republic of Korea is the Banner of Freedom and Independence for our People and a Powerful Weapon for Building Socialism and Communism' (7 September 1968), SW, vol. 5, p. 159.

40. See Kho, 'The Political Economy of the DPRK', pp. 305-8.

41. Article 62, *Socialist Constitution*, p. 19.

42. *The Law of the Democratic People's Republic of Korea on the Nursing and Upbringing of Children* (Foreign Languages Publishing House, Pyongyang, 1978), p. 6. The law was adopted on 29 April 1976.

43. *Report to the Sixth Congress of the Workers' Party of Korea on the Work of the Central Committee, October 10, 1980* (Foreign Languages Publishing House, Pyongyang, 1980), p. 12.

44. 'On Revolutionizing and Working – classizing Women' (7 October 1971), SW, vol. 6, pp. 107-8.

45. 'The Duty of Mothers in the Education of Children' (16 November 1961), SW, vol. 3, pp. 207-9.

46. The central problem of reunification is omitted here because it is primarily political, not ideological. A good scholarly treatment is Gavan McCormack, 'The Reunification of Korea: Problems and Prospects', *Pacific Affairs*, vol. 55, no. 1 (Spring 1982), pp. 5-31.

47. Article 56, *Socialist Constitution*, p. 18.

48. *Let Us Advance*, p. 11.

49. 'Critique of the Gotha Programme', in *Karl Marx and Frederick Engels Selected Works* (3 vols., Progress Publishers, Moscow, 1969-70), vol. 3, p.19.

50. 'The Duty of Mothers', SW, vol. 3, p. 211.

51. 'Theses on Feuerbach', in *Karl Marx and Frederick Engels Selected Works*, vol. 1, p. 14.

52. Kim Jong Il, *On the Juche Idea*, p. 73.

53. 'Warm Greetings to the Sixty-Second Birthday of President Kim Il Sung - the Outstanding Marxist-Leninist of the Present Era Who has Founded Great Kimilsungism', in *The World Historic Significance of the Juche Idea (Essays and Articles)* (Foreign Languages Publishing House, Pyongyang, 1975), p. 4.

54. Kuriki Yasunobu, 'World Historic Significance of the Juche Idea', in *The World Historic Significance*, p. 9.

55. Yasui Kaoru, 'Keynote Report, The Ideological and Theoretical System of President Kim Il Sung and the Basic Viewpoint of Our Studies', in *The Juche Idea is a Great Revolutionary Banner* (Foreign Languages Publishing House, Pyongyang, 1975), p. 17. See also Shawky Ajami, 'The Role of the Leader of the Proletariat in the Development of History, and the Immortal Juche Idea Created by the Great Leader Comrade Kim Il Sung', in *Juche Idea, The Current of Thought in the Present Time* (Foreign Languages Publishing House, Pyongyang, 1977), p. 35.

56. 'The Path of the Korean Revolution', *Works*, vol. 1, p. 9.

57. 'Report to the Fourth Congress', SW, vol. 3, p. 94.

58. *Socialist Constitution*, p. 2.

59. Tai Sung An (*North Korea*, p. 65) scoffs at *juche* as 'simple, eclectic, mediocre, and pedestrian', and concedes no originality to it at all. However, the texture of its priorities and its application to Korea appear to me to justify the word 'innovations'.

60. See also Han Shik Park, ' *Chuch'e*: The North Korean Ideology', in C.I. Eugene Kim and B.C. Koh (eds.), *Journey to North Korea - Personal Perceptions* (University of California Institute of East Asian Studies, Berkeley, 1983), pp. 89-92.

61. Han Shik Park (ibid., p. 84) describes *juche* as 'the driving force behind the solidification of Kim's position and the ideological consensus'. Even Tai Sung An concedes to it the ability to 'bring national pride, and unlock the energy and creativity' of the North Korean people. *North Korea* , p. 66.

62. Since this chapter aims to consider Korean Marxism it deals mainly with the plane of ideology rather than reality. A fair treatment of the problems and reality of the DPRK is Gavan McCormack, 'North Korea: Kimilsungism Path to Socialism?', *Bulletin of Concerned Asian Scholars*, vol. 13, no. 4 (Oct.-Dec. 1981), pp. 50-61. Among very recent detailed general studies is Scalapino and Kim (eds.), *North Korea Today*.

SELECT BIBLIOGRAPHY

An, Tai Sung, *North Korea in Transition From Dictatorship to Dynasty* (Greenwood Press, Westport, Connecticut, 1983). A recent scholarly study which includes four chapters on various aspects of the *juche* idea.

Kim Il Sung, *Selected Works* (7 vols., Foreign Languages Publishing House, Pyongyang, 1975-9). The official translation of selected speeches, addresses and other works by Kim Il Sung, arranged chronologically.

Kim Il Sung The Brilliant Banner of Juche (Foreign Languages Publishing House, Pyongyang, 1981). A series of highly laudatory articles on Kim Il Sung and the *juche* idea written by foreigners. This is one of number of similar books published as propaganda in and for the DPRK.

Kim Jong Il, *On the Juche Idea* (Foreign Languages Publishing House, Pyongyang, 1982). This is the text of a 'treatise sent to the National Seminar on the Juche Idea held to mark the 70th birthday of the great leader Comrade Kim Il Sung', and is dated 31 March 1982. It is a very good summation of how Kim Il Sung's influential son sees the *juche* idea.

Park, Han Shik, ' *Chuch'e*: The North Korean Ideology', in C.I. Eugene Kim and B.C. Koh (eds), *Journey to North Korea - Personal Perceptions* (University of California Institute of East Asian Studies, Berkeley, 1983), pp. 84-98. A preliminary look at the *juche* idea, based partly on personal experience in the DPRK.

Scalapino, Robert A, and Lee, Chong-Sik, *Communism in Korea* (2 vols., University of California Press, Berkeley, Los Angeles, 1972). An early and scholarly account in a Western language on the DPRK and Korean communism. The first volume deals with 'the movement', the second with 'the society'.

Suh, Dae-Sook, *The Korean Communist Movement 1918-1948* (2 vols., Princeton University Press, Princeton, 1967, 1970). The first volume is analytical, the second presents original documents translated into English.

Suh, Dae-Sook, *Korean Communism 1945-1980 A Reference Guide to the Political System* (The University Press of Hawaii, Honolulu, 1981). The nature of this book is explained in the subtitle; the first section gives brief commentary on all Kim Il Sung's works down to his report to the Sixth Congress of the Workers' Party.

7

MARXISM IN JAPAN: THEORY VERSUS TRADITION
Alan Rix

There is no single Japanese strain of Marxism; several types are in fact of interest in discussions of the relevance of Marxist thought and ideology to Japan. Notwithstanding the deep and permanent splits that, almost from the very beginning of the introduction of Marxist thought into Japan, divided the social and political movements which found inspiration in the ideas of Marx and Lenin, that tradition has had an immense impact on Japanese society and politics since the 1920s: it spawned a communist party which is still a vital force in the domestic political system and supported a socialist movement and a strong labour counterpart, from which lineage two large political parties remain. Before and after World War II it inspired successive generations of students and scholars. As an intellectual tradition and world view from outside the Japanese historical experience, it provided a basis for radical critique that went beyond the internal argument of Marxism-Leninism itself which, for the Japanese polity of the 1920s and 1930s, was already radical enough. Marxism was therefore an intellectual, and later a political, movement with long-term significance for Japanese social thought and behaviour.

Japanese strains of Marxism are not easily categorised as systems of thought and ideology. Some writers indeed claim that only a pseudo-Marxism developed. [1] As in many other countries, it was Marxism-Leninism, rather than Marx's own writings, that was of greater direct relevance to the popularising and political use of that ideological tradition. The way Marxism-Leninism has been interpreted and adapted in Japan since the 1890s needs to be looked at in terms of a number of interwoven factors. Firstly, two separate streams, of academic theorising and political activism, gave shape and substance to the early development of Marxism in Japan. The role of individuals was also important in this process and has continued to be influential throughout the history of Marxism and Marxist movements in Japan. Individual writers and thinkers found in Marxism a compelling way to engage in political criticism and personal political action. At the same time as individuals were affected by Marxism, so the development of Marxism in Japan owed much to the commitment and contribution of individuals – the anarchists Kotoku and Osugi, the scholars such as Kawakami, the theorists Yamakawa and Fukumoto, the activist and writer, Sano, and others. For many, the interminable debates within the Marxist movement about the proper course of revolution were a vital element in their personal and political lives.

Alongside the constructive and positive influence of the individual, however, has been its destructive obverse, the faction: this has dogged the history of Marxism-Leninism in Japan and has sapped its organisational energy and impact. A third historical force in Japanese Marxism has been the organised labour movements active since the 1920s and, from a separate political direction, the influence of the international Communist movements. Both of these – one an internal, the other an external pressure – have continually and closely influenced the political development of Marxist ideology. Finally, let us not forget the state, for Marxism-Leninism in Japan achieved its political relevance as an anti-state movement. But it was more than that, since in Japan, for many the epitome of the capitalist-imperialist state, Marxism-Leninism provoked a harsh response. Until 1945, the tolerance of the ideology as separate from its political manifestation was very low; this contributed to the distinctive 'Japanisation' of Marxism.

The Early Development of Marxism in Japan

Marxist thought was first expressed in Japan through a small group of Christian intellectuals who formed the Association for the Study of Socialism in October 1898 as a forum for the discussion of Western socialist thought, including that of Marx. Their socialism was, as Beckmann and Okubo put it, 'an amalgam of Christian humanitarianism, social democracy and pacifism'. [2] They quickly saw the relevance of socialist thought to the rapidly industrialising but imperialist Japan, and formed the Social Democratic Party in 1901, which aimed to achieve fundamental reforms through peaceful means. As well as being immediately proscribed by the state, the movement suffered internal dissension-between the Christians (notably Katayama Sen) and the 'materialist' non-Christians (principally Kotoku Shusui). The two groups espoused, on the one hand, a peaceful social democracy and, on the other, an anarchosyndicalism having its roots in Kotoku's study of Kropotkin and a belief in the value of direct action by workers.

Marxism provided here a framework for social analysis. The socialism of the Meiji era, as it was reflected in both the social democracy movement and the anarchist movement, represented a desire to close the gap between wealth and poverty in Japan. [3] Marxism was recognised by both groups as a means of analysing capitalism and arguing for improved conditions for the working class. The tactics for achieving these ends, however, did not extend to revolution. It took Lenin and the Russian Revolution of 1917 to add that component to Japanese Marxist thought.

The differences between the anarchist and social democratic forces in the Japanese left-wing movement continued in the new Japan Socialist Party (established in 1906) but government suppression of the party forced its leaders into gaol or hiding. Kotoku and some of his followers were executed in January 1911, while Katayama Sen fled to the United States to escape persecution. From there he continued his work, becoming an important figure in the international communist movement and maintaining an input to Japanese debates throughout the 1920s.

One writer regards this early period as representing no more than an 'intellectual movement' of bourgeois academics divorced from the workers movement, and one that descended into a romantic anarchosyndicalism. [4] But World War I changed the climate for radical thought in Japan: industrial growth altered the economic face of the nation and, of all the nations allied against Germany, Japan was one of the few which emerged unscathed and with economic benefit. Industrialisation also provided a stronger basis for the growth of the labour movement, and for labour unrest. The Rice Riots of 1918 in Japan — widespread popular disturbances brought about by the rising price of rice and forcefully put down by the government — and the Bolshevik Revolution of 1917 also added ferment to popular dissatisfaction with government policy towards labour, prices, and the rights of the people generally.

It was this environment and the more liberal atmosphere of the Taisho period that gave rise to new directions in Marxist thought. Fresh attempts were made to organise labour; the revolutionary potential of the proletariat was recognised and used by some anarchosyndicalists who took up Bolshevik ideas. As Large puts it, 'the impact of anarchism on these disputes [within the labour movement over appropriate strategies] was catalytic, sweeping through the Japanese labour movement like an electric shock'. [5] There was also a flowering of Marxist study in intellectual circles which was later to play a central part in debates within the Marxist movement about appropriate strategies. Anarchism flourished only briefly, albeit with romance and notoriety, stemming mainly from the anarchist movement's intellectual leader, Osugi Sakae. He and his mistress were murdered by security police in the aftermath of the Kanto earthquake of September 1923. In the twenty years or so up until World War II the Marxist movement – both Marxist-Leninist and social democratic wings – underwent a testing period of growth, a temporary stability and then gradual dissolution under government policy and repression. The key issues that flowed through the prewar debates about Marxist thought – and which continued after World War II as well-concerned, firstly, the nature of social change and revolution, secondly the role of the proletarian party and, thirdly, the application and adaptation of Marxist and Leninist thought to Japanese society including a thorough assessment of the dynamics of capitalism and imperialism. This agenda constituted the search for 'a scientific characterisation of modern Japan' which, Najita argues

> turned out to be an exceedingly difficult and time-consuming task. It captured the attention of an entire generation of scholars and university students, and their debates and scholarly writings created a distinctive esprit that has had a deep and lasting influence on Japanese intellectual life. [6]

Social Change and the Nature of Revolution

The birth of the Japan Communist Party (JCP) in July 1922 was brought about partly by the Asian activities of the Comintern stemming from Lenin's August 1920 'Theses on the National and Colonial Question'. While the fortunes of the Party are not the concern of this discussion, it is nevertheless important to note that the early years of the Party's life were profoundly influenced by theory and policy imposed by the Comintern and by internal Japanese debates about the proper role of the party. In Japan around 1920, the attractions of Marxism-Leninism were drawing a number of anarchosyndicalists away from direct action towards a more organised revolutionary stance.

Lenin's 'Theses on the National and Colonial Questions' discussed the role of revolution in Asia generally, but did not deal with Japan specifically. Lenin had recognised the need for 'successive periods of development of the revolutionary experience', although this was admittedly designed for colonies that had yet to go through the full bourgeois revolution based on parliamentarism. Lenin, indeed, developed no strategy for the unusual position of Japanese workers – semi-organised, partially exposed to ideology and faced with a repressive state structure.

It was through the influence of Yamakawa Hitoshi and Sakai Toshihiko that the *Communist Manifesto* and Leninist and other Bolshevik ideas gained currency among the left in Japan. Sakai was a journalist who was active with Kotoku in the early dissemination of socialism. Yamakawa had been a student radical and was associated with those others in publishing *The Commoners' News (Heimin shimbun)* since 1907 and he developed into an influential theorist. His most famous statement was his 1922 article 'A Change of Direction for the Proletarian Movement', in which he advocated mass action through a revolutionary proletarian vanguard; this action would be directed to combatting bourgeois politics. Revolution was to come via reform through class politics. Beckmann and Okubo call it 'hardly more than a call to arms for intellectuals', [7] although Yamakawa certainly intended it to be otherwise. But the doctrine of revolution as put forward by Yamakawa was weak and, in any case, written partly for the factional purpose of condemning the anarchists who were influential within the Marxist movement at the time.

The study of Marxism-Leninism had really advanced very little and it needed the ideas of Fukumoto Kazuo to apply Marxist-Leninist revolutionary theory to the Japanese experience. The academic study of Marxism was also developing, and one of Japan's foremost scholars of political economy, Kawakami Hajime, was making Marxism a popular subject in the universities from his base in Kyoto University. Kawakami, an academic economist, recognised the revolutionary relevance of Marx's thought but was not, in the early 1920s, politically activated: he was even, according to Bernstein, increasingly unsure of himself as a scholar of authority on Marxian thought, doubts which were reinforced by Fukumoto's trenchant criticism. [8] Fukumoto's attack on Kawakami and others including Yamakawa for their reformism and inability to promote the struggle, had a strong theoretical and practical impact: it brought Marxist thinking closer to the essence of Marxist-Leninist philosophy. [9]

Yet 'Fukumoto-ism' as it became known, was not a revolutionary strategy and, in many ways, it inhibited the growth of a united proletarian movement. Fukumoto stressed the need for theoretical purity, proper understanding of the theory of revolution, while striving to achieve (as the draft platform of the JCP planned) a bourgeois revolution as the basis for the proletarian revolution. But Fukumoto wanted organisational purity as well, and encouraged notions of splitting off from socialist workers to ensure theoretical correctness within the vanguard party: 'unity through separation' was his slogan. Like Yamakawa, Fukumoto did not in the end provide a revolutionary strategy; rather, he directed his energies towards party ideas and structures.

The so-called '1927 Theses' from the Comintern criticised the Fukumoto approach and accused him of isolating the party from the mass of the proletariat. The Theses reiterated what the Comintern's 1922 draft platform of the JCP had stated, that a two-stage revolution was required in the Japanese case – a bourgeois-democratic one followed by a proletarian revolution. Furthermore, the leadership of the peasantry by the proletariat was seen as essential:

> There are thus in Japan both the objective prerequisites for a bourgeois-democratic revolution (the feudal remnants in the state structure, an acute agrarian problem) and the objective prerequisites for the rapid transformation of the bourgeois revolution into a socialist revolution (the high level of concentration of capital, the growing number of

trusts, the close relationship between the State and the trusts, the approximation of the economy to State capitalism, and the unity of the bourgeoisie with the landed nobility)...For the working class, the bourgeois-democratic revolution is merely a step on the road to a socialist revolution. In leading the bourgeois-democratic revolution, the proletariat does not lose its class consciousness, on the contrary, it is precisely the prospect of transforming the bourgeois-democratic revolution into a socialist revolution that is the decisive factor for the proletariat at all stages of the struggle. [10]

Thus the party, following the 1927 Theses, saw Japan controlled by feudal remnants; this required a first-stage bourgeois-democratic revolution. However, the two-stage theory of revolution had its critics within the communist movement, notably those associated with the journal *Rono*, or *Labour-Farmer* – Yamakawa included. The debate between these militant Marxists, who regarded Japanese capitalism as essentially controlled by the imperialist bourgeoisie, and the Party which saw strong feudal remnants in the Japanese system, stretched from the late 1920s into the postwar period and created, in its wake, an aggressive academic debate on the nature of the development of the Japanese capitalism, a debate which spurred the political level of the discussion. The Labour-Farmer faction regarded the bourgeois revolution as having been completed, and an immediate proletarian revolution was required to overthrow bourgeois monopoly capitalism.

The theoretical debate in Japan about the nature of revolution reflected again the divisions within the Marxist movement in Japan and the tenacity with which those differences were propounded and defended. These divisions spilled into left-wing party politics before and after the war, and the influence of the Labour-Farmer faction was important in the ideological basis of the postwar Japan Socialist Party. [11] But if the domestic approach to revolution was split, the influence of the Comintern did not help matters. The 1931 and 1932 Theses were contradictory on the question of revolution and the place and role of the Party. The 1931 Theses, prepared by party members in Japan in the light of their understanding of Comintern views, criticised the Labour-Farmer faction but advocated a one-stage revolution:

...the fundamental class contradiction in this period is the struggle between the bourgeoisie and the proletariat...the nature of the coming revolution in Japan is a 'proletarian revolution that involves bourgeois-democratic tasks'...the immediate goal of the struggle of our Japanese proletariat is to overthrow the bourgeois-landlord power in the imperial system, under which finance capital holds sway, and to establish the dictatorship of the proletariat.

This view was then strongly criticised by the Comintern, which produced a new set of theses on the Japanese situation within a year. This document was, according to Scalapino, 'to stand as the basic document for the Japanese Communist Party until 1946 and, even then,...certain of its basic provisions were reiterated'. [12]

The 1932 Theses reinstated the two-stage theory of revolution. They argued that the bourgeois state was upheld by the imperial system, which was 'the main pillar of political reaction and of all the relics of feudalism in the country'. The Comintern thus required the abolition of the Emperor system. The Comintern's second important concern was the need to assure a successful agrarian revolution. Therefore the Theses saw 'the character of the forthcoming revolution in Japan as a bourgeois-democratic revolution with a tendency to grow rapidly into a Socialist revolution', under the guidance of the dictatorship of the proletariat.

These concepts of revolution, as originally developed in the prewar Marxist movement, were never entirely appropriate to the conditions in Japan. Part of the problem was that the Comintern was unable fully to take account of the harsh realities of the oppression of the left-wing in the imperial state. Comintern demands for espousing the overthrow of that imperial system were neither practical nor helpful. Internal difficulties were also severe: a tendency towards wrangling over theory and the inability to apply that theory to practice, made the movement disunited and weak. Depredations by police action only furthered the ideological disunity and different individuals and groups were imprisoned or fled. Again, the extent of state direction of Japanese capitalism was such that it was never entirely clear whether the bourgeoisie were the dominant force in the economic structure. This combination of factors bound Japanese Marxists into a revolutionary strategy that, while forced on them by Stalin and the Comintern, could not in the end be effected. The Japanisation of Marxist revolutionary theories (which was not fully carried through until the 1960s and 1970s) thus began when overthrow of the imperial system was advocated and seen to be impossible. While this was in one sense submission to imperialism, factionalism within the Marxist movement in Japan made inevitable the failure of the revolutionary ideal. However, the efficacy of Japanese Marxist revolutionary ideas is related closely to concepts of the role of the proletarian party, and the political objectives of Marxism.

The Role of the Proletarian Party

Marxism and left-wing party politics have been intertwined since the Social Democratic Party was established in 1901 by Kotoku Shusui and his colleagues. But left-wing parties have not all been Communist: the social democratic movement had a strong base both in Marxism and in the Christian humanism of Suzuki Bunji, who founded the Yuaikai, or Friendly Society, in 1912, even though certain elements in that organisation later took on a stronger radical Marxist attitude and Suzuki himself announced in 1919 his conversion to socialism. The debate about Marxism, class and the role of the proletarian party have been extremely important to the development and political expression, of Marxist thought in Japan. In the prewar period the JCP was overridden by the nationalism and imperialism of the 1920s and 1930s while the party's postwar tactics (which will be discussed below) led to the eventual acceptance of the need for a parliamentary role for the achievement of the bourgeois-democratic revolution.

It was in Yamakawa Hitoshi's 'Change of Direction' article in 1922 that a defined role for the proletariat was proclaimed. Very much influenced by the Bolshevik experience in the Soviet Union, Yamakawa hit out at the strongly anarchosyndicalist theories of Osugi Sakae and others, which placed priority on violence and direct action as the keys to the success of the socialist movement. Yamakawa's was not a full programme but the arguments of an intellectual theorist, but he outlined a political role for the proletariat. He identified the interests of the socialist movement with those of the working masses (he also used the prefix 'proletarian' masses), and called for the vanguard minority within the proletarian movement to identify this goal with mass action, and encourage mass support. It was, however, an exceedingly voluntarist approach, for the revolutionary vanguard had to, wrote Yamakawa, 'learn how to activate (*ugokasu*) the masses', [13] without being dissolved into the masses. Yamakawa is saying very clearly here that the proletarian vanguard is essential to the success of the proletarian movement, and that care was necessary to ensure that its existence was preserved. It also gave a concrete political role to the coalition of the vanguard with the proletarian masses: 'we must fight bourgeois politics with a positive spirit. We must throw proletarian politics against the politics of the bourgeoisie'. [14]

Yamakawa spoke of the two elements of the Japanese proletarian movement — the socialist movement and the labour movement — but the Comintern's 'Bukharin Theses' (the 1922 platform for the JCP) placed the party at the centre of widespread revolutionary activity:

> .....the Japanese Communist Party, which has as its aim the struggle on behalf of the dictatorship of the proletariat, must make efforts to mobilise all social forces that are capable of carrying on the struggle against the existing government, because its overthrow is an inevitable stage in the struggle of the working class to achieve dictatorship.

'Yamakawaism', therefore, signalled the beginning of mass activity by the Marxist movement and the pursuance of class struggle, and it was a line given stronger and more focussed political content by directions from the Comintern to the JCP.

In contrast to the JCP, the social democratic parties and the labour movement in Japan emphasised the solidarity of the various classes and rejected the notion of a proletarian vanguard. This did not fit with the notions of equality that ran through their ideology: for them, a large, inclusive, democratic force was required for reform. [15] But for Yamakawa, losing the distinction between the working masses and the vanguard minority 'was not a step towards progress in the proletarian movement, but a fall from revolutionism to reformism and opportunism'. [16]

Despite Yamakawa's call and some impressive inroads made into the labour movement up to 1928, the history of the prewar JCP was such that it never truly became a party of the mass of workers. Even under a revolutionary vanguard the JCP was, on the contrary, a party of socialist sects which suffered from the further disadvantage of being illegal and therefore subject to persecution by the state. Yamakawa began to move away from his support for the JCP. He developed the idea of a 'single proletarian party' which could absorb into itself anti-capitalist elements such as workers and farmers. This was a strategy which ultimately Yamakawa felt the JCP could not achieve.

Fukumoto took a position based firmly on the need for theoretical correctness, and his attitude to the party was that effective unity could only be based on the internal separation of the genuine from the false Marxists. But Fukumoto's approach was again inward-looking and divisive, a further example of the factionalism within the JCP. Fukumoto lambasted Yamakawa for his 'reformism' and 'parliamentarism' and his neglect of the important role of the vanguard communist party. Yamakawa argued that a single legal proletarian party was necessary. Such was the intensity of this debate that one writer later commented that:

> Fukumoto's criticism of Yamakawa certainly explained Yamakawa's defects clearly, but Fukumotoism not only prevented the realising of the problem of unification of the masses raised by Yamakawa; it also thwarted the possibility of the positive benefits for the Japanese labour movement of those things built up in Yamakawa-ism. [17]

The Comintern's 1927 Theses, however, criticised both Yamakawa and Fukumoto and called for a return to the practical business of politics:

> The Communist Party of Japan will be in a position to solve its historical tasks only as a mass party...It must definitely realise that 'without revolutionary theory there can be no revolutionary movement.' But it must just as definitely realise that without a revolutionary mass struggle, without actual and strong connections with the masses, theory is futile.

The 1927 Theses reinstated the party as 'the revolutionary vanguard of the proletariat fighting for the fundamental historical interests of the working class as a whole'. It would thus seek the same sort of general goals as most of the social-democratic parties — an alliance of all proletarian elements — although the was to remain the vanguard and the active leader of the movement because, the Theses stressed, 'the Japanese proletariat has no revolutionary traditions'.

The formal separation of the party from the mass of workers was posed even more clearly by the 1931 Theses. They argued that the 'communist party is a political union of the vanguard of the proletariat' and that all Japanese revolutionary workers must strengthen the JCP. The Theses recognised the organisational task ahead in creating a viable mass struggle:

> The party must strengthen and expand its organisation with a clear view of its task of winning over the majority of the proletariat by independently organising and directing the economic and political struggles of the working masses.

The 1932 Theses determined, in large part, the future JCP attitude to the role of the party: it was to lead the alliance of workers and peasants under the hegemony of the proletariat, to establish the dictatorship of the proletariat after the first revolutionary stage and to lead the proletariat into the socialist revolution. The 1932 Theses drew the JCP further away from the ideology of the other Marxist-based parties, which coalesced under various names and banners throughout the 1930s. [18] In their case, reformism was seen to be achievable through legal processes; revolution was an unacceptable strategy. But the divisions in the Marxist movement drove left and right into tighter and smaller corners over time, to the detriment of the interests of the proletariat. For neither the communists in the JCP nor the social democrats based in the labour movement considered unity a viable option: the 1932 Theses expressly ruled out a balanced union by emphasising the vanguard role of the proletariat. The 1932 Theses were, however, also instrumental in forcing adherents away from the JCP. Sano Manabu, a key JCP figure, for example, claimed that the Theses' attack on the emperor system was the turning point in the process of his renunciation of the Party. In 1933 he and another imprisoned party member, Nabeyama Sadachika, rejected the JCP and the Comintern, claiming that the party was 'a modern representative of

Machiavellianism' and a negative force in Japanese society. [19] While Sano's *tenko*, or his renunciation of an anti-nationalist ideology and return to nationalism, was the beginning of mass defections from the JCP, it did not destroy it permanently. The message of the 1932 Theses was taken up again in the postwar period.

The Application of Marxism-Leninism to Japanese Society

One of the greatest intellectual attractions – and political uses – of Marxist-Leninist thought in Japan has been the critique it has provided from outside the system of Japanese history and society, especially its modern capitalist manisfestations. Yet this, too, has led to a deep and continuing division within the schools of Marxism-Leninism in Japan, and in the communist movement. The ideological split that originated in the late 1920s led to two opposed traditions of communism in Japan, the one official, the other academic-centred but with strong influence over what was to become the radical wing of the Japan Socialist Party. [20] The origins of the split stem from the two major figures who helped spread the political ideology of Marxism in Japan – Yamakawa Hitoshi and Fukumoto Kazuo. The origins of the split also derieving from the differing concepts of revolution as it applied to Japan.

The orthodox view of the JCP was that of the two-stage revolution, as advocated by the 1927 Theses and reaffirmed by the 1932 Theses: the first-stage, or bourgeois-democratic revolution, required a coalition of labour, peasants and the petty bourgeoisie; this would lead quickly into the socialist revolution under the leadership of the proletarian vanguard, the Communist Party. A rival thesis was that espoused by the group which initiated the theoretical Marxist journal *Rono (Labour-Farmer)*, in December 1927. Yamakawa was a member, as were other well known socialists and radical intellectuals such as Inomata Tsunao and Arahata Kanson. They became known as the Labour-Farmer faction. They were challenged by another group of scholars who were involved in the collection of lectures entitled *Nihon shihonshugi hattatsushi koza (Lectures on the History of the Development of Japanese Capitalism)* published in 1932-3. This group came to be known as the Koza-ha or the Lecturer faction. It was this faction which became associated with the orthodox JCP view of Japanese economic development as requiring a two-stage revolution.

This debate, while carried out primarily at an academic level, had far-reaching political implications. The ideological extremism of the Labour-Farmer faction ran them foul of the Comintern, which was itself embroiled in the bitter rivalry between Stalin and Trotsky. The group was expelled from the party in February 1928. Expulsion notwithstanding, the Labour-Farmer faction continued to exert a strong influence on the direction of the Marxist-Leninist theoretical debate in Japan. In fact, the controversy between the Labour-Farmer and the Lecturer factions gave a voluminous historical basis to Marxist debate and helped plant Marxism as an issue firmly in the Japanese intellectual milieu. Previous Marxist scholars had devoted their time largely to explaining rather than developing Marxism. Kawakami Hajime, the best known Marxist scholar in Japan at the time, was an interpreter of Marxian economics; he did not make a significant contribution to the Marxist debate about Japanese economic history, although he did much to provide the knowledge of the tools which others could then apply.

The debate between the two factions turned on interpretation of the Meiji Restoration of 1868. The Labour-Farmer theorists regarded the Restoration as a bourgeois revolution which opened the way for the domination of the Japanese economic structure by capitalism. The imperial system was dominated by capitalist, not feudal forces, since the landlord system – insofar as it had been feudal – had been 'defeudalised' and landlords had become bourgeois capitalists. It was impossible, argued the Labour-Farmer faction, for capitalism to exist on a feudal base, as the Lecturer faction contended. The Labour-Farmer strategy for revolution was based on a coalition between the proletariat and the poor peasants (and also the petty bourgeoisie), not the vanguard role of the communist party:

> What sort of revolutionary strategy is suggested by a dialectical materialist analysis of the present historical conditions in Imperial Japan? In a very short form, we could say the following: (1) The main objective is the overthrow of imperialism; (2) the main revolutionary force is the proletariat; (3) the main reserve force is the poor peasantry; (4) the second reserve force consists of urban semi-proletariat (5) the direction of main efforts is toward the

isolation of the democratic petty bourgeoisie; (6) the focus of force will be the firm alliance between the proletariat and the poor peasants. [21]

The revolution would thus be a single stage proletarian revolution, in a country with a highly developed capitalist system where bourgeois capitalist elements dominated an inherently feudal landlord system.

The conventional view of the JCP, as expressed in the 1927 and 1932 Theses, and as developed in the work of the Lecturer theorists, was that the Meiji Restoration of 1868 was not a thoroughgoing bourgeois revolution, but reflected the prior contradictions within the Tokugawa regime: a group of lower samurai and wealthy merchants alongside a feudal structure based on the imperial and court system, high-ranking samurai and the landlords. The revolution was carried through by the lower samurai, who developed a capitalist industrial base in cooperation with the merchant class, but feudal elements remained in the imperial system and the landlord system. Thus it was necessary to promote a two-stage revolution: the first to eliminate the feudal elements which dominated the absolutist state structure in the Taisho-Showa periods from 1911 onwards, and the second revolution to overthrow the then complete bourgeois capitalist system. One of the leading theorists of the lecturer faction, Noro Eitaro (who organised the series of lectures on the development of Japanese capitalism, became chairman of the JCP's Central Committee in 1933, but died in police custody in February 1934), explained the process of restoration:

The Meiji Restoration was clearly a political revolution but at the same time was a broadly based and thoroughgoing social revolution. This, as is widely known, was not simply a restoration of Imperial Rule but a powerful social change to place the capitalists and capitalist landowners in power.....

The Meiji Restoration was carried out through the conscious cooperation of the reactionary Imperial Court and those of the warrior class who could not in the end throw off their feudal consciousness. Furthermore, right up until today our political organisation has not been able to abandon its reactionary, despotic, absolutist character. However, this did not prevent the development of the Japanese capitalist economy. In fact that despotic political power also cultivated in a hothouse environment the process of change from feudal productive methods to capitalist production methods and, in promoting that change, made possible the surprisingly rapid development of Japan as a capitalist country. [22]

While maintaining that feudal elements had been abolished, the Labour-Farmer theorists found it difficult to explain the nature of imperialism and military rule in the 1920s and 1930s in Japan: it was not easy for them to assess the close and cooperative role of the bourgeoisie in the political arena in Japan. Likewise, the Lecturer faction went to considerable lengths to explain the mechanisms of the 'dual economy', the capitalist system based on a still-feudal peasant agrarian sector.

Some Marxist scholars claim to have found a way through the centre of this dispute. Uno Kozo, for example, developed a theory that isolated a purely theoretical 'capitalism' (as in Marx's *Capital*) from a process developing towards 'capitalism' (one stage of which Lenin analysed in his *Imperialism*). Uno argued that the development of Japanese capitalism in a wider international imperialist phase preserved, rather than abolished, feudal agriculture. This was because, Uno's translator writes,'the form of finance-capital, with its peculiar mode of accumulation through the joint-stock company system, was capable of securing the commoditisation of labour-power without revolutionising the existing form of agriculture'. [23]

Did this debate help the application of Marxism-Leninism to Japanese society? Clearly, the difficulty lay in how Japanese history and society were analysed, and the type of Marxist-Leninist analysis that was being used. A major contradiction lay between the need to justify the use of the universalist methodology of the dialectic and historical materialism, and the unusual and difficult conditions in which Japanese Marxists found themselves in the prewar years: attempting to rationalise Japanese economic history in class terms under an oppressive and imperialist regime, the very existence of which upset the Western European model of development from which Marxist economic analysis sprang. Japan was closer to the Russian model in the way conservative political forces were aligned against revolutionary forces, but Japan's economic development was much further advanced than that of Russia in 1917. The Lecturer theorists argued (as did the Comintern's 1927 and 1932 Theses) that Japanese conditions resembled those of pre-revolutionary Russia, in the combination of 'monarchy... landlordism...and predatory monopoly capitalism'.

Some theorists like Sano Manabu and Akamatsu Katsumaro stressed the peculiarity of Japanese conditions in an attempt to come to terms with the meaning of Marxism for an Asian society such as Japan:

> The coming bourgeois-democratic revolution in Japan will be different in nature from those experienced in the capitalist or in the colonial or semi-colonial countries...The proletariat will carry out the change as the leading force in a violent clash with the imperialist bourgeoisie, which holds hegemony in a political alliance with the landlords. This change will turn quickly into a proletarian revolution-so quickly that the change will mark the beginning of a proletarian revolution...Japan, which is... a reactionary imperialist power in world politics, stands on the eve of a bourgeois-democratic revolution because of the contradictory feudal relations in its domestic life. In the case of Japan, there will be a special type of bourgeois-democratic revolution in the developing process of the world's proletarian revolution. [24]

Sano, as Hoston writes, asked 'What is it that differentiates Marxism from other Eurocentric approaches to development? What is valuable in Marxism for us? And finally, can Marxism still be useful as a theory of development if it is stripped of these prejudicial elements?' [25] Sano developed the theory of 'one-state socialism' for Japan, which had strong nationalist overtones. Monarchy, he thought, was compatible with socialism, as the emperor system was 'an expression of national unity which lessened the brutality of domestic class opposition'. [26] Sano's is the clearest example – but by no means the only one – of the adaptation of elements of nationalism to socialism. But as Wagner writes, he "did not completely renounce his early Marxist-Leninist beliefs. Instead, his brand of Japanese revolutionary socialism was the result of a maturation of his pre–*tenko* ideas and of the post–*tenko* adaptations that he made to Marxism in order to bring his western philosophy into closer conformity with Japanese national customs and institutions'. [27]

However, others who also harboured doubts about the ultimate relevance of Marxism, such as Kawakami Hajime, did not reject the Marxism of the JCP. Kawakami fought hard through many years of scholarship and political activity, to apply Marxism to the truths he held dearest. It was for him an 'academic faith', in Bernstein's words, and one which ultimately did not give him satisfaction. But it did give him a scientific methodology which was appealing to whole generations of scholars. Bernstein puts it most aptly:

> Marxism, however, was different from the other thought systems which the Japanese had adopted throughout their long history, because it was a total system of thought, embracing man, nature, and history in an intricately logical structure whose parts presumably could not be separated and rearranged, like a child's tinker toy. Rather, Marxism presented the Japanese intellectual with a new world view, rigorously materialistic, a monism that challenged the very core of Japanese society and social values with its own interpretation of the nature of social relations and historical development. Marxism insisted upon an end to the coexistence of ideas, in Maruyama Masao's expression, and hence required of the would-be Japanese Marxist a 'bracing-up' of his mental processes. Because Marxism posed as a science, this demand was irresistible. [28]

There is no doubt that Marxism-Leninism was applied to, and accepted as a scientific analysis of, Japanese society. It called forth a huge volume of valuable revisionist scholarship on Japanese economic development but in political terms it was a failure in the prewar period. The attraction was as a critique, not a strategy for revolution despite the underground activities of the JCP. The inability of Marxist theory ultimately to explain the political strength of the imperialist state led in part to its being 'indigenised' to account for imperialist nationalism. But just as there is no Japanese 'Marxism', there was no one scientific analysis of Japanese society by Marxists. Japanese Marxism spawned sects, and orthodoxy was determined by politics as much as by the methodology.

Nonetheless, the attempt to apply the scientific methodology of the dialectic to Japan took place outside, although not too far removed from, the immediate political arena. It was surprising how quickly there developed a strong tradition of Marxist analysis of Japanese modern history after the introduction of Marxism to Japan. This was inevitable, for the revolutionary movement required a theoretical under-pinning based on the Japanese experience, and the political wing of the movement (despite suppression) needed a reference point in the Japanese, not the European or Russian, tradition if the proletarian party movement were to be successful. In the prewar period, that movement was not successful, but not for lack of a Japan-centred ideology. Indeed, rather because of the inability of the movement to agree on appropriate models, the proletarian movement was continually split. Theory, in fact, defeated practice.

Postwar Marxism In Japan

Marxist thought in postwar Japan was firmly rooted in prewar personalities, intra-party politics and ideological disputes. It is therefore treated less fully here. The major difference from the prewar experience has been that Marxism has been legal, and parties and movements based on Marxism have become an accepted and important part of the parliamentary political process in Japan. Furthermore, the postwar period saw the 'Japanisation' of Marxism taken to complete accommodation with the parliamentary process, as a means towards a peaceful bourgeois democratic revolution. But there is still no 'Marxism' in Japan; there remain a multitude of ideologies inspired by Marxism and Marxism-Leninism. The JCP considers itself the vanguard of this ideology, but the Japan Socialist Party boasts a proud prewar lineage, as do the Democratic Socialist Party, which was formed by defecting Socialists in 1960, and the Socialism Association (Shakaishugi kyokai), a radical intellectuals' group within the Japan Socialist Party that derives from the Labour-Farmer faction of the 1930s.

In simple terms, the JCP was heir to the Lecturer tradition and advocated the need for a two-stage revolution, while the left wing of the socialist movement maintained the Labour-Farmer line that Japan was ready for proletarian revolution, being at a well-developed stage of capitalism. The right wing of the socialist movement was only very tenuously related to the Marxist tradition, advocating a 'social evolution' that was 'basically an evolutionary but fundamental change in economic relations among people, enabling them to develop a more moral society...equated with socialism'. [29] It was from the right wing of the Japan Socialist Party that the democratic socialists split in 1959 to form the new Democratic Socialist Party in 1960. For them peaceful, democratic forms are the preferred means of advancing through the stage of democracy to socialism.

The internal debates in the Socialist and Communist parties have been as tortuous and internally damaging as were those in the prewar period. Studies of these debates have been made elsewhere. [30] There are nevertheless some key points in the experience of postwar Marxist thought, notably related to the environment in which Japan found itself in the 1950s and 1960s. A lengthy Allied occupation during which the left-wing was first liberated and encouraged, then heavily controlled, overlapped a war in the Korean Peninsula which exacerbated a cold war spirit and solidified Japan's role in the American strategy of containment of communism on the Asian mainland. Japan was bound to the United States by a Security Treaty which the left-wing regarded as representing their own oppression and as a derogation of Japanese sovereignty. At the same time, conservative political rule in Japan became entrenched as economic prosperity strengthened middle-class values, and brought Japan into the society of nations on an equal basis. In this social climate, the appeal of Marxist-Leninist ideology was restricted and the chief problems for theory revolved around the nature of the transition to proletarian rule on the one hand, and the successful adaptation of Marxist ideology as a whole to Japanese conditions on the other.

The first postwar attempt to adapt Marxism-Leninism to Japanese conditions was that of Nosaka Sanzo, a member of the JCP Central Committee, after his return from exile in January 1946. The Nosaka line tried to relate communism to the fact of the Occupation: he wanted a mass party, dedicated to a 'peaceful' revolution. This revolution was to be the completion of the bourgeois-democratic revolution, for he saw the postwar constitutional reforms as externally imposed and unable to come to terms with the 'feudal' remnants in Japanese society: the bureaucracy, the monopoly capitalists and the rural elite. Nosaka felt that it was essential for the party to draw to itself the peasants, small and medium business and the petty bourgeoisie. This form of revolution was consistent with that of the 1932 Theses, without the violence espoused therein: Japanese capitalism still harboured feudal elements, which resisted democratic processes, and abolition of the emperor system, land reform and civil liberties were required. While this programme was orthodox, the tactics of the 'lovable' JCP invited Cominform criticism of the Nosaka views. The Cominform's claim that Nosaka was 'naturalising' Marxism-Leninism on Japanese soil was quite appropriate, for Nosaka was indeed trying to make the theory fit the undeniable facts of military occupation and growing distrust of the communist cause by the US. He began what eventually became the programme for the JCP's popularisation and political success of the late 1960s and 1970s.

A new direction in party theory appeared in the 1951 Theses prepared by the party's Secretary General, Tokuda Kyuichi, which drew heavily on Maoist and Stalinist ideas in its approach to revolutionary tactics. Tokuda aimed at the establishment of a national-liberation democratic government based on an alliance of workers, peasants and small-medium businessmen, through armed struggle and the overthrow by violent revolution of the existing regime based on American imperialism. [31]

But the advocation and practice of armed struggle, while fine in theory, was not helpful to the communist cause in postwar Japan. The party was weakened and factionalised in this period, and it was not until the 1958 Seventh Party Congress that a return to theoretical pragmatism was solidified. The Eighth Congress in 1961 assured a return to the Nosaka tradition of the peaceful path. The Japanese revolution was, in these terms, to be two-stage and uninterrupted, an 'anti-imperialist, anti-monopolist capitalist revolution'. The JCP would lead a multi-class national democratic united front, through the electoral and parliamentary process.

This 1961 programme, says Fukui, 'remains the basic guideline for the JCP's ideology and policy commitments'. [32] It also took Nosaka's naturalisation further, being particularly nationalist in its tone, as Ueda Koichiro (currently a parliamentarian and leading theorist of the Party) shows:

The Report of the Central Committee of the Japan Com-

munist Party to the Eighth Party Congress said the following about the meaning of revolution in Japan: 'This
revolution will be a people's democratic revolution based
on the working classes. As a democratic revolution against
imperialism and monopoly capitalism, it will be a new democratic revolution. It will also be a step towards victory for
an international united front against imperialism, and will
be internationally significant in forming the basis of a firm
peace in Asia...' The revolution will break the hold of
American imperialism and Japanese monopoly capital, and
establish people's democratic power. It will decisively alter
the path of Japan. This will change the Japanese path from
the path of 'American imperialism and Japanese monopoly
capital that relies on America and revives Japanese militar-
ism and imperialism', to the 'popular path of restoring Japanese autonomy, achieving real independence and democracy and aiming for peace and social progress'. It will bring
about a Japan of independence, democracy, peace,
neutralism and prosperity, will move towards a socialist Japan through a popular revolution. Japan has grown into a
modern heavy industrial economy as a result of productivity advances from the socialisation of labour, the high levels
of culture and technology and a hard working people. Under correct Marxist-Leninist leadership by the Japan
Communist Party this will make possible the necessary conditions for rapid progress in building socialism in Japan . [33]

Since the 1961 Program was enunciated, the JCP has been
dominated by Miyamoto Kenichi. [34] The JCP has become a parliamentary party, throwing off its violent revolutionary theory altogether, bent on forming a coalition of classes to effect the
democratic revolution. It has won success at the polls, and a
large measure of respectability amongst the general public, and
its theoretical basis- while firmly Marxist-Leninist originally-has
been 'naturalised' [35] to suit domestic conditions. It has thus isolated itself from both the Soviet and Chinese Communist parties.
It has removed the term 'cell' from its vocabulary along with
'dictatorship of the proletariat', and in 1976 the word 'Marxist-
Leninism' officially became 'scientific socialism'. This was said
to be a return to the original terminology of Marx and Engels,
but it served a clear domestic purpose in removing the

party another step from the violence surrounding its past. The theory of Marxism as used by contemporary communists in Japan is, in form at least, well adapted to the social and political climate of that country.

The Japan Socialist Party is also a Marxist party, but it has never been revolutionary. Again, the theory of socialist Marxism has been peculiarly 'naturalised', but the left wing of the Socialist Party has always been anti-Communist, partly because of its Labour-Farmer legacy but also because of the JCP's tactic of violent revolution in the 1950s and, conversely, its later electoral success.

The theory of 'structural reform' has dominated Socialist Party Marxism in the postwar period. This theory argues that within Japan's monopoly capitalist system, peaceful revolution is required through democratic reform and restructuring of the present capitalist society. The objective is the socialist revolution through gradual changes to the means of production (such as the nationalisation of industry) and an end to class conflict (especially via the parliamentary process and effective social policies to redress income differentials). [36]

It is ironic that it has been differences over the nature of Japanese capitalism and the related strategy of revolution — a debate going back to the 1920s — which has influenced the way the two Marxist parties have adapted to the parliamentary road. The JCP's emphasis on the need for a democratic revolution *before* a proletarian revolution has no doubt aided its electoral success and given purpose to its policies. The Socialists, on the other hand, have found it difficult to relate their inflexible brand of 'structural reform' to a staunchly capitalist, competitive and changing society. The goal of proletarian revolution seems much further away than that of 'popular parliamentarism' and the democratic revolution.

Conclusion

The postwar experience of Marxist thought in Japan is neither limited nor negligible. It is the end result of a long process of adaptation of European ideas to an Asian culture. Those ideologies built in the heyday of European revolutionary movements were introduced initially to a Japan ruled firmly by a regime founded on an elitist revolution and supported by a popular naturalistic deism. Marxism—or the various strands of it which found root in Japanese intellectual circles – did not sit easily in this climate and has been slowly moulded since the 1920s to fit the national circumstances.

But Marxism has been the most important critique of the Japanese polity to appear in the last century in Japan. Not only did it give a world view to the Japanese that was alien enough to be considered subversive *per se*, but it provided a critique which could not be refuted theoretically from within the Japanese tradition. Likewise, it gave a methodology that appeared to be scientific, the first to have appeared in Japan in the field of ideas. It was also inherently reformist if not, in some circumstances, revolutionary, and for that reason inspired generations of scholars to a new approach to the social sciences in Japan. Marxism's intellectual contribution has been as profound as its political legacy.

But is Marxism in Japan Marxist? In a way, it hardly matters. Marxism reached its full flower as an ideological and revorevolutionary influence in Japan when the state least wanted it – for that reason, its effects may have been all the greater, since the resulting clash between official and radical ideologies left deep and enduring marks in the fabric of Japanese political, social and intellectual life.

NOTES

* I wish to thank several colleagues for their comments on an earlier draft of this chapter.

1. John Crump, *The Origins of Socialist Thought in Japan*(London, Croom Helm, 1983).

2. George M. Beckmann and Okubo Genji, *The Japanese Communist Party 1922-1945* (Stanford University Press, Stanford, 1969), p. 1.

3. Takeuchi Yoshitomo (ed.), *Marukishizumu II, Gendai nihon shiso taikei vol. 21* (Chikuma Shobo, Tokyo, 1965), p. 13.

4. Ibid., p. 15.

5. Stephen S. Large, *Organized Workers and Socialist Politics in Interwar Japan* (Cambridge University Press, Cambridge, 1981), p. 32.

6. Tetsuo Najita, *Japan, The Intellectual Foundations of Modern Japanese Politics* (University of Chicago Press, Chicago, 1974), p. 123.

7. Beckmann and Okubo, *The Japanese Communist Party*, p. 54.

8. Gail Lee Bernstein, *Japanese Marxist, A Portrait of Kawakami Hajime, 1879-1946* (Harvard University Press, Cambridge, 1976).

9. Takeuchi, *Marukishizumu II*, p. 25.

10. The full text of the 1922 Draft Platform and the 1927, 1931 and 1932 Theses are in Beckmann and Okubo, *The Japanese Communist Party*, pp. 280-357.

11. Robert A. Scalapino, *The Japanese Communist Movement 1920-1966* (University of California Press, Berkeley, 1967), p. 33 and J.A.A. Stockwin, *The Japanese Socialist Party and Neutralism* (Melbourne University Press, Melbourne, 1968).

12. Scalapino, *The Japanese Communist Movement*, p. 42.

13. The full Japanese text of this article is in Okochi Kazuo (ed.), *Shakaishugi, Gendai nihon shiso taikei vol. 15* (Chikuma Shobo, Tokyo, 1963), pp. 332-43. This quote is at p. 343.

14. Ibid., p. 342.

15. George Oakley Totten III, *The Social Democratic Movement in Prewar Japan* (Yale University Press, New Haven, 1966), p. 184.

16. Okochi, *Shakaishugi*, p. 343.

17. Takeuchi, *Marukishizumu II*, p. 27.

18. See Totten, *The Social Democratic Movement*.

19. Jeffrey Wagner, *Sano Manabu and the Japanese Adaptation of Socialism* (University Microfilms, Ann Arbor, 1980), p. 101.

20. Summaries of the general debate are contained in Najita, *Japan*, pp. 123-5 and George M. Beckmann, 'Japanese Adaptations of Marxism-Leninism', *Asian Cultural Studies*, vol. 3 (October 1962), pp. 103-14.

21. Suzuki Masa, *Nihon no marukusu shugisha* (Nagoya, Kubosha, 1973), p. 62.

22. Uchida Yoshihiko, Otsuka Hisao and Matsushima Eiichi (eds.), *Marukishizumu I, Gendai nihon shiso taikei vol. 20* (Chikuma Shobo, Tokyo, 1966), pp. 82-3.

23. Uno Kozo, *Principles of Political Economy, Theory of a Purely Capitalist Society*, translated by Thomas T. Sekine (Harvester Press, Sussex, 1980), p. xiii.

24. Beckmann and Okubo, *The Japanese Communist Party*, p. 177.

25. Germaine A. Hoston, 'Marxism and Japanese Expansionism, Takahashi Kamekichi and the Theory of Petty Imperialism', Paper for 1982 meeting of American Political Science Association, p. 3.

26. Wagner, *Sano Manabu*, p. 100.

27. Ibid., p. 15.

28. Bernstein, *Japanese Marxist*, p. 166.

29. Allen B. Cole, George O. Totten and Cecil H. Uyehara, *Socialist Parties in Postwar Japan* (Yale University Press, New Haven, 1966) p. 87.

30. Refer to Cole, Totten and Uyehara, *Socialist Parties*; Scalapino, *The Japanese Communist Movement*; and Stockwin, *The Japanese Socialist Party and Neutralism*.

31. Scalapino, *The Japanese Communist Movement*, p. 82. Readers are referred to Scalapino's book for a full treatment of this period.

32. Haruhiro Fukui, 'The Japanese Communist Party, the Miyamoto line and Its Problems', in Morton A. Kaplan (ed.), *The Many Faces of Communism* (Free Press, New York, 1978), p. 283.

33. Ueda Koichiro et al. (eds.), *Koza, Gendai nihon to marukusushugi iv, ideorogii* (Aoki Shoten, Tokyo, 1966), p. 60.

34. See Fukui, 'The Japanese Communist Party'.

35. This aspect is discussed in Paul F. Langer, *Communism in Japan, A Case of Political Naturalization* (Hoover Institution Press, Stanford, 1972).

36. I have not discussed the radical left-wing of the Marxist movement in Japan – the heavily factionalised, student-based groups that emerged from the struggle within the postwar movements. They are partly a reaction to the

moderation of the JCP's brand of Marxism and, while they have been influential in some celebrated anti-government campaigns (such as over Narita airport), their extreme factionalism has limited their ideological and political impact.

SELECT BIBLIOGRAPHY (English-language sources only)

Beckmann, George M. and Okubo Genji, *The Japanese Communist Party 1922-1945* (Stanford University Press, Stanford, 1969). The standard work on the origins and prewar experience of the JCP. Detailed, clear and an invaluable sourcebook.

Bernstein, Gail Lee, *Japanese Marxist, A Portrait of Kawakami Hajime, 1879-1946* (Harvard University Press, Cambridge, 1976). A sympathetic biography of a central figure in the Japanese Marxist tradition, which excellently portrays the flavour of the times.

Cole, Allen B., Totten George O. and Uyehara H. Cecil, *Socialist Parties in Postwar Japan* (Yale University Press, New Haven, 1966). A follow up to the prewar analysis, and an excellent treatment of the conflict between the Socialist parties up to the mid-1960s.

Crump, John, *The Origins of Socialist Thought in Japan* (Croom Helm, London, 1983). A detailed and very personal analysis of the first few decades of socialist thought in Japan. Very useful in assessing Kotoku's role.

Langer, Paul F., *Communism in Japan: A Case of Political Naturalization.* (Hoover Institution Press: Stanford, 1972). A short and handy account of the postwar JCP.

Large, Stephen S., *Organized Workers and Socialist Politics in Interwar Japan* (Cambridge University Press, Cambridge, 1981). As the title indicates, very useful on the interplay of socialism and trade unionism.

Scalapino, Robert A., *The Japanese Communist Movement 1920-1966* (University of California Press, Berkeley, 1967). Overlaps Beckmann and Okubo, but takes the JCP story into postwar years. It is not as good as Beckmann and Okubo on ideological analysis of the Japanese communist movement.

Totten, George, *The Social Democratic Movement in Prewar Japan* (Yale University Press, New Haven, 1966). The standard work on this subject and is followed by the Cole, Totten, Uyehara book.

Wagner, Jeffrey, *Sano Manabu and the Japanese Adaptation of Socialism* (University Microfilms, Ann Arbor, 1980). An excellent analysis of the conflict between Marxism and Japanese tradition and ideology.

8

THE APPLICATION OF MARXISM-LENINISM TO VIETNAM

Sean Kelly and Colin Mackerras

The Vietnamese revolution is of particular significance because it was the first to take place in a colony of a European power. The Vietnamese experience held many lessons for other anti-colonial revolutionaries. Furthermore the Vietnamese revolution faced unparalleled resistance, first from France and then the military might of the United States. The success of their protracted revolutionary struggle against seemingly unbeatable opposition highlights the significance of Vietnamese revolutionary doctrine. Hence the body of Marxist-Leninist theory which guided Vietnam's communists to ultimate victory is worthy of close examination.

A key feature of Vietnamese Marxism-Leninism which contributed greatly to the success of the revolution is the unity of the Party and the continuity of its leadership. Large-scale purges are conspicuously absent in the history of the Vietnamese Party, and although conflicts have occurred, they have never degenerated into factional struggles involving the defeat and humiliation of individuals. The Politburo apparently operates on consensus decision-making and once a clear majority emerges on an issue, the Politburo as a whole accepts the decision in the interest of unity. As a result, violent clashes accompanying changes of line, such as that occasioned by the fall of the gang of four in China, are not a feature of the history of Vietnamese communism. Furthermore, this emphasis on unity has resulted in unparalleled continuity in the Party's leadership; with the exception of natural attrition due to death or old age, the membership of the Politburo has remained the same for forty years.

The unity of the Vietnamese Party, the consensus style of leadership and the theoretical pluralism which results from it, the continuity of leadership and the absence of major internal turmoil as features of the Party all result in a rich body of innovative and flexible Marxist-Leninist theory, a key strength of the revolution.

Not peculiar to Vietnam, but nevertheless a very powerful source of its revolution's success is patriotism. The father of the Vietnamese revolution Ho Chi Minh (1890-1969) has acknowledged that the primary cause of his conversion to socialism, in Leninist form, was his passionate love for Vietnam. In April 1960 he wrote:

> At first, patriotism, not yet communism, led me to have confidence in Lenin, in the Third International. Step by step, along the struggle, by studying Marxism-Leninism parallel with participation in practical activities, I gradually came upon the fact that only socialism and communism can liberate the oppressed nations and the working people throughout the world from slavery. ... Leninism is .... the radiant sun illuminating our path to final victory, to socialism and communism. [1]

In the early 1920s, then living in France under the name of Nguyen Ai Quoc (Nguyen the Patriot), he had joined the French Socialist Party through his friend Jean Longuet, a nephew of Karl Marx. But Ho found the Socialist Party inadequate for his real primary purpose, which at that time was the liberation and independence of Vietnam from French colonialism. It was reading Lenin's 'Theses on the National and Colonial Questions' which gave Ho Chi Minh a real enthusiasm for socialism. Here was the prescription for Vietnam's liberation and independence. [2] It remained equally relevant when later the issues changed from independence from French colonialism to reunification of Vietnam in the face of American imperialism.

One contemporary scholar describes the history of Vietnamese communism 'as the product of a graft'. [3] Ho Chi Minh, he argues, 'grafted Leninist ideology and Bolshevik revolutionary methods onto the youthful patriotic movement of the 1920's'. [4] In June 1925 Ho founded the Vietnamese Revolutionary Youth League, 'the first truly Marxist organization in Indochina'. [5] The eventual success of this graft was due to its combination of a vitally important internal factor, patriotism, and an imported one, proletarian internationalism, the latter taking its roots not so much from Marx as from Lenin. As one writer puts it more specifically, 'the seminal document in Vietnamese Communism is probably not *Das Kapital*, or even the *Communist Manifesto*, but Lenin's Theses on the National and Colonial Questions'. [6]

Clearly the central appeal of Leninism to the Vietnamese is its hostility to colonialism and imperialism. The opposition takes its roots from, and also fosters, Vietnamese patriotism as well as the distinct though related factor of nationalism. [7] The power of these several spirally and mutually supporting phenomena - hatred of imperialism, patriotism, nationalism - has surprised, alarmed and also defeated successive imperialists such as the French and Americans.

Ho Chi Minh is acknowledged as the founder of Vietnamese Marxism-Leninism, but is by no means its only, or even principal contributor to ideology. In theoretical terms Le Duan, Truong Chinh and Vo Nguyen Giap are his equals or superiors. There is indeed a Vietnamese Marxist-Leninist theory which, though initially influenced strongly by China, bears its own characteristic stamp.

One of the strengths of Vietnamese Marxism-Leninism, connected with its plurality of really significant and influential ideological leaders, is the relative lack of personality cult. Ho has never been the subject of a cult anything like that of Stalin, Mao or Kim. Correspondingly, Ho has not been debunked after death as have Stalin and Mao.

Analysis of Vietnam's Class Antagonisms

As Vietnam's communist movement is led by orthodox Marxists, their body of theory begins from a scientific investigation of Vietnamese society and the class antagonisms upon which the revolutionary process is to be based. However, while their methodology may be orthodox, their 'creative application of Marxist-Leninist theory to Vietnam's concrete conditions' yielded quite unconventional results. In part this was because the Vietnamese revolution was the first communist revolution to take place in a completely colonial and semi-feudal country, the first breach of the colonial system of imperialism at its weakest link in Southeast Asia. In part this was also because of the integration of indigenous Vietnamese features into the revolution.

The Vietnamese proletariat was naturally identified as the most advanced revolutionary class which must lead the revolution, but as Le Duan explained, the colonial and semi-feudal society produced a proletariat with rather different characteristics:

> ...the Vietnamese proletariat was born earlier than the bourgeoisie because it was a product of the colonial policy of French imperialism...[Furthermore] the Vietnamese proletariat was imbued with a high revolutionary spirit. This was because it was linked with the most advanced form of economy and suffered from the triple oppression and exploitation of imperialism, feudalism and domestic bourgeoisie. [8]

It is important to note that Vietnam's economy was essentially feudal with externally created capitalism grafted upon it. Hence in Vietnam there was no problem of trying to prove that they had passed into the stage of capitalism (a prerequisite to achieving socialist revolution) as there had been in Russia. Vietnam was part of France's undeniably capitalist system. (This partially accounts for the importance Ho and others attached to proletarian internationalism, discussed below). The main implication of this is that because Vietnam's proletariat was created as part of an international system of capitalism, not domestic capitalism, the principal class antagonism for the Vietnamese proletariat was not with the Vietnamese bourgeoisie but rather with the French colonial bourgeoisie.

What about the Vietnamese bourgeoisie? Lenin and, at various times, the Comintern, argued that the national bourgeoisie was a revolutionary force in colonial and semi-colonial societies, and that both the national bourgeoisie and the proletariat had interests in a national-democratic revolution against imperialism. Lenin therefore counselled a policy of class alliance, and the Comintern issued directives on united front strategies. However, Le Duan contends that colonialism, as it operated in Indochina, created a different type of bourgeoisie:

> After World War I, the French colonialists carried out their policy of exploiting Indochina, completely subordinating the economy of the countries in this area to the French

economy. The economic conditions of Viet Nam at the time could only produce an economically weak bourgeoisie which politically compromised with imperialism and followed a policy of reformism. The Vietnamese bourgeoisie was, therefore, unable to lead the national-democratic revolution. [9]

Unlike most other colonial powers, France did not make extensive use of locals in its administration. The French preferred to bring Frenchmen to Indochina to take up any positions of importance, and the only way for a Vietnamese to advance was to be French educated and gain French citizenship. Hence the Vietnamese bourgeoisie and Vietnamese in administrative positions were for the most part Francophiles and did not identify their interests with those of the Vietnamese people. For this reason the Vietnamese bourgeoisie did not take a prominent role in Vietnam's revolution, although the Vietnamese communists did, from time to time during the 1930s and 1940s, enter into united fronts with patriotic bourgeois elements at the directive of the Comintern. [10]   Even in the 1980s Vietnam maintains the semblance of united front in the form of the Vietnam Fatherland Front, but the bourgeoisie does not play a major role in it.

Vietnam is an overwhelmingly agrarian country, and the question of the role of the peasantry is of some importance. Ho Chi Minh, the father of Vietnamese Marxism, recognised the revolutionary potential of the peasantry of the colonies. Through the Comintern Ho pressed the importance of the Peasant International and at the Fifth Congress of the Communist International in July 1924 Ho presented a 'Report on the National and Colonial Questions' in which he declared:

> The native peasants are ripe for insurrection. In many colonies they have indeed risen up but their rebellions have all been drowned in blood. The reason for their present passivity is the lack of organisation and leaders. The Communist International must help them to reorganise, supply them with leading cadres and show them the road to revolution and liberation. [11]

This advocacy of the peasantry as a revolutionary force appears to predate that of Mao Zedong. While Vietnam's communists adhered to the premise that the proletariat must lead the revolution, they also recognised the importance of mobilising the peasantry and solving the peasant question. Hence the Indochinese Communist Party adopted a 'land to the tiller' programme similar to that of China and worked actively in rural areas.

This conviction led Party theoreticians Truong Chinh and Vo Nguyen Giap to conduct an investigation into the peasantry, similar to Mao's, entitled *The Peasant Question (1937-1938)*. They concluded that the peasantry was neither proletarian (because they usually owned some land and tools) nor bourgeois (because they worked to support themselves and did not exploit others). In fact they decided that 'peasants belong to the petty-bourgeois class, between the bourgeoisie and the proletariat'. [12] Like Mao, they identified some stratification among the peasantry and noted that the interests of rich peasants tended to be similar to those of the bourgeoisie, while the poor and landless peasants had interests closer to the proletariat. [13] This implies an alignment of class interests between the urban proletariat and the peasantry, almost an attempt to 'proletarianise' the peasantry. Chinh and Giap argue that peasant support was important to the French bourgeois revolution in 1789, that the peasantry joined workers in demanding democratic freedoms in France in 1793, and claim that peasants supported the Russian October Revolution. From this they conclude that 'any large-scale social reform must have peasant participation in order to succeed'. [14]

Ironically, since the break with China in 1978, one of the grounds on which Vietnamese ideologues have attacked Maoism most strongly has been 'that it pays lip service to, but *denies in practice, the historic role and mission of the working class*'. Mao was never a true Marxist because he made the role of peasants into an absolute one. Vietnamese and Chinese can alike agree that it is necessary to 'set great store by the role of the peasants and the countryside' and 'to advocate building base areas in the countryside in the national democractic revolution in a country like China'. But it remains a fundamental thesis of Marxism-Leninism, which 'is absolutely correct in all circumstances', that the communist movement can never start from the countryside; 'communism can only be born from big industry and from the class which is the special product of big industry - the working class'. [15]   The   accuracy   or   fairness   of   the   judgement on Mao is not the issue here. What is clear is that Vietnamese Marxist-Leninists are still most vehement that 'solution of the peasant question' in no way implies a leading role in the worker-peasant alliance for any but the workers. They are adamant that in their own history communism comes from the cities, not the countryside.

The importance of the various classes in actual history, as distinct from theory, is the subject of an excellent paper dealing with the Vietnamese revolution down to 1945. The conclusions reached are that the worker-peasant alliance was a reality by the end of 1930 and that the peasants provided the mass base of the Vietnamese revolution, but that 'the proletariat made a major contribution' to its development. [16] The proletariat was the creation of the French who introduced modern industry to Vietnam,[17] and was consequently a new class. The Vietnamese revolution was not simply a peasant revolution because 'its leaders were those who were familiar with modern organization, technology, and ideas, namely revolutionary intellectuals and workers'. [18] In other words, workers were not the only leaders but it is not invalid to claim that the leadership was urban. Whether one can legitimately go further and claim proletarian leadership depends on precisely what leadership means and whether revolutionary intellectuals can be defined as part of the proletariat. Vietnamese Marxist thinkers have declined to make this jump.

What implications does the Vietnamese analysis of their own class relations have for Vietnam's revolutionary process? Leading Party theoretician Truong Chinh has explained that:

> ...in Viet Nam two fundamental contradictions had to be solved: *first*, that between the Vietnamese people and the imperialists who had robbed them of their country; and *second*, that between the broad masses of the people, the peasants especially, and the feudal landowner class. *The essential contradiction*, for the solution of which all forces should be concentrated, *was that between the Vietnamese people on the one hand, and the imperialist aggressors and their lackeys on the other* [our emphasis]. Imperialism was relying on the feudal landowner class to rule over our country; on the other hand, the feudal landowner class was acting as an agent of the imperialists and relied on their protection to maintain its interests and privileges. That is

why two tasks were set for the Vietnamese revolution:

1) To drive out the imperialist aggressors and win national independence - its anti-imperialist task.
2) To overthrow the feudal landowner class, carry out land reform, and put into effect the watchword 'Land to the Tiller' - its anti-feudal task.

These two tasks were closely linked together and could not be separated: to drive out the imperialists one had to overthrow the feudal landowners; conversely, to overthrow the feudal landowners, one had to drive out the imperialists. [19]

Because the Vietnamese proletariat identified its primary contradiction as being with the French colonial bourgeoisie, and because the weak Vietnamese bourgeoisie and the feudal landowner class had compromised with and were dependent on the French, the Vietnamese national revolution and the social revolution were one and the same. Although the Vietnamese went through the motions of a national democratic revolution, as the period of anti-French resistance from 1945 can be defined, it is essentially true that a single patriotic revolution against the French overthrew both colonialism and feudalism. This has three main theoretical implications.

Firstly, as noted earlier, capitalism had not developed in Vietnam nor had a significant bourgeoisie; Vietnam was essentially a feudal-agrarian country with colonial capitalism grafted upon it. Despite this, the Vietnamese made no serious attempt at engendering a period of capitalist development. In his 1976 Political Report to the Fourth Congress of the Vietnam Communist Party (VCP), Secretary-General Le Duan noted that:

It is clear that our country is still in the process of advancing directly from a society whose economy remains essentially one of small-scale production to socialism, by-passing the stage of capitalist development. This is the most oustanding characteristic reflecting the nature of the process of socialist revolution in our country and conditioning the main contents of this process. [20]

How can this be consistent with the orthodox Marxist tenet

of five historical periods of development: primitive communism, slave society, feudalism, capitalism, and communism? Clearly it is not. Whitmore, in his study of Vietnamese Marxist historiography, notes that during the ideological liberalism of Khrushchev's reign, the Vietnamese instigated a debate on the question of the Asiatic Mode of Production and in particular the universality of the five-stage periodisation. [21] Vietnamese Marxist historians have also expressed doubts about the existence of a slave society in Vietnamese history. Noted historian Professor Pham Huy Thong argued that while slavery existed, it did not play a decisive part in production and so could not be regarded as a social system. [22] After the fall of Khrushchev the debate was dropped with the Vietnamese coming to the rather uncertain conclusion that although Asian societies like Vietnam did indeed evidence a degree of distinctiveness, they also conformed loosely to the univsersal theory.

Whitmore suggests, however, that the Marxist dialectic of history is of less significance in Vietnamese Marxist historical writings; instead he identifies a theme of continuity of the struggle for national identity.

> Where the Chinese Communists have, of necessity, forced a separation between socialist present and oppressive past, the Vietnamese Communists have recreated the link between this present and a disrupted past and forged a meaningful bond between their acts and the flow of their civilization. The Chinese had to struggle against their past; the Vietnamese had to find theirs. [23]

Vietnamese history was characterised by repeated struggles against foreign domination—Chinese, French, Japanese, American, and now Chinese again. As Professor Thong explained, 'our struggle to maintain our culture for thousands of years up until now has become second nature'. [24] It almost seems that for the Vietnamese the dialectic is not a struggle between social systems but rather between continuation of Vietnam's national identity and threats of foreign domination. This view conforms with the anti-imperialist character of class struggle mentioned above and explains the remarkably resilient theme of nationalism and patriotism which permeates all facets of Vietnam's socialist revolution. Ho repeatedly linked past struggles with the present, and persistently used traditional images and literary forms. For example, in 1941 Ho wrote this passage to stir resistance to the French and the Japanese:

> A few hundred years ago, in the reign of the Tran, when our country faced the great danger of invasion by Yuan armies, the elders ardently called on their sons and daughters throughout the country to stand up as one man to kill the enemy. Finally they saved their people and their glorious memory will live forever. Let our elders and patriotic personalities follow the illustrious example set by our forefathers. [25]

Such appeals to patriotism were not just a revolutionary tactic or an attachment to their Marxism; patriotism and nationalism were a logical extension of their analysis. References to traditional viewpoints or historical precedents interlace Vietnamese theory on a wide range of topics, in a way which harmonises socialist revolution with the continuation of the best elements of Vietnamese tradition.

This leads to the second theoretical implication: because the task of socialist revolution is achieved by the patriotic revolution, nationalism and socialism are harmonised. We already saw that it was patriotism and nationalism which had led Ho to communism. Le Duan declared in an address to the National Assembly in June 1976 that 'nation and socialism are one'. 'For us Vietnamese', he explained, 'love of country now means love of socialism'. [26] Had Vietnam passed through a two-phase revolution, the second struggle against the national bourgeois democratic state would have diminished, although not eliminated nationalism as a motor of socialist revolution. Because the two revolutions were combined, the strident nationalism of the anti-colonial struggle was not diminished by socialism. Professor Thong asserts that in Vietnam the revolution must be recognised to be both socialist *and* Vietnamese. [27] A Western scholar notes that the Vietnamese 'are conscious of the national imprint on their revolution and believe this imprint to be one of its virtues'.[28] Nobody would question that it is also a source of great strength.

Finally, the class analysis outlined above has implications for the theory of proletarian internationalism. As noted earlier, the key contradiction upon which the revolution was based was that between the Vietnamese people and colonialism, and more specifically, between the Vietnamese proletariat and the French colonial bourgeoisie. The Vietnamese revolution had a distinctively international dimension. Ho firmly adhered to the belief that because of the colonial system, revolutions in the colonial world and the capitalist world were interdependent. In his 1924 'Report on the National and Colonial Questions at the Fifth Congress of the Communist International', Ho warned:

> ...it is not an exaggeration to say that so long as the French and British Communist Parties do not apply a really active policy with regard to the colonies, and do not come into contact with the colonial peoples, their vast programmes will remain ineffective, and this because they go counter to Leninism....the victory of the revolution in western Europe depends on its close contact with the national liberation movement against imperialism in the colonies and dependent countries; the national question, as Lenin taught us, forms a part of the general problem of proletarian revolution and proletarian dictatorship. [29]

Ho's Leninist faith in proletarian internationalism remained the cornerstone of Vietnamese analysis of the international situation, the basis of their position on the Sino-Soviet split and was the origin of their formulation of a theory of foreign relations, the 'three revolutionary currents in the world'. According to Pike, Vietnamese leaders see these as three major forces dominating the world scene.

> The first force is the ever-growing economic strength and ever-expanding military capability of the socialist world, emanating from the superiority of the socialist system over the 'bankrupt' capitalist system. The second force is the rise of new national attitudes of independence, an outgrowth of the previous generations' anti-colonial sentiment....The third dominating force is the solidarity perceived among the so-called Third and Fourth World nations (i.e., nations both small and poor) which are bound together by grievances against the established West and by the determination to redress existing economic imbalances.[30]

These clearly reflect an abiding faith in proletarian internationalism, although it is interesting to note the way Third World nationalism is harmonised with other internationalist revolutionary currents. Proletarian internationalism remains the basis of Vietnamese foreign policy.

Revolution: People's War

Ho Chi Minh discusses the 'national revolution' by citing two good examples, the Socialist Revolution of October 1917 by which Lenin brought the Bolsheviks to power in Russia and the August Revolution of 1945 which led up to his own famous Declaration of Independence of 2 September. He lists five features of both cases, which amount to prerequisites for the success of a national revolution: (i) reliance upon 'a broad national front against imperialism'; (ii) solution of the peasant question; (iii) organisation of a people's army; (iv) the 'brotherly support of the people and proletariat of other countries'; and (v) the leadership of the Party of the working class. [31]

Most of these specifications are discussed elsewhere. Perhaps the most significant innovation in Vietnamese revolutionary theory was the development of their theories on the conduct of revolution and resistance. As was noted before, Vietnam's revolution was aimed primarily at colonial oppression - it was a war of national liberation which would result in a socialist revolution. It was Vietnam's approach to revolution which enabled it to defeat both the French and the Americans so spectacularly and it is that success for which the Vietnamese revolution is famous.

Initially the Vietnamese derived their revolutionary theory from the experiences of the Russian revolution and of the resistance in China. Theoretician Truong Chinh produced two of the earliest works on revolutionary warfare. In *The August Revolution* (1946) he compared the Vietnamese August Revolution of 1945, which was an essentially bloodless urban seizure of power after a protracted resistance, with the Russian October Revolution; in *The Resistance Will Win* (1947) he essentially summarised Mao's 1938 treatise 'On Protracted War' as a guide for the resistance against the French. Neither work shows great originality; both represent a literal acceptance of the views of Lenin and Mao, although probably leaning more towards the Chinese view. According to Boudarel, many Vietnamese communists during the 1940s and 1950s regarded Maoism as a concrete adaptation of Marxism-Leninism to colonised and semi-colonised countries [32] (although they rejected the Maoism of the 1960s). Vietnam's theory of people's war originated from the Chinese theory, but the Vietnamese later altered and innovated to the extent that the theory became their own.

The first significant departure from Maoist doctrine can be found in a Resolution of the Central Committee of the Indochina Communist Party in October 1951, which advocated the '... utilisation of all forms of struggle adapted to the circumstances, from the weakest to the strongest, from the legal to the illegal, from economic demands to armed action'. [33]

The 'total war' approach to people's war advocated and practised by Vo Nguyen Giap descends directly from this position; a people's war involved the total participation of the whole population, both in armed struggle and politics. In 1963 Le Duan reassessed the August Revolution in *Raise High the Revolutionary Banner of Creative Marxism-Leninism*. By this analysis, the Russian revolution was an armed insurrection in the cities which spread to the countryside; the Chinese revolution was a protracted revolutionary war in the countryside leading eventually to the surrounding and ultimately the seizure of the cities. However Le Duan wrote:

> In Vietnam, our revolution is a protracted revolutionary war in which political struggle is coordinated with armed struggle and the creation of local guerrillas and military bases in the countryside is coordinated with the political mobilization of the masses in order to bring about, at a favorable moment, an armed insurrection in both urban and rural areas to seize power. [34]

Therefore, in line with the 1951 Resolution calling for the utilisation of all forms of struggle, the Vietnamese opted to fight the revolution in all theatres and by all means. This was because of their belief that 'oppression engenders struggle and struggle engenders forces-in-place'. Consequently urban-based struggle or rural-based struggle was replaced in Vietnamese theory by coordinated struggle in three strategic areas - the mountains, the plains, and the cities. [35] This represents a radical departure from Mao's strategy of the countryside encircling the cities. Boudarel notes, however, that this occurred without a renunciation of people's war or its being openly criticised; rather, alien concepts were incorporated into it.

One of the principal features of Mao's revolutionary strategy to be abandoned was the importance of numerical combat superiority to the extent of nine to one, and the superiority of the mass peasant army. By the mid-1960s military strategist Vo Nguyen Giap had reversed this principle in favour of extolling the virtue of using 'few against many'. Clearly 'Mao bet on quantity; Giap, who did not hesitate to speak of an elite army, on quality'. [36] This change from quantity to quality was due to the devastating effects of American military firepower which was rapidly expanding at that time and which forced a reappraisal of strategy. Another change forced by the American intervention was the abandonment of the Chinese counsel of revolutionary forces springing from the local population and living off the land. To defeat the Americans the Vietnamese must have better weaponry, secure supplies and nationwide direction of the struggle. What is more, this necessitated constant arms and material supplies which only the Russians could guarantee. Boudarel suggests that 'the increasingly sharp tilt towards Moscow after 1965, in spite of sympathy with some theses hitherto advanced by Beijing, resulted from the fact that the Soviet Union offered the only meaningful capability for solving Vietnam's problems'. [37]

In fact Vietnam's tilts to one side or the other during the 1950s and 1960s were directly related to the Soviet and Chinese positions on the task of reunification. For example, Vietnam tilted decidedly away from the Soviets in the early 1960s because of the implications of Khrushchev's peaceful coexistence policy to the task of liberating the south.

The most spectacular example of Vietnam's new form of revolutionary war was the 1968 Tet Offensive.

> Consisting of a general offensive in the rural areas coordinated with a general uprising in the major cities, Tet represented an effort to destroy a significant proportion of the South Vietnamese military forces and at the same time to shake the political stability of the Thieu regime in Saigon... Hanoi was realistic enough not to count on total victory, however, and the offensive had a minimum goal as well: to accelerate opposition to the war in the United States and to transform the Vietnam crisis into a major issue in the

American presidential campaign. [38]

This last political aspect of strategic planning was one of the most innovative aspects of the total war concept; not only did the Vietnamese fight a military war and political war in the south, they were also conscious that the political battle could be taken to the United States. Indeed, if a small country like Vietnam was to win over a superpower like the United States, the victory must be a moral–political one.

A final innovation of the new Vietnamese revolutionary doctrine was the role of negotiated peace. Neither the Soviets nor the Chinese had envisaged a negotiations phase of people's war, but for the Vietnamese it became a key part of their strategy. As early as 1947 Truong Chinh suggested the possiblity of a negotiating phase, [39] and throughout the 1950s, 1960s and into the 1970s the Vietnamese made good use of diplomacy as part of their combat effort. Duiker explains that

> Recognition of the importance of diplomacy led Party strategists to make use of a new variation of the old Maoist three-stage hypothesis: from a first stage of purely military conflict, to a second stage of simultaneous fighting and negotiating, and on to a final stage of negotiations and peace. The key requirement for success was to delay the opening of serious negotiations until an advantageous situation had arisen on the battlefield which could stimulate the sense of war-weariness in Saigon and erode support for the war in the United States. [40]

There are numerous examples of coordination of military and diplomatic struggle. The most significant battles in the siege of Dien Bien Phu were timed to affect the Geneva peace negotiations; also the 1972 Easter offensive was timed to affect negotiations underway in Paris as well as the US Presidential election campaign. [41]

Vietnamese theory of people's war, or total war, involves the coordination of all forms of struggle. Coordination of rural guerrilla offensives with urban insurrections; coordination of Vietnamese People's Army regulars with National Liberation Front guerrillas; coordination of military struggle with political struggle; and coordination of military strategy with political and diplomatic strategy. Every means at their disposal was coordinated towards the overriding goal of independence and reunification.

The doctrine of people's war implies a recognition that the triumph of the revolution can come only through violence. But Ho Chi Minh is a little less absolute than this. He talks of 'recognizing that in certain countries the road to socialism may be a peaceful one', but goes on to declare that the proletariat must always prepare for armed struggle.

> While recognizing the possibility of reunifying Viet Nam by peaceful means, we should always remember that our people's principal enemies are the American imperialists and their agents who still occupy half our country and are preparing for war; therefore we should firmly hold aloft the banner of peace, and enhance our vigilance. [42]

In other words peaceful means are in theory possible but in practice most unlikely to lead to success. He explains that this is because the enemies of the revolution are bound to inflict violence in a vain bid to preserve their interests. Ho's is a sober and, in retrospect, an unfortunately realistic judgement in Vietnam's case, tending towards the Chinese view in the Sino-Soviet debate over the peaceful transition to socialism.

Just after the Tet offensive of 1968, Truong Chinh put forward a similar but even less optimistic point of view. He paid lip service to the possibility of a peaceful transition to socialism, but also stated clearly the need for 'the masses' revolutionary violence to smash the counter-revolutionary violence of the exploiting ruling classes' in order to build a new society. No exploiting class, he explains, ever renounces its power of its own consent. The lesson is simple: 'in no case should they [the Communists] nurture illusions about an easy peaceful transition'. [43] It would have needed an astonishing abandonment of realism to write otherwise considering the immense scale of bloodletting which the Tet offensive had involved.

The Party, the State and Socialist Transformation

Revolutionary analysis and the strategies of people's war in Vietnam represent a prelude to the ultimate objective of the Vietnamese revolution - a thorough-going transformation of Vietnamese society. Vietnam's Marxist-Leninists have produced an extensive body of theoretical innovations which reflect their approaches to socialist transformation and organisation of the state. These descend from the Russian and Chinese revolutionary experiences but also retain a certain Vietnamese distinctiveness.

The leading organisation at all times is the party, a highly Leninist concept. The Indochina Communist party was set up in Hongkong in February 1930 and dissolved itself on 11 November 1945. It was revived under the name Vietnam Workers' Party early in 1951 and at the Fourth Congress, of December 1976, was renamed the Vietnam Communist Party.

Apart from its proletarian leadership, the key feature of the Vietnamese Party is its high degree of organisation and centralisation. This follows from its Leninist nature. According to Le Duan, 'The hallmark of the revolutionary movement led by the proletariat is its high organisational standard'. He continues that 'all activities aimed at bringing the masses to the point where they will rise up and topple the ruling classes' really boil down to one point: 'to organize, organize, organize'. To do this requires propaganda, for it is only thus that the masses can be educated to support the revolution actively. Thus 'propaganda, organization, and struggle must go hand in hand'. [44]

An important part of the Party-led social transformation is land reform which deprives the landlords and rich peasants of their material base, and transfers it to the peasant masses. A thorough-going land reform took place in the north from late 1953 to mid-1956, and collectivisation of agriculture in the south after 1975. In the second half of 1980 Le Duan reported to a Plenum of the Party Central Committee on a new draft Constitution, which was in fact formally adopted the following year. He emphasised 'a crucial point': the provision 'for the ownership of all the lands by the entire people'.

> This point conforms with the law of advance to socialism, with the situation of land in our country, with the interests of the entire society, and also with the interests of the peasants themselves. Indeed, one of the principles of socialism is the common ownership of all the principal means of production. [45]

This principle is an essential part of the system of 'collective mastery' (*lam chu tap the*), the central and overriding theme of the Vietnamese state. A theoretical innovation of Party Secretary-General Le Duan, the idea of collective mastery includes many pre-existing concepts: the dictatorship of the proletariat, socialist democracy, socialist legality, agricultural collectivism, democratic centralism, and even elements of the mass line. Le Duan explains:

> To build the system of socialist collective mastery is actually to build a comprehensive system of social relations reflecting more and more fully the mastery of the working people.... [It is] a state organised by the working class and the working people themselves to exercise their right to collective mastery, a state which is really of the people, by the people and for the people, through which the Party exercises its leadership over society. [46]

Collective mastery describes 'a system of correct relationships between the Party, the State, and the people' in which 'the party is the leader, the people are the master and the state is the manager'. At times, collective mastery also described a mass line approach in which:

> ...the Party always starts from the aspirations, interests and degree of consciousness and understanding of the masses. After lines and policies are put forward, the Party should propagate them among the masses, put them to discussion by the masses so as to transform those Party lines and policies into the masses' own ideas. Through the masses' ideas and revolutionary actions, the Party sums up experiences and perfects its lines and policies. [47]

It should be noted, however, that, as Turley points out, the degree of mass participation fluctuated according to the needs of the state at that time. Mass participation, in general, was designed primarily to promote greater mass identification with the Party's policies, not to influence or modify them. [48] The perfection of collective mastery through the Party and the State accrues to the Party and the State the right to exercise the collective mastery of the people. Hence collective mastery also includes democratic centralist dimensions. Because the State is the expression of the collective mastery of the working people, the State deserves the support of the people. As Le Duan points out:

> Political collective mastery involves both duties and rights: duties are corollary to rights. We must ensure the citizens rights and individual freedom while requiring that each citizen and each individual fully discharge his duties to society, the state and the collective such as the duty to work, the duty to defend the motherland, the duty to respect and defend socialist property, respect the rules of collective life, etc. [49]

Refugee reports suggest that, in the south since 1975, political reeducation has placed great emphasis on those duties associated with collective mastery. The theory of collective mastery has also been described as the basic content of the new (1980) constitution.

'Collective mastery', emphasises Le Duan, 'is not only an attitude and an institutional system but is also a fixed organizational structure'. [50] The Vietnam Communist Party was formed along Leninist lines, and so great emphasis has always been placed on organisation; their faith in organisation as the key to a successful revolution was strengthened by their experiences in revolution and resistance. This principle of revolution has become part of the Vietnamese theory of socialist transformation. 'Organization', wrote Le Duan 'is a basic *measure* for ensuring implementation of [the] line. Whether the organization is right or wrong determines the success or failure of the line'. [51] According to Elliott, this reflects a general belief that institutions mould man, and so socialist transformation in the ideological field can be achieved by a correct organisational framework. [52] The result of this belief in organisation is what may be described as the 'administrative state', which Elliott argues has three main characteristics:

> (1) the faith in organizational solutions to political and economic problems, (2) a commitment to 'socialist legality'- a framework of laws and regulations that defines the standards of performance and spheres of institutional competence, and (3) a tendency to establish highly centralized

and frequently redundant institutions as a means of ensuring that central policies are effectively implemented. [53]

This highly bureaucratic organisation holds with it the dangers of bureaucratism and commandism. Ho condemned these faults at the Second Congress of the Vietnam Workers' Party in February 1961. Bureaucratism 'shows in fondness for red tape, divorce from the masses of the people...and reluctance to learn the experiences of the masses'. Commandism Ho described as the use of compulsion against the people, without explanation, and without allowing them to 'work on their own initiative and own accord'. [54] Bureaucratism and commandism ran contrary to the right of collective mastery and so the Party at various times organised mass criticism campaigns. These campaigns, however, were very different from such mass campaigns in China as the Cultural Revolution. Turley notes:

> The purpose of the campaign was not to curtail the Party's authority or to place it under popular control but to improve the interpersonal skills of cadres who had to deal with the people face-to-face, enhance the legitimacy of local Party organs, and heighten popular support for Party objectives. [55]

Hence mass criticism was in effect orchestrated to strengthen the Party and State, not to attack it. Comparison with China shows that the Vietnamese never organised such vehement attacks on the Party and bureaucracy as did Mao, and the idea of inviting the masses to launch a full-scale attack against the Party like the Cultural Revolution has always been anathema to the Vietnamese. Mass criticism was viewed as a tool for perfecting the organisation of collective mastery.

The establishment of socialist collective mastery and the achievement of a thorough-going socialist transformation 'is a process of carrying out the three revolutions: the revolution in relations of production, the scientific and technological revolution, and the ideological and cultural revolution, in which the scientific and technological revolution is the king pin.' [56] Truong Chinh provides a detailed explanation of the three revolutions which first begins with the establishment of collective mastery in the economy. He explains:

The revolution in relations of production should not be confined to transforming the ownership of means of production but should also include the system of management and distribution. The aim...is to establish the collective ownership of the labouring people over the essential means of production as well as production and distribution, thereby developing socialist democracy, and promoting the labouring masses' spirit of initiative and creativeness in production work.

After the basic completion of the transformation of relations of production in the system of ownership, the *technological revolution* holds a key position....We must carry out *socialist industrialization* and wage a *technological revolution* in order to make our economy truly independent and sovereign. We must set up a modern Vietnamese industry capable of transforming the present production, which relies mainly on handicraft labour, into a large-scale mechanized production....Parallel to these two revolutions and with a view to effectively serving them, we carry out an *ideological and cultural revolution*. In the field of *ideology* we must foster and strengthen proletarian ideology, fight all forms of bourgeois ideology, criticize petty-bourgeois ideology and continue to do away with all vestiges of feudal and other erroneous ideologies. In the field of *culture*, we inherit in a critical way the national culture, build for Viet Nam a new culture, socialist in content and national in character. [57]

The three revolutions do not include any radical breaks from theoretical orthodoxy, but they do represent a reformulation of theory. A few points can be made here about the three revolutions. Firstly, the revolution in the relations of production is a matter of organisation, a specific organisational framework. Also, as was noted above, the ideological and cultural revolution is related to proper organisation. Secondly, the emphasis placed on a scientific and technological revolution as the road to socialist transformation places the Vietnamese revolution firmly in line with the Stalinist policy of industrialisation, and implicitly rejects the Maoist low-technology style of industrialisation such as that seen in the Great Leap Forward. Thirdly, the blending of positive aspects of the national culture with socialist culture is another example of continuity in the Vietnamese revolution.

One problem arising from the idea of 'collective mastery' is whether class struggle continues under that system which follows the victory of the revolution. Nguyen Duc Binh, expressing the official view, ridicules Mao's notion that class struggle does indeed persist in the new society; as well as the related concepts of the bourgeoisie's existing within the party itself and of the continuing revolution under the dictatorship of the proletariat. But he stops short of denying directly that class struggle can persist into the new era. Contradictions exist in all societies, he argues, and that includes socialist society. 'How can one imagine the bourgeoisie still existing and existing as such through all the periods of development of socialism!', he demands. He thus implies that it exists in some of them, but not others, so opening the possibility of class struggle. What is crystal clear, however, is that he regards the formulae of Mao's late years as stirring up unnecessary and very harmful social conflicts under the guise of class struggle. [58] It appears that, for all the disagreements, the Vietnamese share at least one important view with their archenemies, the Chinese Deng Xiaoping leadership.

Among the most important changes which should emanate from the social revolution caused by the establishment of the system of collective mastery is the restructuring of the family and equality between the two sexes.

As in other countries of East Asia the background of the family in Vietnam was, firstly, that it was the central social and economic core of the political culture and, secondly, that women held a low position in society and suffered gross inequalities, discriminations and maltreatment, although there is an important tradition of patriotic heroines. It was part of the programme of Ho Chi Minh and his followers to right the injustices practised against the female sex and the ten slogans put forward by the Communist Party of Indochina on its foundation in February 1930 included one 'to implement equality between man and woman'. [59] Women began to take an interest in the activities of the Party. Central Committee resolutions of 1937 and 1938 'stressed the female constituency and instructed all Party echelons to establish specialized women's committees', [60] with some positive results. No sooner was the Democratic Republic of Vietnam set up than on 11 September 1945 the first general conference of the Women's Association for National Salvation was convened, the precursor of the Vietnam Women's Union which still functions very strongly today.

The two factors of French colonialism and the Vietnamese revolutionary process caused the family to lose its economic centrality. On the other hand, it continued strongly as a social unit. On 28 December 1959 the National Assembly adopted a new law on marriage and the family which laid down freedom of marriage, monogamy, equality between the sexes and defence of children's rights and interests.

Ho Chi Minh took a close interest in matters relating to the family. Apart from its social importance he justified his attitude by saying he did indeed have a family - the world's working class and the Vietnamese people. His views are strong and urge thorough-going liberation for women.

> *Women make up half of society. If they are not liberated, half of society is not freed.*

> *If women are not emancipated only half of socialism is built....*

> *The law on marriage to be presented to the National Assembly is a revolution*, an integral part of the socialist revolution.

> *Therefore we shold adopt the proletarian stand to understand it.* It is not correct if our understanding is based on feudal, bourgeois or petty-bourgeois stand. [61]

He also calls on women to organise themselves without waiting for government or Party directives.

Le Duan also advocates women taking part in the management of society and production. Their emancipation 'is essentially to ensure their fullest participation as collective masters in all three respects *masters of society, masters of nature and masters of themselves*' (italics in original). [62] Their burdens of housework must be reduced. On the other hand, a 'new woman' is one who 'carries out her duty as a socialist citizen, one who fulfils satisfactorily her noble function as a mother towards her children, and as a wife in the family.' [63]

The Women's Union has been very active in endeavouring to bring about progress towards equality between the sexes not only in theory but in fact. Women have joined the labour force in a big way. In particular, in 1979, they made up 43.8 per cent of all workers in the state sector, including 65 per cent in light industry, 61.5 per cent in public health and 60 per cent in education.[64] Whereas 95 per cent of women were illiterate before the revolution, [65] girls were 47 per cent of the total number of schoolchildren in 1979-80, or 5,557,400 out of 11,804,000; [66] women made up 25.6 per cent of all faculty staff in colleges and universities in 1981. [67] Women account for less than 20 per cent of membership of the Party, and the official view is that the proportion is not nearly high enough. [68]

Nobody, including the Vietnamese, [69] is claiming that full equality between the sexes has been reached. Even at senior government levels sexist attitudes persist. [70] The statistics offered above suggest that women have been encouraged to enter the workforce in particular 'female' areas, so that sex roles are in no sense disappearing.

One study of women in Vietnam claims that despite enormous strides towards equality after 1945, their position actually worsened since 1975. They have retreated from public life with the return of the men from the front. Polygamy has actually increased because of the heavy predominance of women due to the anti-American war. Women who join the workforce often find themselves also burdened with all the domestic chores and are thus seriously overworked. However, modernisation is likely to go some way towards solving these problems in the future because mechanisation of agriculture and industry will to some extent relieve women of back-breaking labour and education will help them develop their talents more than at present. [71]

Conclusion

Vietnam's revolutionaries have made a significant contribution to the body of Marxist-Leninist thought. While their theory has been innovative and flexible, the Vietnamese Party has never strayed radically from Marxist-Leninist orthodoxy. As true Marxists, they begin from a scientific investigation of the class antagonisms upon which their revolution must be based, then proceed to formulate a revolutionary doctrine appropriate to their situation, and finally implement a thorough-going restructuring of their society.

The ideologues of the Vietnamese Party have been and remain fully aware of the Marxist-Leninist theories which should lead to social equality. The stages of social development, class struggle, and analysis of classes in society, the leadership of the working class, the dictatorship of the proletariat all hold their place in Vietnamese socialist ideology.

In particular, Ho Chi Minh and the Party he led give the necessary due to the vital place of theory.'We must teach everybody Marxist-Leninist theory', declares Ho. 'He who knows theory but does not put it into practice is good for nothing... Only with theory can we understand all that happens in society and in the mass movements'. [72]

Yet several Western authors have commented on Ho's *lack* of theoretical grounding. One suggests tartly that the 'uncle' shunned and eschewed theorising and that he was thus able to twist the line to suit his needs; he 'showed uncommon talent for political maneuver within the strictures of orthodoxy'. [73]

Certainly Ho was no theoretician; he was first and foremost the leader of the Vietnamese Party and revolution, but unlike other revolutionary leaders, Ho did not expect to take on ideological primacy. Rather the Vietnamese Party drew upon the considerable talents of a number of innovative theoreticians within the Politburo, including Le Duan, Truong Chinh and Vo Nguyen Giap. As was noted earlier, Ho chose Leninism as the best weapon to achieve his nationalist aims, and under his leadership the Vietnamese Party reformulated Marxist-Leninist theory appropriate to Vietnam's situation and in order to achieve their final goal. The flexibility and innovativeness with which the Vietnamese absorbed Russian and Chinese theory clearly demonstrates that they did creatively apply Marxism-Leninism to Vietnam.

So collective mastery stems in a real sense from collective leadership. And that depends to a great extent on unity, of their record in which the Vietnamese are very proud. In May 1969, not long before he died, Ho Chi Minh remarked that '*unity* is an extremely precious tradition of our Party and people'. He called on 'all comrades, from the Central Committee down to the cell' to 'preserve the unity and oneness of mind in the Party like the apple of their eye'. [74]

Ho also expressed the hope that the Vietnamese Party

would 'do its best to contribute effectively to the restoration of unity among the fraternal parties on the basis of Marxism-Leninism'. [75] There is considerable poignancy in the aged revolutionary's making such a plea in his last testament, just after the Sino-Soviet border clashes of March 1969 had revealed a new depth to the bitterness in the two largest socialist powers. Had Ho been able to view developments over the succeeding fifteen years or so, he would doubtless have been happier over the continuing unity in his own Party than over 'the restoration of unity among the fraternal parties'.

NOTES

1. Ho Chi Minh, 'The Path Which Led Me to Leninism', *Selected Works*, vol. 4, p. 450. The four volumes of Ho Chi Minh's *Selected Works* in English were published by the Foreign Languages Publishing House in Hanoi in 1960 (vol. 1), 1961 (vols. 2 and 3), and 1962 (vol. 4).

2. See William J. Duiker, *The Rise of Nationalism in Vietnam, 1900-1941* (Cornell University Press, Ithaca and London, 1976), pp. 196-7.

3. Huỳnh Kim Khánh, *Vietnamese Communism 1925-1945* (Cornell University Press, Ithaca and London, 1982), p. 20.

4. Ibid., pp. 57-8.

5. Duiker, *The Rise of Nationalism*, p. 201.

6. William J. Duiker, 'Vietnamese Revolutionary Doctrine in Comparative Perspective', in William S. Turley (ed.), *Vietnamese Communism in Comparative Perspective* (Westview Special Studies on South and Southeast Asia, Westview Press, Boulder, 1980), p. 45.

7. Huỳnh Kim Khánh (*Vietnamese Communism*, p. 27) insists on the distinction in the Vietnamese experience. He writes: 'Patriotism, an inward-looking, kinship-oriented concept with sentimental connotations, reflects the attachment of a people. Nationalism, on the other hand, emphasizes a nation's perceived legitimate rights and is often the political expression of a society's elite elements.'

8. Le Duan, 'Hold High the Revolutionary Banner of Creative Marxism, Take our Revolutionary Cause to Complete Victory!', Le Duan, *Selected Writings* (Foreign Languages Publishing House, Hanoi, 1977), p. 67.

9. Ibid., pp. 66-7.

10. See Duiker, 'Vietnamese Revolutionary Doctrine in Comparative Perspective', in Turley (ed.), *Vietnamese Communism*, pp. 47-54.

11. Ho Chi Minh, 'Report on the National and Colonial Questions at the Fifth Congress of the Communist International' (July 1924), Ho Chi Minh, *Selected Writings (1920-1969)* (Foreign Languages Publishing House, Hanoi, 1973), p. 36.

12. Truong Chinh and Vo Nguyen Giap, *The Peasant Question (1937-1938)*, trans. Christine P. White (Cornell University Data Paper No. 94, Ithaca, January 1974), pp. 16, 19.

13. Ibid., p. 19.

14. Ibid., p. 20.

15. Nguyen Duc Binh, 'The Reactionary Nature of Maoism', in *Against Maoism Dossier - Beijing's Expansionism and Hegemonism* (Vietnam Courier, Hanoi, 1980), pp. 31-5.

16. Christine Pelzer White, 'The Vietnamese Revolutionary Alliance: Intellectuals, Workers, and Peasants', in John Wilson Lewis (ed.), *Peasant Rebellion and Communist Revolution in Asia* (Stanford University Press, Stanford, California, 1974), p. 91.

17. Ibid., p. 87.

18. Ibid., p. 95.

19. Truong-Chinh, 'Forward Along the Path Charted by Karl Marx', in Truong-Chinh, *Selected Writings* (Foreign Languages Publishing House, Hanoi, 1977), p. 584.

20. Le Duan, 'Bring Into Full Play the Right to Collective Mastery' (excerpts from the Political Report to the Fourth Congress of the Vietnam Communist Party), in Le Duan, *On the Right to Collective Mastery* (Foreign Languages Publishing House, Hanoi, 1980), p. 11.

21. Whitmore, John K., 'Communism and History in Vietnam', in Turley (ed.), *Vietnamese Communism*, p. 27.

22. Pham Huy Thong, quoted in ibid., pp.27, 28.

23. Ibid., p. 29.

24. Pham Huy Thong, quoted in ibid., p. 30.

25. Ho Chi Minh, 'Letter From Abroad' (6 June 1941), Ho Chi Minh, *Selected Writings (1920-1969)*, p. 45.

26. Quoted in Whitmore, 'Communism and History', in Turley (ed.), *Vietnamese Communism*, p. 38.

27. Pham Huy Thong, quoted in ibid., p. 32.

28. William S. Turley, 'Introduction' in Turley, ed. *Vietnamese Communism*, p. 3.

29. Ho Chi Minh, *Selected Writings (1920-1969)*, p. 25.

30. Douglas Pike, 'Vietnam's Military Assistance', in John F. Copper and Daniel S. Popp (eds), *Communist Nations' Military Assistance* (Westview Press, Boulder, 1983), p. 165.

31. 'The October Revolution and the Liberation of the Peoples of the East' (6 November 1957), *Selected Works*, vol. 4, p. 277.

32. Georges Boudarel, 'Influences and Idiosyncracies in the Line and Practice of the Vietnam Communist Party', in Turley (ed.), *Vietnamese Communism*, p. 142.

33. Quoted in ibid., p. 151.

34. Quoted in ibid., p. 144.

35. Ibid., p. 151.

36. Ibid., pp. 150-1.

37. Ibid., p. 154.

38. Duiker, 'Vietnamese Revolutionary Doctrine', in Turley (ed.), *Vietnamese Communism*, p. 63.

39. Boudarel, 'Influences and Idiosyncrasies', in Turley (ed.), *Vietnamese Communism*, p. 142.

40. Duiker, 'Vietnamese Revolutionary Doctrine', in Turley (ed.), *Vietnamese Communism*, p. 62.

41. Ibid., pp. 62-4.

42. 'Speech Closing the 9th (Enlarged) Session of the Central Committee of the Viet Nam Workers' Party' (24 April 1956), *Selected Works*, vol. 4. p. 154.

43. 'Forward Along the Path Charted by Karl Marx', in Truong-Chinh, *Selected Writings*, pp. 598, 600.

44. Le Duan, 'The Vietnamese Revolution: Fundamental Problems, Essential Tasks', Le Duan, *Selected Writings* (Foreign Languages Publishing House, Hanoi, 1977), pp. 198-9.

45. *Vietnam News Bulletin* 01,81 (7 January 1981), p. 3.

46. Le Duan, 'Bring into Full Play the Right to Collective Mastery', in Le Duan, *On the Right to Collective Mastery*, pp. 15-16.

47. Le Duan, 'Promote Socialist Legality, Ensure the People's Right to Collective Mastery' (Speech to the National Conference of the Central Branch, 22 March 1967), in Le Duan, *On the Right to Collective Mastery*, p. 87.

48. Turley, 'Political Participation and the Vietnamese Communist Party', in Turley (ed.), *Vietnamese Communism*, p. 187.

49. Le Duan, 'Bring into Full Play the Right to Collective Mastery', in Le Duan, *On the Right to Collective Mastery*, p. 17.

50. Le Duan, quoted in David W.P. Elliott,'Institutionalizing the Revolution: Vietnam's Search for a Model of Development', in Turley (ed.),*Vietnamese Communism*, p. 210.

51. Ibid.

52. Ibid.

53. Ibid., p. 201.

54. 'Political Report Read at the Second National Conference of the Viet Nam Workers' Party Held in February 1961', *Selected Works*, vol. 3, p. 255.

55. Turley, 'Political Participation and the Vietnamese Communist Party', in Turley (ed.), *Vietnamese Communism*, p. 187.

56. Le Duan, 'Bring into Full Play the Right to Collective Mastery', in Le Duan, *On the Right to Collective Mastery*, p. 14.

57. Truong-Chinh, 'Forward Along the Path Charted by Karl Marx', in Truong-Chinh, *Selected Writings*, pp. 593-5.

58. See Nguyen Duc Binh's lengthy discussion in 'The Reactionary Nature of Maoism', pp. 58-70. The direct quotation is on p. 64.

59. Ho Chi Minh, 'Appeal Made on the Occasion of the Founding of the Communist Party of Indo-China (February 18, 1930)', *Selected Works*, vol. 2, p.148.

60. David G. Marr, *Vietnamese Tradition on Trial, 1920-1945* (University of California Press, Berkeley, Los Angeles, London, 1981), p. 246. Marr deals in some depth with 'the question of women' pp. 190-251.

61. Ho Chi Minh, 'Excerpt from a Talk at a Cadres' Meeting Debating the Draft Law on Marriage and the Family' (October 1959), *Selected Works*, vol. 4, p. 371. (Italics in original).

62. Le Duan, 'The Role and Tasks of Vietnamese Women in the New Stage of the Revolution', in Le Duan, *On the Right to Collective Mastery*, p. 106.

63. Ibid, p. 108.

64. *Women of Viet Nam Statistical Data, Femmes du Viet Nam Données statistiques* (Viet Nam Women's Union, Hanoi, 1981), p. 18.

65. This is the claim of the current government. See 'The Miraculous Changes in the Life of the Vietnamese Women', *Women of Vietnam*, 3 (1975), p. 3.

66. *Women of Viet Nam Statistical Data*, p. 39. The total population of Vietnam in 1979 was 52,462,000, 51.5 per cent female, 48.5 per cent male. Ibid., p. 11.

67. Ibid., p. 31.

68. David Jenkins, in *Far Eastern Economic Review*, vol. 126, no. 45 (8 November 1984), p. 28.

69. See, for instance, 'The Miraculous Changes', pp. 1-4. especially p. 3.

70. See Marr, *Vietnamese Tradition*, pp. 250-1.

71. Sophie Quinn-Judge, 'Vietnamese Women: Neglected Promises', *Indochina Issues*, 42 (December 1983), pp. 1-7.

72. Ho Chi Minh, 'On Training Work and Study' (May 1950), *Selected Works*, vol. 3, p. 195.

73. Boudarel, 'Influences and Idiosyncracies' in Turley (ed.), *Vietnamese Communism*, p. 142.

74. 'Testament', in Ho Chi Minh, *Selected Writings (1920-1969)*, p. 360.

75. Ibid., p. 362.

SELECT BIBLIOGRAPHY

50 Years of Activities of the Communist Party of Vietnam (Foreign Languages Publishing House, Hanoi, 1980). A brief history of the Vietnamese Party, from the point of view of the Vietnamese government, in five parts: birth of the Party, the August 1945 revolution, the war against the French, the period 1954-75 leading to victory over the US, and the years 1975-80.

Ho Chi Minh, *Selected Works* (4 vols., Foreign Languages Publishing House, Hanoi, 1960-62). Articles and speeches of Vietnam's revolutionary leader arranged chronologically.

Huỳnh Kim Khánh, *Vietnamese Communism 1925-1945* (Cornell University Press, Ithaca and London, 1982). This work of ideological history covers some non-communist groups, but focuses on the development of communism. Its author, in the preface, calls it 'a history of the transplantation and adaptation of an imported revolutionary ideology' and 'an analysis of one response to Western imperialism'.

Le Duan, *On the Right to Collective Mastery* (Foreign Languages Publishing House, Hanoi, 1980). Contains ten articles by Vietnam's leading contemporary ideologue on the central concept of Vietnamese Marxist governance.

Le Duan, *Selected Writings* (Foreign Languages Publishing House, Hanoi, 1977). Contains nine tracts, by far the longest being 'The Vietnamese Revolution - Fundamental Problems, Essential Tasks'.

Marr, David G., *Vietnamese Tradition on Trial, 1920-1945* (University of California Press, Berkeley, Los Angeles, London, 1981). The leading account of Vietnamese intellectual history of the period stated, this work covers, among other topics, 'ethics and politics', 'the question of women', and 'harmony and struggle'.

Truong-Chinh, *Selected Writings*(Foreign Languages Publishing House, Hanoi, 1977). Includes some of the main works by this key Vietnamese ideologue such as 'The Resistance Will Win' and 'Forward along the Path Charted by Karl Marx'.

Turley, William S. (ed.), *Vietnamese Communism in Comparative Perspective* (Westview Special Studies on South and Southeast Asia, Westview Press, Boulder, 1980). This work, originally a set of conference papers, assembles some leading Vietnam specialists of the West and covers political, ideological and other issues.

Vo Nguyen Giap, *Selected Writings*(Foreign Languages Publishing House, Hanoi, 1977). A collection 'of the most important speeches and writings' between 1969 and 1972 of Vietnam's major military thinker. The publisher's note calls them 'a valuable aid for understanding the general line, strategy and tactics of the national liberation war' in Vietnam.

9

KAMPUCHEA AND STALINISM
Ben Kiernan

After returning home in 1980 from Kampuchea, where I had spent much time photographing the prison records of the ousted Pol Pot regime (1975-9), I read Robert Conquest's *The Great Terror* [1] on the Soviet purges of the 1930's. One particular passage caught my attention:

> For the 1936 Trial, Molchanov had prepared for Stalin 'a special diagram...a system of many-coloured lines on the diagram indicated when and through whom Trotsky had communicated with the leaders of the conspiracy'. [2]

My mind was immediately cast back to the charts I had photographed of alleged rebel or foreign agent 'contact networks' drawn up by Security cadre of Pol Pot's Democratic Kampuchea, at Tuol Sleng prison in Phnom Penh. Their 'many-coloured lines' connecting rows of boxes with data on each person implicated seemed almost a direct imitation of the Soviet technique of the 1930's. [3] Further, Conquest's statement that the dossiers of the 'leading figures' targeted by Stalin 'have the low numbers: Pyatakov I, Radek V, Sokolnikov VIII, Drobnis XIII', took me back to my notes on the Tuol Sleng dossiers, where I had written: 'Roman numerals used by prison interrogators for top prisoners', the names of Nos. I-XIX of whom I had copied down.

Now the use in each case of Roman numerals, and even of similar diagrams, may well be coincidence. But it is tempting to suspect otherwise, given the 'confessional' nature of the Kampuchean prison records. [4] They resemble what we know of the archives of Stalinism in nearly every way, with the important exception that the records were kept secret; not even show trials were held in Democratic Kampuchea (DK), and the existence of Tuol Sleng only became known to the outside world after that regime was overthrown.

That aside, could Kampuchean Security personnel have been formally trained in the bureaucratic (and other) interrogation techniques of the Stalinist purge (perhaps in Mao's China of the early 1970's)? This question may never be answered, but other possible parallels and connections are very much worth pursuing, particularly in the realm of ideology. To what extent was Pol Pot's regime Marxist, and to what extent did it consider itself so?

It should be emphasised that what follows is largely tentative; much work remains to be done in what has turned out to be a broad field of enquiry, now that large numbers of DK internal documents and confidential CPK's publications have been made available by the successor government, that of Heng Samrin. [5] The ideology of the DK state and of its ruling party, the CPK, is also an important field of enquiry, given that they presided over the deaths of more than a million Kampucheans in less than four years of power, [6] a period begun by the evacuation of all cities and towns.

The most impressive attempt so far to come to terms with the role of Marxism-Leninism in DK has been that of Michael Vickery. After a detailed comparative study of non-communist revolutionary upheavals in many other rural societies, Vickery concludes that in DK as well, 'nationalism, populism and peasantism really won out over communism', and even that the CPK led 'a victorious peasant revolution, perhaps the first real one in modern times'. [7] In the absence of a good deal more evidence from peasant sources than Vickery presents, I am unconvinced by the second statement. But it should be possible to begin to examine the first, at least on the ideological level, through internal CPK documents.

In early 1977, the Communist Party of Kampuchea's (CPK) third-ranking leader, Ieng Sary, told foreigners in Singapore: 'We are not communists, we are revolutionaries.' [8] This was of course disinformation; the CPK was officially unveiled later that same year. But Ieng Sary's statement was also a signal of a conscious departure from Marxist orthodoxy. As the CPK's internal magazine, *Tung Padevat ('Revolutionary Flag')* had put it in late 1976:

> Left or not left, we must stand by the movement. We must not stand by the Scriptures. [9]

This injunction appeared in an article which also announced, to some consternation among Party cadres, that the CPK was not, after all, twenty-five years old, but only sixteen. [10] The first nine years of organised communism in Kampuchea (1951-60) were thenceforth deemed invalid by the CPK leadership. Party seniority could no longer extend further back than 1960, when Pol Pot (and Ieng Sary) joined the Central Committee. Prior to that the Party was alleged to have been controlled by Vietnamese. This new official doctrine was kept secret for another year (until September 1977), while the Party was subjected to a series of massive and violent purges, especially of its veteran and dissident or suspected dissident members. This period of great convulsions was effectively launched with the appearance of the September-October 1976 issue of *Tung Padevat* (quoted above), which included discussions of socialist revolution, class contradictions, state power and the dictatorship of the proletariat, private and collective property relations, and dialectical materialism. [11] In this paper I will attempt to explain the relationship between some of these theories and the formulation and implementation of the policies of the CPK leadership.

The CPK leadership waited two and a half years after their 1975 victory to declare their communist credentials to the world. [12] The silence was the result, not only of the CPK's obsessive secrecy and factionalism, but also of its tenuous relationship to orthodox Marxism-Leninism. This relationship was increasingly questioned by the dominant (and victorious) Party faction, as can be seen in a range of actions and policies derived from (or justified by) what it claimed to be its Marxist-Leninist philosophy.

In fact, an examination of CPK philosophy, as expressed in Party documents, suggests that its philosophy was a truncated and ill-understood version of Stalin's mechanical dialectical materialism, whose materialist aspects were expunged in an obsession with voluntarism and the role of subjective will. Over time, the communist currents of the CPK's thinking were displaced or overshadowed by nationalist and racist ones which, in Kampuchean conditions at least, demanded an extreme voluntarism and which were unable to coexist with orthodox Marxism.

It is at this point, for the pragmatic requirements of CPK ultra-nationalism, that some elements of Maoist-style politics filled the Party's need. (In the same way, Chinese influence in general was sought to counter-balance that of Hanoi.) But little evidence has yet been uncovered from CPK texts of a far-reaching Maoist influence over the Party's philosophy. Mao's writings *On Practice* and *On Contradiction*, which also discuss dialectical materialism, were not referred to or even plagiarised in any recognisable form.

For example, the CPK slogan of a 'Super Great Leap Forward' [13] was obviously formulated in an exaggerated imitation of Maoist policies of the late 1950's, but again this seems to have been a result of the CPK's perceived need to demonstrate Kampuchean superiority over Vietnam in socialist construction, rather than of an ideological imperative. And the ideology of the Cultural Revolution, on the other hand, while sometimes recognisable in CPK documents, is never explicit or permeating.

Dialectical Materialism

According to the September-October 1976 issue of *Tung Padevat* dialectical materialism is 'the most basic document of Marxism-Leninism'. [14] How then, did the CPK approach this topic which it claimed to be fundamental to its own ideology as well?

In 1950, Stalin had republished his 1938 study, *Dialectical and Historical Materialism*, which divided the subject into three sections: the dialectical method, philosophical materialism, and historical materialism (see Chapter 2). The first section, the dialectical method, Stalin described as having four principal features, namely that:

> 1) All phenomena are organically inter-related. 2) Nature is in continuous movement, change and development. 3) Development involves quantitative changes becoming qualitative ones. 4) Internal contradictions are inherent in all things. [15]

In its 1976 issue cited above, *Tung Padevat* presented a 'Review of Dialectical Materialism' that revealed the influence of Stalin's work (but without mentioning his name). It sum-marised, however, only the first section of Stalin's outline of the subject (as above), although calling its features 'the four laws of dialectical materialism'. [16] In other words, what for Stalin was only the *method*, became for the CPK the 'essence' of the phi-losophy itself, with the exclusion of his two materialist sections. What resulted was a kind of dialectical *voluntarism* rather than materialism (and incidentally, perhaps closer to Hegel's meta-physics than to Marx). Stalin's discussion of the material nature of the world, the primacy of matter, objective truth, modes of production, productive forces, and relations of production was all omitted in the *Tung Padevat* review of the subject. What was apparently considered more important than objective conditions was the subjective method (or approach or tactics?) adopted. We will now turn to the CPK's version of this.

The first point of what Stalin called the 'Marxist dialectical method' is that all phenomena are organically inter-related. The *Tung Padevat* article noted this, and then gave what it said was an example 'to illustrate the law of dialectical materialism' (in Khmer, *patice:samuppad*, or 'counter-collection' is the translation for 'dialectics'). This example is revealing:

> Example: In the situation of a person who has injured a buffalo's leg. We must analyse ... We must ask if the child or the old man who tends the animal injured it, or who else did, and if it was done, why? Was it unintentional, or was it to oppose the cooperative? Look for a person who has something to do with this matter... The cowherd, what composition [background?] is he, what class stand, what political stand, which milieu is his stand in contact with? ... We follow up. Following up is a measure. If we cannot find out in one or two days, we will find out in two or three days. [17]

In this way, the first feature of the Marxist dialectical method, that all phenomena are organically inter-related, was perceived in CPK ideology in terms of the rationale for a witch-hunt.

Such CPK witch-hunts are in fact reminiscent of Stalin's against 'wreckers' who allegedly sabotaged production lines in the USSR in the 1930's. [18] And there is a kind of mechanical materialism in the CPK's preoccupation with the class background of suspects, displayed in the quotation. But overshadowing this, perhaps, is the CPK's firmly-held, if degenerate, philosophy of voluntarism; its assumption being that if the people have correct consciousness, any objective or material obstacles can be overcome. In fact *Tung Padevat* instructed them to:

> Pull out weeds, add water and fertiliser *by pushing the socialist revolutionary consciousness and stance.* [19]

This is voluntarism *à l'outrance*. The person who fails to add water, who breaks a ploughshare, or injures a buffalo's leg must be (and was) suspected of *deliberate* treason. [20] For he had it well within his power to do otherwise, by adopting a different 'consciousness and stance'. One does not look at objective conditions to explain a buffalo's leg injury: excess or unseasonal work patterns, for instance, are not admissable as explanations. Instead, one must 'look for a *person* who has something to do with this matter'.

A second example given by *Tung Padevat* of the point that 'everything is inter-related' concerns 'contradictions' (*tumnoas*, a word really meaning 'conflicts' and used here in the sense of 'disputes') between two agricultural cooperatives. Dialectical materialism, the magazine informs us, teaches that the specific traits of each cooperative must be analysed objectively and from a collective point of view, so that when the offending cooperative is identified, it can be 'purified'. This second example, too, has little to do with the creative tension of the dialectics and a lot to do with witch-hunting. (The substance of its approach, in other words, is personal and metaphysical rather than materialist.) Questions immediately arise about the political function of this *Tung Padevat* article, and the uses to which Marxist theory was put to legitimise the Party's domination.

Three further examples are given. All are used to suggest that the good points, weak points and strong points of both the Party and its enemy must all be taken into account in any given situation or difficulty. The dialectical approach here is clear enough: one's strength is partly related to the weakness of one's enemy, and so cannot be evaluated in isolation.

Still closely following Stalin's outline of the dialectical method, *Tung Padevat* goes on to note its second and third features, that 'everything undergoes transformation' and that this includes 'transformation from quantity to quality'. This means that accumulated piecemeal or everyday developments can have *essential* significance. Now in a materialist framework, in which 'man's social being determines his consciousness', accumulated material development brings about a transformation in his view of the world. But *Tung Padevat* appears to reverse this Marxist prediction, in a clearly implied anti-materialist direction. Its first example of these two features is of a person's incorrect *attitude* 'regarding morality' which may eventually lead to an incorrect *action*, and the transformation is from quality to quantity rather than vice versa.

> This property [attitude?] is evolving. At some point, it will not stay correct with consciousness; it will become a concrete action... Consciousness will not remain still; we must beware not to let the consciousness change into a quantity [*sic*]. [21]

What is particularly striking about this quotation is the final word, which substitutes for Stalin's predicted change 'to quality'. As this substitution is consistent with *Tung Padevat's* replacement of the materialist transformation ('social being determines consciousness') with a metaphysical one (accumulated attitudes determine 'concrete action'), we may presume that it represents a *deliberate* departure from the theory stated a few lines earlier in the article.

All this of course adds more weight to the CPK's deletion of Stalin's discussion of materialism. But its significance would probably end there but for the use to which such theoretical passages were put in DK. The broad, partly incomprehensible theories were applied in three ways: 1) to individuals rather than to historical classes, 2) future 'treason' was considered discernible in minor displays of attitude or could even be considered as merely hidden if undiscerned, and 3) such predicted developments, although in a sense 'metaphysically determined', were still considered preventable, by human vigilance.

> For instance, a bud of material property: do not nurse it. Eliminate it immediately. Therefore, we will be masters

over ourselves. [22]

Two other examples given concern individuals who 'have some hard feelings towards each other', and the tactics of the revolution in its early years (when it capitalised on the tendency for change). The assumption behind them is, again, voluntarist. Objective conditions can be overcome by purely political means. To say otherwise would be to 'remain as observers': 'We cannot just let something go its own way... Do not put the blame on the objective [conditions],' [23] an injunction that was also applied to the buffalo's injured leg, as we have seen.

Stalin's fourth and final feature of the dialectical method is that 'internal contradictions are inherent in all things'. *Tung Padevat* dutifully notes this, but then describes 'internal contradictions' as 'secondary'. The principal ones are 'life-and-death [antagonistic?] anti-Party contradictions'. [24] This latter category apparently derives not from Stalin but from Mao's analysis of antagonistic and non-antagonistic contradictions (see Chapter 4); however, *Tung Padevat* seems to mix this up with Mao's separate analysis of 'principal' and 'secondary' contradictions. [25]

The CPK's discussion of 'internal contradiction' is closer to Mao's theory of 'contradictions among the people' than to Stalin's dialectics. [26] And *Tung Padevat's* illustration is again by means of an example of consciousness or attitude (rather than any material or social tension): 'a heavy property standpoint'. But the border line is perilous: 'going just a bit further becomes an anti-Party contradiction'. Party members are warned not to confuse the two types of contradiction, but the greater risk is said to be mistaking the serious for the less serious.

If we have a life-and-death contradiction, we cannot think it is an internal contradiction. [27]

The converse, which interestingly is what Mao chose to warn against, [28] is not spelled out in this way by *Tung Padevat*. It was obviously not so dangerous for the party to treat an internal contradiction as a life-and-death one. It was, of course, very dangerous for the society, especially one run by a bureaucratic and rigidly hierarchical Party whose cadres would feel safe overfulfilling their quotas of contradictions 'resolved' than underful-filling them. One slogan of the period, used to describe policy towards urban evacuees (as testified by many survivors), was consistent with the view that there was little danger in mistaking internal contradictions for 'life-and-death' ones:

Spare them, no profit; Remove them, no loss. [29]

This chilling epigram is quite unique, even for the more ruthless communist regimes. It is of course a classic anti-dialectical statement, which proclaims that no relationship whatever exists between a dissident and his or her environment. (It even implies the same for the party and *its* environment, that the party can be defended whatever the human cost to the society.)

In conclusion, then, the officially proclaimed CPK view of dialectical materialism excludes any consideration of philosophical materialism or historical materialism. What is left betrays a close adherence to the *form* or outline of Stalin's discussion of dialectical method, while grossly distorting its theoretical content, with occasional forays into selected but unrelated tenets of Maoism. Some aspects of the CPK approach, as we have seen, are indeed dialectical; others definitely are not. Materialism appears only in the preoccupation with the class background of individuals, as an adjunct to state suspicions of them that arise basically out of a metaphysical approach. Beyond this, the Marxist concern with the material forces of history is replaced by a concentration on dialectical method alone. In a political context this translates into tactics and attitudes. In the words of *Tung Padevat*, 'the essence is the class standpoint' of an individual, not the material basis of that class or of his or her standpoint. [30]

What is most interesting is the apparent deliberation with which elements of various Marxist-Leninist theories and writings were selected and combined (or re-shuffled) to form a new ideological framework that suited the CPK leadership's needs, preoccupations, and claims. These were largely nationalist (or chauvinist) in content, as the process of selection itself suggests, even if they were expressed in Marxist terminology, as in the DK Four-Year Plan:

We have leapt over the neo-colonial and semi-feudal society

of the American imperialists, of the feudalists and all types of capitalists, straight to a socialist society. [31]

Kampuchea's material qualifications for such a historic 'leap' were not explained. But the comparisons with other communist countries suggest that it was considered more a matter of leadership policy.

> This situation, compared to other countries, is completely different from them. For example, China was liberated in 1949; they prepared to terminate the people's democratic revolution first, before they went on to prepare the transition to socialism. It took a long period of time; in 1955 they started forming general cooperatives. In 1958 they started the people's communes. For example, Korea was liberated in 1945. Not until 1958 did they establish cooperatives in general in the rural areas, and at that time cooperatives consisted of only 20 or 30 families. So after liberation it took them a long time, the transition to socialism. They did not carry out socialist revolution in general until 1958. The transition required fourteen years. North Vietnam was the same. Now it is the same also in South Vietnam. Their transition takes a long time.
>
> As for us, we have different characteristics... we are six or eight years ahead of them. We have new relations of production, nothing complicated like them. [32]

Finally, several pages later we read:

> Technology is not a determining factor. The determining factors of the revolution are politics, revolutionary people and the revolutionary system. [33]

This statement obviously owes a great deal to Maoist ideology in its preference for 'red' over 'expert', expressed here in a very simplistic form. It seems to me that this is the response of the CPK to the fact that, compared to China, Korea and Vietnam, 'we are very much weaker than them industrially'. [34]

Nationalism and Internationalism
But the neglect of materialism was also interwoven with the

CPK's stand on internationalism, and with its relations with other communist parties (like Mao's) which did claim to 'stand by the Scriptures'. The connection is clear enough in the notes of a senior CPK cadre, apparently transcribed into his diary in August 1978:

> Ever since 1957 our Party has stood on the standpoint of politics... We did not stand on technology as was the experience [all] over the world, whether in the area of the imperialist Western countries *or in the area of revolution.* This experience has emerged [in Kampuchea] very long before [it has in the rest of] the world. [35]

This is an implicit rejection of all previous communist models of revolution. (It also helps explain how Democratic Kampuchea became the first communist regime to provoke a full-scale war with another communist regime — Vietnam.) [36] Indeed, Pol Pot told Yugoslav journalists in March 1978: 'We have no model in building up our new society'. [37] This statement obviously applied to China as much as anywhere else, just as the cadre's private diary tacitly wrote China off as an 'area of revolution' where the experts dominate, just as they do in the imperialist West. In many ways Pol Pot's Kampuchea regarded itself as the centre of world political experience; and this applied whether the CPK followed a line that was 'left or not left'.

In CPK pronouncements, Kampuchea's relationship with the outside world was largely a matter of the example it provided other countries. The DK Four-Year Plan, for instance, claimed that 'we have no foreign assistance':

> We have no assistance from outside either for industry or for agriculture. North Vietnam, after liberation in 1954, was assisted by China and Russia a great deal. It is the same at present. China and Korea after liberation were also greatly assisted by Russia... For us, at present, there is some Chinese aid. Realistically, it is nothing much compared to other countries. This matter is our Party's policy. If we beg around we would certainly get some, but it would affect the political line of our Party. [38]

The implication is that foreign aid is a liability: 'If we allowed foreigners to move in, we would have capital but we would be tied politically.' [39] This suspicion of foreign countries, even friendly ones like China, is a key element of CPK ideology, which springs in large part from its view of Kampuchea's historical experience.

An interesting but little studied phenomenon of the Pol Pot regime is its ideological undercurrent of irredentism. CPK cadres all over the country at various times expressed determination to reconquer the Mekong Delta, which had been seized by Vietnam in the eighteenth century. The Delta has since been known to Khmers as Kampuchea Krom (or 'Lower Kampuchea'), and it retains a large minority of ethnic Khmer, perhaps one million or so. A similar number of Khmers inhabit the southern part of northeast Thailand, an area ruled by Bangkok from the sixteenth century. CPK cadres spoke of regaining this territory also. [40]

As early as 1973, leading CPK representatives (including the current Chief of the General Staff of Democratic Kampuchea, Mok), expressed a historically preoccupied view of relations with Vietnam. According to a witness:

Mok said that Kampuchean territory... included Kampuchea Krom, which Vietnam had taken. The Kampucheans would fight to get it back, Mok said.

Around the same time, other CPK cadres identified Vietnam as a 'hereditary enemy'. [41] This phrase was also used publicly by Pol Pot himself in early 1979. [42] The CPK is one of the few communist parties, if not the only one, to target its political or military opponents in such terms, encompassing an entire nation-state.

Within Kampuchea itself, the most severe treatment of all, perhaps, was reserved for an ethnic minority with an unfortunate history that the CPK wished Kampuchea to avoid repeating (and also to erase from memory). This was the Cham community, survivors of the Vietnamese southward onslaught in the fifteenth century, whose ancestors had fled to Kampuchea and adopted Islam. In 1970 they numbered several hundred thousand.

It seems that at least half of the Cham population of Kampuchea were executed or worked to death in the Pol Pot period. All suffered obliteration of their culture, prohibition of their language, dispersal of their villages, and enforced assimilation with the Khmer population. A Cham woman who survived said the CPK cadres had told her:

> The Chams are hopeless. They abandoned their country to others. They just shouldered their fishing nets and walked off, letting the Vietnamese take over their country. [43]

The modern descendents of such fifteenth-century 'losers' would find no refuge in Democratic Kampuchea; as an autonomous ethnic group they were considered a weak point in the state. This view was reportedly expressed by the CPK leadership as follows:

> There is only one revolution; in Kampuchea there is only one nation and there is only one language, the Khmer language. [44]

The results were particularly disastrous for the Cham, but the effects of Khmer chauvinism were more wide-ranging still. As the internal situation went from bad to worse after 1975, and more and more *Khmers* became disillusioned and embittered by what the CPK leadership was doing, the racism turned in on itself. Khmers who did not share the view that the 'nation' had priority over the rights of its citizens were now branded as not really 'Khmer' at all. With ever widening divisions in the CPK and the resultant uprising by the Party's Eastern Zone branch in May 1978, the entire population of the Zone (about 1.5 million people), bordering Vietnam, were described as having 'Khmer bodies with Vietnamese minds'. This led to the largest massacre of Khmers in recorded history - by their own government. Probably over 100,000 easterners perished in a matter of months. [45] The material and historical links between the Eastern Zone and Vietnam - in terms of border trade, intermarriage and other contacts, and a shared experience (on the part of some) labouring in the rubber plantations there - were all subsumed by official CPK ideology in a metaphysical process of *thinking like Vietnamese.* This ideological approach rationalised the political and military suppression of the Zone's population. It could be said that historical materialism was displaced by a tragic and paranoid historical *voluntarism*, echoing the fate of dialectical materialism in CPK ideology.

All this might lead one to suggest, as Michael Vickery has done, that the CPK was much more a traditionalist revival, an old-fashioned movement of racial irredentism, than a Marxist one. There is a good deal of truth in this. Yet one cannot ignore the sectarian political quality of the Pol Pot leadership, which shared two of the features of modern sectarian communism in this context. Firstly, political movements which were ideologically closer to the CPK were perceived as the greater enemies. Thus, communist Vietnam attracted the violence of CPK rhetoric and action to a much greater extent than capitalist Thailand, although both suffered Kampuchean border raids. Secondly, the Pol Pot leadership's enmity towards its eastern neighbour was magnified by the longstanding Vietnamese influence in the CPK itself, which was perceived as a threat to the leadership. One of Pol Pot's colleagues even claimed in 1980 that 'most of the people in the Party were all Vietnamese agents'. [46] Traditional chauvinism and communist sectarianism seem to have fed off one another, at the expense of both internal and external peace.

Peasantry and Proletariat

No communist party apart from the CPK has emptied all the working class areas under its control and turned their inhabitants into peasants, although there are some (relatively muted) anti-urban strands in Maoist thinking. [47] Nor is it likely that any other communist party could have produced the following statement, which can be found in a 1977 CPK text on the Party's history:

> Concretely, we did not rely on the forces of the workers. The workers were the overt vanguard, but in concrete fact they did not become the vanguard. In concrete fact there were only the peasants. Therefore we did not copy anyone.[48]

This was not merely a practical assessment of the historically small size of the Khmer proletariat. (It may have been this in part.) The CPK's laconic attitude to the working class continued after victory in 1975, as the following statement in the September-October issue of *Tung Padevat* makes clear:

> There is a worker class which has some kind of stand. We have not focussed on it yet. [49]

The magazine even went on to define class struggle in such terms:

> We evacuated the people from the cities which is our class struggle. We develop and strengthen [rural] cooperatives as class struggle... If there were no cooperatives, the true revolutionary traits would be gone. The true imperialist traits would come back. Revisionism would come back. There would be markets, there would be cities, confusion. Slavery. [50]

This passage, which ends the discussion of the dictatorship of the proletariat in *Tung Padevat*, is of particular interest for the way in which Marxist theoretical concepts such as 'revisionism' quickly give way to the almost millenarian final note. This is relatively uncommon in CPK theoretical texts, although its practical effect was probably greater than that of the lip-service usually paid to the importance of the proletariat. Another example is relevant: 'it is not possible that old assets can serve in new duties', [51] according to *Tung Padevat*. What this means seems to have been spelled out in the Four-Year Plan:

> We do not use old workers. We do not use them because if we use the old workers without careful selection and purification, there will be many political complications which will lead to many difficulties for us... We do not want to tangle ourselves with old things. [52]

The former working class, like foreign connections, was regarded as something of a liability to an essentially millenarian nationalist revolutionary project.

It would probably be unfair to avoid the question of whether the anti-worker, anti-internationalist thinking of the CPK leadership, even in its theoretical publications, disqualifies it from membership of the movement that adopted the slogan 'Workers of the World Unite!' I believe, on the evidence reviewed so far, that it does. But careful attention remains to be given to CPK texts and actions that have yet to be analysed. It is true that the only document of established Marxist-Leninist theory to be translated and published in Khmer by the DK regime was Lenin's 'The State'. [53] But very little was published at all under DK. And although none of Mao's works was published, there are occasional (unacknowledged) glimpses of the ideology of the Cultural Revolution, for instance in this passage from *Tung Padevat*:

> There are the revolutionary ranks. These revolutionary ranks are a strata, too. It is a power-holding layer. We must not forget it; it will be hidden. Then it will expand and strengthen as a separate strata, considering itself as worker-peasant; in fact, it holds power over the worker-peasants... We do not want them to expand and strengthen themselves to hold power outside of the worker-peasants. Someday they will oppose the worker-peasants. [54]

Given the tragic history of Democratic Kampuchea, this was a remarkably accurate prediction of the role played by the CPK leadership itself. Whether this warning was a feint, or whether the theory itself represented genuine conviction but was hopelessly inappropriate to Kampuchean conditions is a question that, in the absence of a full review of the evidence, is best left to the reader. However, it appears evident that the distorted Stalinist ideology of the CPK under Pol Pot was far removed from orthodox Marxism-Leninism, and that grotesque and unfortunate consequences flowed from this particular adaptation of Marxism to an Asian context.

NOTES

1. Pelican, 1971.

2. Ibid.,pp. 496-7.

3. One of the first journalists to give detailed attention to the Tuol Sleng records, Anthony Barnett, described 'fantastic charts of lines ... drawn up, in coloured inks.' *New Statesman*, 2 May 1980, p. 671. In a longer article in the same issue, Chanthou Boua and I compared Tuol Sleng with the archives of Stalinism. 'Bureaucracy of Death', pp. 669-676, at p. 670.

4. See for instance, *L'Aveu* (' *The Confession*') by the Czech, Artur London (Paris, 1969).

5. I have described the documents in my possession in 'An Exchange on Cambodia', *New York Review of Books*, 27 September 1984, pp. 63-4.

6. Ben Kiernan and Chanthou Boua (eds.), *Peasants and Politics in Kampuchea, 1942-81* (Zed Press, London, 1982).

7. Michael Vickery, *Cambodia 1975-1982* (George Allen and Unwin, Boston, South End, and Sydney, 1984), pp. 290, 66. See in particular pp. 253-90, 'The Nature of the Cambodian Revolution'.

8. *Far Eastern Economic Review*, vol.96, no.17 (29 April 1977), p 11 .

9. *Tung Padevat*, special issue, September-October 1976, pp. 33-97, 'Sharpen the Consciousness of the Proletarian Class to be as Keen and Strong as

Possible', at p. 40. This article has been elegantly translated from the Khmer by Timothy Carney and Kem Sos, and will appear in full in a forthcoming book edited by Karl Jackson. I am grateful to Timothy Carney for permission to quote from the translation.

10. See David P. Chandler, 'Revising the Past in Democratic Kampuchea: When Was the Birthday of the Party?', *Pacific Affairs*, vol. 56, no. 2 (Summer 1983), pp. 288-300.

11. *Tung Padevat*, op.cit.

12. Phnom Penh Radio, 28 September 1977. See BBC *Summary of World Broadcasts*, 1 October 1977, FE,5629,C2,1ff.

13. Ben Kiernan, 'Pol Pot and the Kampuchean Communist Movement', in Kiernan and Boua, op.cit., pp. 227-317 at p. 228.

14. *Tung Padevat*, op.cit., p. 85.

15. J. Stalin, *Dialectical and Historical Materialism* (September 1938) (Foreign Languages Publishing House, Moscow, 1951), pp. 7-13. Interestingly, Pol Pot was a student in Paris at the time this booklet was published, and was affiliated to the very pro-Stalinist French Communist Party.

16. *Tung Padevat*, op.cit., pp. 84-97.

17. Ibid., pp. 87-8.

18. 'Then, there was the need to find scapegoats for everything that had gone wrong during and after the collectivisation campaign...Livestock were crippled on the orders of the "wreckers"...' Adam B. Ulam, 'The Price of Sanity', in G.R. Urban(ed.), *Stalinism* (London, 1982), p. 121.

19. Ibid., pp. 44-5.

20. See Y Phandara, *Retour a Phnom Penh* (Metaille, Paris, 1982), p. 100: 'The most minor technical faults caused by inexperience were immediately considered as attempts to serve the interest of the enemy', and p. 117: 'the technical faults made on the masonry work were denounced as a sabotage carried out by hidden enemies'.

21. *Tung Padevat*, op.cit., p. 93.

22. Ibid., p. 95.

23. Ibid., pp. 94-5, 48. The latter quotation continues: 'And say that someone offered the private chair to us to sit in. No one gave it to us. Because the private chair is everywhere around us. We must look for the collective chair and grasp it tightly.' The emphasis is on human will struggling against the objective tide.

24. Ibid., pp.95-6.

25. Mao Tse-tung, *Four Essays on Philosophy* (Foreign Languages Press, Peking, 1968). See in particular 'On Contradiction'.

26. Ibid. 'On the Correct Handling of Contradictions Among the People'.

27. *Tung Padevat*, op.cit., p.96.

28. Mao Tse-tung, 'On the Correct Handling', p. 96: 'Those with a "Left" way of thinking magnify contradictions between ourselves and the enemy to such an extent that they take certain contradictions among the people for contradictions with the enemy, and regard as counter-revolutionaries persons who are not really counter-revolutionaries.'

29. Author's interviews with Khmer refugees in France, and with Kampucheans who remain in their country, 1979 and 1980.

30. *Tung Padevat*, op.cit., pp. 56-7. The quotation reads in full: 'The essence is the class standpoint, class character, sentiments, habits reminding it of the desire to oppress...'

31. *Kumrung Pankar Buon Chhnam Sangkumniyum Krup Phnaek Rebos*

Pak, 1977-80 (' *The Party's Four-Year Plan to Build Socialism in All Fields, 1977-80*'), 110 pages, dated July-August 1976, p. 3. The translation is by Chanthou Boua.

32. Ibid.

33. Ibid., p. 5.

34. Ibid., p. 4.

35. Document photographed by the author in Tuol Sleng prison, 1980, dated 18 August 1978.

36. See Ben Kiernan, 'New Light on the Origins of the Vietnam-Kampuchea Conflict', *Bulletin of Concerned Asian Scholars*, vol. 12, no. 4 (1980), pp. 61-5.

37. 'Interview of Comrade Pol Pot... to the Delegation of Yugoslav Journalists in Visit to Democratic Kampuchea', Phnom Penh, Ministry of Foreign Affairs, March 1978, p. 5.

38. *Kumrung Pankar Buon Chhnam*, op.cit., p. 4.

39. Ibid.

40. Kiernan, 'New Light...'

41. Author's interviews with former CPK cadre Yos Por and Kim Kai.

42. Statement of the Government of Democratic Kampuchea, Phnom Penh, 2 January 1979, p. 10-11: 'The whole Kampuchea's people are against Vietnam which is a hereditary enemy.'

43. Ben Kiernan, 'Wild Chickens, Farm Chickens and Cormorants: Kampuchea's Eastern Zone under Pol Pot', in David P. Chandler and Ben Kiernan(eds.), *Revolution and its Aftermath in Kampuchea: Eight Essays* (Southeast Asia Monograph no. 25, Yale University, 1983), pp. 164-6.

44. 'Report on the Genocide Crime Committed by the Pol Pot-Ieng Sary Clique against Religions and Believers in Kampuchea', People's Revolutionary Tribunal, Phnom Penh, August 1979, document presented to the United Nations by the Vietnamese representative Ha Van Lau, 12 October 1979, 14 pp., at p. 9. The CPK document allegedly went on: 'The Cham nation therefore no longer exists on Kampuchean soil belonging to the Khmers. Accordingly, the Cham mentality, Cham nationality, the Cham language, Cham usages and customs, and Cham religious beliefs must be immediately abolished. The Chams must change their names and take names similar to those of the Khmers. Those who fail to obey this order will suffer all the consequences for their acts of opposition to Angkar [the CPK].' I should stress that I have not seen the original of the document, but its contents conform with the accounts of many Cham survivors of DK.

45. See Kiernan, 'Wild Chickens', p. 136-211.

46. Stephen Heder's interview with Thiounn Mumm, 4 August 1980.

47. See Maurice Meisner, 'Utopian Socialist Themes in Maoism' , in by John W. Lewis (ed.), *Peasant Rebellion and Communist Revolution in Asia* Stanford University Press, 1974.

48. *Rien saut daoy songkep nu prowatt chollana padevatt Kampuchea kroam kar duk noam rebos pak kommyunis kampuchea*, undated, 1977 (?), 23 pp., at p. 7. The translation is mine.

49. *Tung Padevat*, op.cit., p. 52.

50. Ibid., pp. 61, 72.

51. Ibid., p. 71.

52. *Kumrung Pankar Buon Chhnam*, op.cit., p. 4.

53. In Khmer, *Ompi Rott*, 1976, 35 pp.

54. *Tung Padevat*, op.cit., p. 53.

SELECT BIBLIOGRAPHY

Carney, Timothy M., *Communist Party Power in Kampuchea (Cambodia): Documents and Discussion* (Cornell University Southeast Asia Program Data Paper No. 106, 1977). A valuable collection of primary documents on the Khmer Rouge movement in the early 1970's, with a thoughtful introduction.

Chandler, David P., *A History of Cambodia* (Westview Press, Boulder, Colorado, 1983). A first general history of Kampuchea in the English language; essential reading for the background to the 1970's revolutions.

Chandler, David P., and Kiernan, Ben (eds.), *Revolution and its Aftermath in Kampuchea: Eight Essays* (Southeast Asia Monograph no. 25, Yale University, 1983). Includes chapters by the editors and Anthony Barnett, Chanthou Boua, Gareth Porter, William Shawcross, Serge Thion, and Michael Vickery.

Kiernan, Ben and Boua, Chanthou (eds.), *Peasants and Politics in Kampuchea, 1942-1981* (Zed Press, London, 1982). Presents accounts by Western and Kampuchean writers and participants in the country's politics and society from the colonial period to the Heng Samrin government.

Kiernan, Ben, *How Pol Pot Came to Power: A History of Communism in Kampuchea 1930-1975* (Verso, London, 1985). A history of the origins, development and internal conflicts of the Kampuchean communist movement, largely based on primary sources.

Ponchaud, François, *Cambodia Year Zero* (Allen Lane, London, 1978). The first serious attempt to describe life under the Pol Pot regime, focussing on 1975-6.

Shawcross, William, *Sideshow: Kissinger, Nixon and the Destruction of Cambodia* (Andre Deutsch, London, 1979). A history of US involvement in Kampuchea to 1975, including the most detailed account of the Lon Nol regime (1970-5).

Vickery, Michael, *Cambodia 1975-1982* (George Allen and Unwin, Sydney, 1984). The most comprehensive account of the Pol Pot regime and its successor, that of Heng Samrin, including an attempt to analyse the nature of the revolution of the 1970's.

10

THE INDONESIAN MARXIST TRADITION
Robert Cribb

Marxism has a longer tradition of formal organisation in Indonesia than in any other country discussed in this book. The first Marxist association in the Netherlands Indies was established in 1914, three years before the October Revolution in Russia; the Indonesian Communist Party (*Partai Komunis Indonesia, PKI*) was founded in 1920, the first communist party in Asia outside the borders of former Tsarist Russia. This seniority, together with sheer physical distance from the centres of Marxist authority, enabled Indonesian Marxists to develop a distinctive indigenous application of Marxism-Leninism to the circumstances in their country.

Indonesian Marxists, however, have been persistently unable to carry out a successful Marxist-Leninist revolution. During three separate periods, 1920-6, 1945-8, and 1951-65, the party operated in an environment of relative political freedom, drawing wide popular support. Each period of legality ended, however, with the party's implication or involvement in an ill-prepared and wholly unsuccessful uprising. On each occasion, government repression following the uprising has effectively removed the PKI from the Indonesian political arena. The party has now been illegal since 1966 and the only sign of its activity is the odd government warning against the 'latent danger' it presents. An underground party almost certainly exists, but its efforts must be devoted largely to survival rather than revolution. The party's few attempts to engage in protracted guerrilla warfare on the Chinese or Vietnamese model have been entirely unsuccessful.

The present low ebb of Marxism in Indonesia, and the fact

that surviving members of the party outside Indonesia are dependent for the most part on the financial support of the Eastern European or Chinese Communist parties, has encouraged a general tendency to see the PKI's indigenous Marxist interpretation of Indonesian society as mistaken and ultimately responsible for the party's eclipse. It is probably more accurate, however, to regard this indigenous interpretation as responsible rather for the party's temporary political successes in a society which, despite certain resemblances to the societies of China and Indochina, does not permit the uncritical application of any externally derived interpretation of the thought of Marx.

The attrition in PKI ranks brought about by repression and by the longevity of the party has led to a number of changes in leadership over the years. The party moreover has been wracked from time to time at critical junctures in Indonesian history by serious disputes over tactics. Nonetheless there is a continuity in Indonesian Marxist thought which constitutes a distinctive Indonesian tradition in the application of Marx's thought to Indonesian conditions. The PKI's interpretation of Marxist-Leninist thought has enabled it to survive extended periods of repression, without the territorial base enjoyed by the Chinese and Vietnamese communists, and to blossom when conditions were favourable, coming within striking distance of power. If, by botanical analogy, Vietnamese communism is the product of a graft, Indonesian communism is a desert plant which survives hostile wind and sun by staying underground until the right climatic opportunity enables it to shoot forth and spread with great rapidity. This pattern of survival and efflorescence was made possible by the emphasis which the party placed on the preservation and spread of Marxist-Leninist ideas rather than on direct revolutionary action. This aspect of Indonesian Marxism is the basis of persistent allegations, especially since 1965, that the PKI was revisionist. As will be argued below, however, the PKI was never a social democratic party in the European sense; nor for that matter was it an Asian representative of Eurocommunism, despite its striking parallels with the Italian communist party. With its attention to the importance of ideas, it more closely resembles the emphasis of recent Western Marxism on subverting the ideological hegemony of the capitalist system as a prerequisite for revolution. [1] Even that parallel, however, is not exact; the party's willingness to work within the framework of the Indonesian state reflected rather its interpretation of the role of that state as a vehicle for the ultimate victory of the proletariat.

The proletariat, of course, occupied the central role in Indonesian Marxist theory. 'The Indonesian revolution will not succeed unless it is under the leadership of the Indonesian proletariat', wrote D.N. Aidit, the PKI's foremost leader of the 1950's and early 60's. [2] As in other largely agrarian societies of East and Southeast Asia, however, the Indonesian proletariat has never been more than a small proportion of the total population. Aidit estimated in 1958 that the proletariat numbered twenty million people, one quarter of the population, but this figure included workers in a wide range of occupations, from plantation labourers to workers in craft industries, together with their families. The modern industrial proletariat in a strict sense he estimated to be well under one per cent of the population. [3]

Marxists seeking to make revolution in these societies have accordingly sought to identify the allies on whom the proletariat may call in its struggle for power. The Dutch Marxists who in 1914 founded the ISDV (Indies Social Democratic Association), the Marxist organisation which preceded the PKI, were amongst the first to recognise that a key ally in the struggle was the peasantry and that the bourgeois nationalist parties were the means by which the peasantry could be first reached and then recruited. Members of the ISDV infiltrated the first mass nationalist organisation in Indonesia, the Sarekat Islam, from about 1916 and were successful in taking over many of its local branches. This practical experience was carried by the ISDV's founder, Henk Sneevliet, to the Second Congress of the Comintern in 1920, where it became a major basis for Lenin's 'Theses on the National and Colonial Questions'. [4]

The Indonesian Marxists who succeeded to control of the ISDV, however, and who subsequently formed the PKI, cast class alliance in a rather different light. The first chairman of the PKI, Semaun, was one of the pioneers of communist infiltration of the Sarekat Islam and was a close associate of Sneevliet. Yet his report to the First Congress of the Toilers of the East in Irkutsk in 1921 made no mention of this as a strategy. In fact it made very little reference to class or class structure in Indonesian society at all, but rather provided the following analysis of Indonesia's condition:

...from 1908...a powerful upsurge of European imperialism
had revolutionized the masses. The development of capitalism in Europe, overproduction, and a surplus of goods
caused the capitalists to seek salvation in the colonies. The
Netherlands Indies had been conquered three hundred years
before, and since that time had suffered under the yoke of
European rule; but the consequences of an imperialist policy only made themselves felt since 1900, that is, since the
time the country was opened to international capital.... The
year 1900 saw great changes: the growth of capitalism had
brought the exploitation of the natives and with this their
proletarianization. [5]

This analysis, arguing that colonialism had proletarianised
Indonesian society, goes some way beyond Lenin's argument that
colonial exploitation had enabled European capitalists to em-
bourgeoise important sections of the European working class.
For while Lenin maintained that the success of the national revolution in the colonies was an important element in the success of
the proletarian revolution in the advanced capitalist countries of
the West, he had insisted that the proletarian revolution in the
West was in turn necessary to bring socialism to the East. Semaun's argument that Indonesians had been proletarianised
meant that proletarian revolution could take place in Indonesia
itself and implied that it could take place independent of proletarian revolution in the West. While Semaun's analysis did not
deny the possibility of cooperation with other proletarianised colonial people in Asia, it clearly foreshadowed the theoretical and
practical self-sufficiency which characterised the PKI through
much of its history.

In arguing that Indonesians were proletarianised by colonialism, Semaun was asserting that colonialism oppressed all Indonesians in the same way. While he recognised the existence of
different classes in Indonesian society, and could not fail to be
aware that the massive unevenness of historical development in
Indonesia had led to the existence side by side of primitive communism, slavery, feudalism and late capitalism, he argued that
the cooperation between classes in the anti-colonial struggle was
not simply a tactical and temporary alliance but rather was based
on a longterm identity of interest. Semaun in fact made no

reference to class conflict within Indonesian society. He mentioned 'native landowners', but described them as 'acting, where possible, on behalf of the native rural population'. [6] Later Marxist theorists in Indonesia modified this analysis considerably, identifying feudal landowners and the compradore bourgeoisie as indigenous class enemies of the proletariat, alongside its foreign, capitalist-imperialist enemies, but they retained the emphasis on the identical nature of these enemies for all Indonesians. 'The Indonesian proletariat', wrote Aidit, 'is exploited by three forms of brutal exploitation, that is, imperialism, capitalism and feudalism'. [7]

The suggestion that a proletariat could be oppressed by feudalism reflects a general theme in Indonesian Marxism that human history has been telescoped in Indonesia so that a single revolution, led by the proletariat, could take place, simultaneously combining, embodying and bypassing the normal succession of historical stages outlined by orthodox Marxism. Semaun suggested that while colonialism had brought parts of Indonesia to the stage of mature capitalism, much of the colony remained in a state of primitive communism.

> The peasantry comprised about 95% of the population; the Netherlands Indies was and to a significant degree still is a country of primitive communism. The land belonged to the community, which at an assembly apportioned it among its members for a set length of time, at the end of which period it was redistributed.... The 'open rural assembly' represented in its way a primitive soviet and embodied the highest administrative and legislative power of the village. [8]

At the meeting at which the PKI formally decided to join the Comintern in 1920, the party explicitly demurred at the Comintern resolution calling for the redistribution of land, not on the grounds that the party should avoid antagonising potential allies, but on the grounds that there was no large scale land-holding in Indonesia. [9] In fact this analysis of rural society in Indonesia reflected a romantic idealisation of village life rather than any knowledge of rural conditions, and it was not until the early 1950's that Indonesian Marxists undertook the detailed rural research which enabled them to recognise the strength of feudalism, especially in rural Java. Nonetheless, the strategic unity of the proletarian and other revolutions remained a fundamental principle of Indonesian Marxism. [10]

Since colonialism, according to Semaun, was the prime proletarianising force in Indonesia, it followed that the national revolution against colonialism would be the vehicle for proletarian victory. Indonesian Marxists did not generally argue for a two-stage revolution, for a bourgeois nationalist phase to be followed by a socialist phase. Rather, they argued that, since the two revolutions were one, they had to be achieved together. In the 1950's, therefore, when the national revolution appeared to many observers to be over, leaving power in the hands of the bourgeois nationalists, PKI theorists argued that the national revolution against imperialism had in fact not yet been won, that Indonesia remained *de facto* a colonial country. As evidence they pointed to the Netherlands-Indonesian Union imposed on the Indonesian Republic in the negotiations which ended the national revolution in 1949, and to the Dutch retention of West New Guinea (now Irian Jaya), which all Indonesian nationalists regarded as an integral part of the national territory. Although they regarded the Indonesian state as being at least partly controlled by colonial and neo-colonial interests, the Indonesian Marxists argued that the state could be freed from this burden not only by revolutionary action from below, but also by action initiated within the state apparatus itself. The twin issues of the Union and Irian Jaya played an important role in PKI campaigns in the 1950's. It was the logic of this position and the fact that the Indonesian Republic under Sukarno did in fact succeed in ridding itself of both the Union and Dutch rule in Irian, as well as of Dutch domination of the economy, which led Aidit to articulate his theory of the dual nature of the state. This theory was simply that the state had both a pro-people aspect and an anti-people aspect.

> [The] realities pertaining to the basis also find their reflection in the superstructure, including state power and chiefly in the *cabinet*. In the state power, a policy against imperialism, feudalism, bureaucrat-capitalists and compradors is reflected alongside the policy which defends imperialism, vestiges of feudalism, bureaucratic-capitalists and compradors. [11]

The task of the party was to bring about the dominance of the pro-people aspect.

This element in Indonesian Marxism has caused some discomfort amongst foreign Marxists sympathetic to the PKI. Mortimer, for instance, referring to the 'ingenuity and flexibility' of the Indonesian communists and to their 'hardheaded political judgement' in a political situation in the early 1950's whose prospects for the PKI were 'dismal', avoids addressing the ideological implications of the PKI's political programme. [12] For, although the nature of the state is still a matter of widespread debate amongst Marxists, Aidit's formulation appears to stray far beyond the orthodox Marxist instrumentalist assessment of the state as a tool which one class uses to oppress another class.[13] While it is true, however, that the dual nature theory of the state was not publicly articulated as such until 1963, it reflected an ambivalent attitude to the state which was deeply rooted in the history of the PKI and of Marxism within the Indonesian nationalist movement.

From the earliest years of nationalist organisation, Marxism had been a major intellectual influence within the movement. There had been no Indonesian state before the Dutch established their empire in the archipelago. Whereas Vietnam and China, like Japan and Korea, had long traditions of statehood and cultural identity which underpinned their respective patriotisms, Indonesia was a creation of Dutch colonial rule. Although bourgeois nationalists energetically created a nationalist mythology of statehood and cultural identity, [14] the revitalisation of traditional Indonesian political forms was too unspecific a goal to form a significant part of the nationalist critique of colonial rule; Indonesia could have no Phan Boi Chao, no Meiji Emperor. The Marxist critique of colonialism, by contrast, was not only powerful but unambiguously modern, and it was consequently influential in nationalist thinking and discussion far beyond the confines of the PKI. Indonesia's first prime minister, Sutan Syahrir, for instance, argued an essentially Marxist analysis of Indonesian society which identifed feudalism and international capitalism as the twin enemies of the Indonesian people. [15] Only Islam offered a comparably influential critique of colonialism, and during the 1910's and 20's there was even a briefly influential Islamic Communist stream of thought whose leaders argued that the principles of Islam and Communism were essentially the same.

One leader of this stream of Islamic liberation theology, for instance, suggested:

> The righteous teacher, our Lord the Prophet Mohammad, was the man who removed all inequality between the sexes, did away with the difference between ruler and subject, between rank and class. And all these changes were brought about by the Socialist par excellence, by our Prophet Mohammad. [16]

Tan Malaka, the PKI's most prominent theorist in the 1920's, also consistently rejected the Comintern's hostility to Pan-Islamism, arguing that Islam, like nationalism, represented a force which could be used to mobilise the oppressed peoples of Asia. Even after overt Islamic Communism disappeared as an intellectual force, Marxist categories of analysis continued to influence the thought of Muslim politicians such as Mohammad Hatta, Indonesia's first vice-president, who laid considerable stress, for instance, on the condemnation of capitalism by both Islam and Marxism. [17]

The most important synthesiser of nationalism and communism was Sukarno, who subsequently became first president of the Indonesian Republic. Sukarno freely used and adapted Marxist ideas in his own thought. He attributed Indonesia's ills to capitalism as manifested in colonialism, but he considered the result of this to be the impoverishment of the Indonesian people rather than their proletarianisation. Similarly, he turned the PKI's idea of a revolution which encompassed different historical stages into one which merely encompassed different ideological and social groups: the nationalists who fought foreign rule, the Muslims who fought the infidel and the *marhaen* [18] who fought their exploiters and oppressors. His 1926 essay, *Nationalism, Islam and Marxism*, was a passionate assertion that the traditional antagonisms between the three ideologies did not apply in the Indonesian case and that supporters of all three could work together for a national independence which would simultaneously fulfil the aims of all three. [19] In the 1950's and 60's this proposition was expressed in the formula NASAKOM (Nationalism, Religion, Communism) which gave to Marxism official sanction while ensuring at the same time that it remained only one element amongst three in the official pantheon. Sukarno's ideas were also echoed in a variety of forms by a wide range of non-communist politicians on the left, notably those from the Murba (Proletarian) Party and the left wing of the Indonesian Nationalist Party (PNI) under Ali Sastroamijoyo. Murba in particular argued that there were no serious class divisions within Indonesia and that the primary contradiction lay between Indonesia and the capitalist, imperialist West.

The strength of such quasi-Marxist ideas in the intellectual make-up of Indonesian bourgeois nationalism reached a peak under Sukarno's Guided Democracy (1959-65), when the PKI rose to become the largest communist party outside the communist world. It led Indonesian Marxists towards the conclusion that the national movement, and later the national state, might be captured by Marxism through peaceful means and, having been captured ideologically, would naturally admit Marxists to positions of power. In the 1920's and 1950's, the party fought major battles over ideological issues, seeking to make a Marxist view of the world the natural and orthodox way of thinking for the Indonesian people. In this the PKI was probably influenced by deeply rooted ideas in traditional Javanese political thought on the nature of power. There is in classical Javanese cosmology a close relationship between knowledge and power, connected ultimately perhaps to Buddhist and Hindu ideas of enlightenment and transcendent knowledge. [20] If the concepts and intellectual structure can be perfected, it is felt, then power will flow as a matter of course. Ruth McVey has pointed out the influence of this world view in the composition of Aidit's *Indonesian Society and the Indonesian Revolution*, the PKI's chief text on the Indonesian revolution during the eleven years following the fifth party congress in 1954. The text is flat and plain, remarkably free of the rhetoric and traditional imagery one finds in Chinese Marxist writings and in the contemporary political language of Sukarno. In this very spurning of traditional forms, however, the party was working within a traditional belief that control of new ideas leads to power. This, argues McVey, was one of Marxism's major attractions:

> ...it was not so much its radical anti-imperialism or its call for social justice (though it was certainly these things too) as it was its promise that by associating and thinking in a new way one could gain strength and become, in the end,

invincible.... It provided [cadres] with a charter as a counter-elite, a basis on which they could top the post-revolutionary establishment's claims to cultural and social superiority and ultimately the right to rule. [21]

A major tool in the PKI's battle to inculcate a socialist way of thinking in a state which was not yet wholly in progressive hands was the party's cultural affiliate, Lekra (*Lembaga Kebudayaan Rakyat*, Institute for People's Culture) founded in 1950. Lekra acted on one level as a sponsor of artists and writers, defending their professional interests as a kind of cultural trade union, as well as organising cultural exchange programmes with communist countries. Its principal function, however, was to transform the terms of artistic discourse in Indonesia into terms compatible with Marxism.

> ...Lekra gives active support to everything that is new and progressive, Lekra actively assists in the demolition of the remainders of colonial 'culture' which has left a part of our people in dark ignorance, with feelings of inferiority and with weakness of character. Lekra accepts our ancestral heritage critically and studies carefully all its aspects... and thus creatively endeavors to further the great tradition of our history and our nation, directing it toward a new culture which is rational and scientific.... In short, in repudiating the antihuman, antisocial character of the culture that is not-of-the-people, in repudiating the violations of truth and beauty, Lekra helps shape a new society capable of self-advancement, a society developing its individuality which is both multifaceted and harmonious. [22]

Reflecting the party's dualist approach to the state, Lekra distinguished between Art for the People and Art for Art's sake, the latter being regarded as dangerously reactionary, and it waged a protracted campaign in universities, the press and cultural circles against art and literature which it considered to be dangerous to the broad programme for creating the new communist human being in Indonesia by means of ideas. In the 1940's Tan Malaka, although then no longer a member of the PKI, expressed a similar need for creating first a new way of thinking based on what he termed *Madilog* (materialism, dialectics, logic).[23]

The PKI's interpretation of the state as partly pro-people effectively closed it off from the path of armed revolution which brought its Chinese, Vietnamese and Kampuchean counterparts to power, although Aidit's writings are ambiguous on the question of whether revolutionary violence can be avoided in the long term. The only national revolt which the party unambiguously launched, namely the risings of 1926 and 1927, had the character of a putsch rather than a prolonged people's war. The role of the PKI leadership in planning the 1948 Madiun rising and the 1965 coup is much debated. The party's leader in 1948 was Musso, one of the leaders of the 1926-7 risings, and he talked openly of a 'Gottwald Plan' to seize power in a bloodless coup along the lines of the communist takeover in Czechoslovakia, [24] while in 1965 there was at least a wide public presumption that the party was planning a pre-emptive strike against the army leadership in a bid for greater political power. On the other hand there is also evidence that both events were at least in part the work of groups hostile to the PKI who wished to implicate it in an act of revolt. Whatever the facts of either matter, those affairs, too, were attempts to seize power by a swift strike at the centre of authority rather than by guerrilla war. In the aftermath of the 1965 coup, remnants of the party did commence a guerrilla struggle in the Blitar area in East Java, and this strategy was justified in a document known as the *Otokritik (Self-criticism)*, which purports to be a post-coup evaluation and condemnation of the philosophies and strategies of the Aidit years produced by Indonesian Marxist revolutionaries still active in Indonesia. [25] Specifically, the document criticises the party for adopting the two aspects theory of the state, which it sees as the Soviet-style revisionism of the 'peaceful road' to socialism, and it calls for armed revolution in the countryside, based on a worker-peasant alliance under the leadership of the proletariat. The guerrilla struggle in East Java appears in fact to have ended by the early 1970's. This may, however, reflect not a change in strategy but simply military defeat and the fact that the geopolitical realities of Indonesia make revolution on the models of mainland Asia unlikely to succeed. The fact that Indonesia is an archipelago immeasurably complicates lines of supply and prevents the use of outlying regions as a base area for a march on the capital, while the main island of Java, the only region geographically suited to prolonged guerrilla warfare, happens to be strongly Muslim and in recent times unsympathetic to communism.

It is this general repudiation of armed revolution as the technique for achieving the victory of the proletariat which has opened the PKI to charges of modern revisionism. Whether Indonesian Marxism lies wholly within the orthodox Marxist tradition may indeed be legitimately debated; it should be clear, however, that its analysis was not a variety of the so-called modern revisionism of Tito, or Khrushchev or the Eurocommunists, for it was not through the formal institutions of the bourgeois state that the PKI hoped and expected to march to power. Rather, the state itself could be transformed by the creation of pro-people institutions, such as a new parliament or new cabinets with different social bases, to replace the old anti-people institutions which previously dominated it. The accession to positions of power of communists such as Amir Syarifuddin, who became first defence minister and then prime minister of the Republic during the early years of the revolution, might appear to refute this generalisation, and Amir is known personally to have been an admirer of Tito. Nonetheless Amir's rise to power appears to have been an unexpected fruit of his refusal to collaborate with Japanese fascism and even he appears to have attached limited significance to holding office, for he resigned from power in 1948 after a parliamentary vote of no confidence, without having explored all the possible avenues for retaining office. The proposition that the PKI should seek power by parliamentary means was then decisively defeated in the power struggle between Tan Ling Djie, who briefly led the party from the Madiun affair to 1951, and Aidit who succeeded him. [26]

Although the role of the party in Indonesian Marxist analysis was not as leader of an armed revolution, the anti-people aspect of the state made the party an essential strategic element in the struggle, as reservoir and disseminator of Marxist ideas and understanding. From the earliest times, Marxists in Indonesia faced government harassment, and they became acutely aware of their vulnerability to repression, especially in the aftermath of the razzias or round-ups which followed the abortive 1926-7 uprisings. Tan Malaka, one of the party's chief theoreticians, who had split with the PKI leadership over his opposition to the risings, organised a new party, called Pari (*Partai Republik Indonesia*), which almost immediately became a clandestine organisation. Its members flitted in and out of the Netherlands Indies, concentrating on propaganda, recruitment and above all survival by means of a tight cell structure which enabled the party to survive vigorous Dutch repression for at least ten years after the 1926-7 risings. Although the party's constitution of 1927 provided for a democratic centralist structure, its committees never met and it was held together principally by the force of the ideas it transmitted. [27]

Much the same applied to the network of activists who remained loyal to the PKI and who were reassembled by Musso in 1936 into the so-called 'illegal PKI'. This party survived the closing years of Dutch rule and the even greater repression of the Japanese occupation by employing a cell structure similar to that of the Pari and by passing from one leader to another, sometimes just a few steps ahead of the Japanese secret police, a mandate to direct party activity. [28] Even when the party could operate legally once more after the declaration of independence in 1945, it chose to form only a relatively small open party and to disperse its members amongst a variety of left wing parties. The most notable of these was the ostensibly socialist Amir Syarifuddin, who as defence minister and later prime minister reached a position of greater power than any Indonesian communist before or since. [29] Reliable information on the fifties and after is difficult to obtain, since clandestine activity by its very nature was not discussed openly except by the PKI's opponents, who persistently alleged that the party maintained an illegal organisation for the purpose of launching a revolutionary putsch.[30] The correct degree of clandestinity was certainly discussed extensively in the party in the early 1950's, with Tan Ling Djie becoming the straw man in a debate with his successor over the merit of maintaining working class parties other than the PKI. [31] Although Aidit argued on this occasion that the working class was sufficiently politically conscious and the party's political opponents sufficiently weak to permit an open campaign by the party, the perennial threat of repression by hostile sections of the armed forces meant that the situation in Indonesia was far from being so favourable that the PKI leaders were likely to consider totally abandoning the clandestine organisation which was their guarantee of the party's long-term survival.

The debate over Tan Ling Djie-ism was conducted within the broad PKI assumption that the primary role of the party was as a reservoir and vessel for Marxist ideas rather than as a simple tool for revolutionary action. At issue in the debate was the question of how favourable conditions were in Indonesia for a florescence of the party; the victory of the optimists around Aidit opened the way for a vast expansion in PKI membership which took the party to an eventual membership of around three million. Party membership under such circumstances became the first rather than the final step in the development of commitment to Marxist ideas, and the party became a giant educational institution, not only for society but for its own members, running innumerable training and theoretical courses, maintaining a wide network of party schools, and even establishing a college for advanced theoretical study, the Aliarcham Academy.

This emphasis on education had, in turn, major implications for the relationship of the party to the proletariat and of the proletariat to the rest of society. In selecting cadres and leaders the PKI characteristically emphasised commitment to Marxism over class origin. 'An ex-feudalist or ex-bourgeois', argued Soerjono, a junior party cadre during the revolution, 'who sides with the people's struggle is far better than a "proletarian" who bourgeoisifies himself.' [32] Indeed one of the persistent features of the PKI was its domination by individuals who were not proletarian in their class background, but rather came from petty bourgeois families. [33] The effect of this was to blur in practice the normally strict and careful categorisation of classes characteristic of Marxist thought. It was based theoretically, however, on the argument that the class nature of the mass of the party membership was more important than that of its leadership, because the party functioned primarily as a tool for raising consciousness.

While affirming the importance of Marxist ideology as a tool in the struggle, the PKI nonetheless recognised the class base of the anti-people aspect of the state and the need for an explicitly cross-class alliance to combat it. Although Semaun had made no reference in his 1921 report to a strategy of class alliance, it was the practical experience of the PKI in its dealings with Sarekat Islam which underpinned Sneevliet's 'bloc within' strategy. Under this strategy, small, weak Asian communist parties were urged to infiltrate larger mass nationalist parties in order to win over their mass following in the long term and to displace their bourgeois nationalist leadership. [34] The terms of this cross-class alliance varied from period to period, but it remained a national united front in conception, that is an alliance of Indonesian social groups with long term identical interests. An exception to this generalisation may be the illegal PKI of the late 1930's and 1940's, which appears from the limited evidence available to have closely followed the Dimitrov anti-fascist popular front doctrine which contributed significantly to Amir Syarifuddin's somewhat unexpected rise to power during the early revolution. [35]

It was under Aidit that the nature of this class alliance was most clearly spelt out in terms of a national united front. Aidit attributed this formulation to Musso, who had returned to Indonesia again in 1948 to take charge of the party shortly before the Madiun Affair and had set out the idea of a national front in a pamphlet entitled *A New Road for the Indonesian Republic*. [36] The details of Aidit's united national front, however, bear the strong imprint of Mao Zedong's concept of the four-class alliance. Aidit expressed the PKI doctrine as follows:

The revolutionary forces in Indonesia are composed of all classes and groups suffering from imperialist and feudal oppression. They are the *proletariat (the working class), the peasants, the petty bourgeoisie, the national bourgeoisie and other democrats*. They must be united in an anti-imperialist and anti-feudal national united front based on the worker-peasant alliance and led by the working class. [37]

In practice, as Mortimer has pointed out, Mao's four-class alliance could not easily be applied to Indonesia, for the categories of petty bourgeoisie and national bourgeoisie bore no clear resemblance to existing socio-economic groups in Indonesia; the petty bourgeoisie included for instance both doctors and impoverished fishermen. Nor did the categories of feudal landowner and comprador bourgeoisie adequately encompass the forces opposed to the PKI, for they omitted the entrenched civil bureaucracy and the largely anti-communist army. The party was later to classify these separately as 'bureaucratic capitalists'. In fact the PKI identified the components of its national united front by their political attitudes rather than by their social class, as indeed is implied by the term 'other democrats' in Aidit's statement above. The PKI's distinction between its supposed ally, the national bourgeoisie, and its opponents the comprador bourgeoisie and the feudal landowners was based on the hostility of the latter to the party, irrespective of their landholdings or ties with Western imperialism. [38]

The four-class alliance, therefore, functioned less as a guide to practical action than as a simple public affirmation of the PKI's acceptance of what was at the time of 1954 party congress the accepted model for communist victory in Asian countries. There was indeed much in the party's theory and practice which is difficult to reconcile with the four-class alliance as it is commonly understood. Although the PKI controlled Indonesia's main trade union organisation, SOBSI, the PKI had within its original programme virtually no demands which directly addressed the interests of the proletariat. Those interests, the PKI argued, would be met by the ultimate socialist victory, not by direct action. Even the nature of that ultimate socialist victory was couched in the vaguest terms.

In the countryside, too, the PKI pursued a programme which was scarcely realistic in terms of the four-class alliance. Aidit had introduced for the first time a serious consideration of the peasantry as a major element in PKI strategy, to the point of saying that 'the agrarian revolution is the essence of the people's democratic revolution in Indonesia'. [39] The party, however, chose the redistribution of land as its principal programme in rural areas. While this was clearly of interest to the peasants, there was simply not enough land in most areas on Java for redistribution to make a significant contribution to solving problems of rural production. Moreover, while there were significant differences in wealth in rural society, these differences were small by the standards of many Asian countries and they were blurred further by the existence of an intricate and subtle gradation of wealth and social status within the village. Polarisation was under way, but it fell far short of a clear division between an exploited peasant class and an oppressive landlord class. When the PKI, therefore, applied its criterion of sympathy or antipathy to the communist cause to rural Javanese society, it tended to coincide with a pre-existing division in society which was cultural rather than social. The PKI became identified with the *abangan* cultural stream within Javanese society, that is those whose belief, while nominally Muslim, is in fact a blend of Sufism, Hinduism and native Javanese mysticism, as opposed to the more orthodox Muslim *santri*. The party accepted as members *abangan* landlords and petty bureaucrats who saw it as an opportunity to fight long standing battles with the *santri* rather than to wage class war. Inconsistent as such activity may be with a strictly interpreted four-class alliance, it is eminently consistent with a programme of attracting people into the orbit of the party in order to educate them and to establish Marxism as a natural way of viewing the world within broad sections of society.

The discontinuity between the four-class alliance, with its Maoist overtones, and the actual theory and practice of the PKI is consistent with the party's tradition of independence in its foreign relations. While recognising the international dimension of the struggle against imperialism, Indonesian Marxists have generally placed little emphasis either practically or theoretically on proletarian internationalism. Independence, even defiance, of the Comintern was a characteristic of the PKI in the 1920's. On joining the Comintern in 1920, the PKI executive stated:

> As has previously been explained, we have followed the Communist tactic here before there existed 'orders from Moscow' concerning it. We therefore need change nothing following our affiliation as far as our tactics or method of struggle are concerned. [40]

Tan Malaka, although he had been Comintern representative in Southeast Asia in the early 1920's, shared this view, arguing that the Pari could best ensure the survival of the Indonesian people's movement 'by relying in the first place on our own strength, and secondly, by marching independently but on a parallel course with the international proletarian movement.' [41]

This lack of enthusiasm for the Comintern was based both on the theoretical self-sufficiency of the Indonesian revolution which derived from the thesis that Indonesians had been proletarianised by colonialism, and at times on more practical considerations. During the national revolution, in particular, PKI leaders wished to avoid provoking American intervention on the side of the Dutch and they sought accordingly to minimise their already meagre public connections with the Soviet Union. [42] This pessimism concerning the power of the PKI's imperialist enemies was associated, like pessimism over indigenous opponents, with

Tan Ling Djie, and it was modified somewhat by the Aidit leadership of the party, which felt confident, for instance, in attacking the United States as an imperialist power. Nonetheless, the party under Aidit, while it drew on ideas and terminology from other Marxist parties, insisted that it alone could undertake the task of 'welding the truths of Marxism-Leninism with the concrete practice of the Indonesian revolution itself.' [43] Aidit in particular argued that there was an important distinction to be made between the universal laws of Marxism, which were accessible to Marxists everywhere, and the particular laws which applied in individual countries and which could be grasped only by Marxists working under local conditions. [44] Thus the party, for instance, stayed largely aloof in the Sino-Soviet split, though it established an important tactical alliance with the Chinese in the later Guided Democracy period. [45]

The elements of Indonesian Marxist theory which centre on the national united front and the four class alliance lie comfortably in the broader application of Marxism to Asian conditions as developed by Mao Zedong, Ho Chi Minh and others. Indonesian Marxism, however, departed from this broad consensus in ignoring protracted armed struggle as a means by which the local communist party might eventually achieve power. This departure has traditionally been regarded by observers as a realistic and intelligent, though ultimately disastrous, tactical response to the political situation in which the party found itself in the 1950's. Neither Mortimer, sympathetic to the PKI, nor van der Kroef, definitely unsympathetic to it, regarded this eschewal of armed revolution as having any great theoretical significance. A much smaller number of observers have treated this aspect of PKI policy as central to party theory, but they have done so largely in order to portray the party as revisionist in the Khrushchev manner and in order to use the party's demise as a stick with which to beat revisionism.

In the context of the longer term history of Indonesian Marxism, however, the PKI's abstention from violent revolution in the 1950's and early 60's was neither simply tactical nor an expression of revisionism. On the contrary, it reflected a long tradition within the party which derived ultimately from the proposition that history need not follow the strict chronological succession of historical stages outlined by orthodox Marxism; in particular, that two or more stages could and did exist within the one society. From this proposition, Indonesian Marxists could argue during the colonial period for an identity of interest between the proletariat and the nationalist movement. After the achievement of formal independence, then, they could consider Indonesian society to be not only semi-feudal and semi-colonial but also partly people's democratic, by virtue of the increasing ideological hegemony of Marxist thought within the state. [46] It is this partial shift of the arena of struggle from the barricades to the world of ideas which represents the most significant contribution of Indonesians to the application of Marxism to Asia.

NOTES

1. See Perry Anderson, *Considerations on Western Marxism* (Verso, London, 1979), pp. 92-4.

2. D.N. Aidit, *Indonesian Society and the Indonesian Revolution* (Jajasan Pembaruan, Jakarta, 1958), p. 62.

3. Ibid., p. 61.

4. Michael Williams, 'Sneevliet and the Birth of Asian Communism', *New Left Review*, no. 123 (September-October 1980), pp. 85-6.

5. Semaun, 'The Indonesian Movement in the Netherlands Indies', in R.T. McVey (ed.), 'An Early Account of the Independence Movement', *Indonesia*, no. 1 (1968), pp. 50-1.

6. Ibid., p. 51.

7. Aidit, *Indonesian Society and the Indonesian Revolution*, p. 62.

8. Semaun, 'The Indonesian Movement in the Netherlands Indies', p. 51.

9. Ruth T. McVey, *The Rise of Indonesian Communism* (Cornell University Press, Ithaca, N. Y., 1965), p. 74.

10. Aidit, *Indonesian Society and the Indonesian Revolution*, p. 53.

11. D.N. Aidit, *The Indonesian Revolution and the Immediate Tasks of the Communist Party of Indonesia* (Foreign Languages Press, Peking, 1964), p.41. Emphasis in original.

12. See, for example, Rex Mortimer, *Indonesian Communism under Sukarno, Ideology and Politics, 1959-1965* (Cornell University Press, Ithaca, N.Y., 1974), pp. 402-4.

13. For an example, strongly condemning Aidit on these grounds, see John Gerassi, *Towards Revolution, Volume I, China, India, Asia, the Middle East, Africa* (Weidenfeld & Nicolson, London, 1971), pp. 157-8.

14. See especially the writings of Muhammad Yamin, for example his *Gadjah Mada, Pahlawan Persatuan Nusantara (Gajah Mada, Hero of the Unity of the Archipelago)* (APA, Jakarta, 1953), which portrayed the prime minister of a fourteenth century Javanese kingdom as a forerunner of Indonesian nationalism.

15. This argument is developed more extensively in Ruth T. McVey, 'The Enchantment of the Revolution, History and Action in an Indonesian Communist Text', in Anthony Reid and David Marr (eds.), *Perceptions of the Past in Southeast Asia* (Heinemann, Singapore, 1979), pp. 344-6. For Syahrir's analysis, see Sutan Sjahrir, *Our Struggle* (Cornell University Modern Indonesia Project, Ithaca, N.Y., 1968), pp.24-8. For an example of this penetration of Marxist categories and terminology into everyday nationalist usage, see Mas Marco

Kartodikromo, *Three Early Indonesian Short Stories*, edited by Paul Tickell (Monash University Centre of Southeast Asian Studies, Clayton, Vic., 1981).

16. Hasan Ali Surati, at the First National Congress of the Sarekat Islam at Bandung in 1916, quoted in McVey, *Rise of Indonesian Communism*, pp. 363-4.

17. McVey, *Rise of Indonesian Communism*, pp. 160-2, Mohammed Hatta, *Past and Future* (Cornell University Modern Indonesia Project, Ithaca, N.Y., 1960),pp. 1-7.

18. The term *marhaen* was one of Sukarno's many coinages. It refers to an individual who owns only sufficient means of production to maintain himself or herself at subsistence level. It thus refers to impoverished peasant small holders, pedicab drivers, street vendors and the like. Although Sukarno was inclined to suggest that the *marhaen* was the Indonesian proletarian, the *marhaen* exists as an individual, not as a member of a class.

19. Two major statements of Sukarno's position are his 1926 essay, *Nationalism, Islam and Marxism* (Cornell University Modern Indonesian Project, Ithaca, N.Y., 1969) and his 1957 speech, *Marhaen and Proletarian* (Cornell University Modern Indonesia Project, Ithaca, N.Y., 1960).

20. See Benedict R. O'G. Anderson, 'The Idea of Power in Javanese Culture', in Claire Holt *et al.* (eds.), *Culture and Politics in Indonesia* (Cornell University Press, Ithaca, N.Y., 1972), pp. 43-7.

21. McVey, 'The Enchantment of the Revolution', p. 344.

22. From a mimeographed statement accompanying application for membership of Lekra, June 1956, in Claire Holt, *Art in Indonesia, Continuities and Change* (Cornell University Press, Ithaca, N.Y., 1967), p. 247.

23. The Lekra campaign is discussed somewhat unsympathetically in Justus M. van der Kroef, 'Indonesian Communism's Cultural Offensive', *Australian Outlook*, no.18 (April 1964), pp. 40-61; on Madilog, see Harry A. Poeze, *Tan Malaka, Strijder Voor Indonesië's Vrijheid, Levensloop van 1897 tot 1945* (Martinus Nijhoff, The Hague, 1976), pp. 499-514.

24. George McTurnan Kahin, *Nationalism and Revolution in Indonesia* (Cornell University Press, Ithaca, N.Y., 1952), p. 275.

25. A full text of the *Otokritik* was published in *Build the PKI along the Marxist-Leninist Line to Lead the People's Democratic Revolution in Indonesia, Five Important Documents* (Delegation of the CC PKI, Tirana, 1971). The *Otokritik's* content is summarised from a Hsin Hua news bulletin in Michael van Langenberg, 'A Maoist View of the Indonesian Communist Party (P.K.I.)', *Review of Indonesian and Malayan Affairs*, no.2 (April-June 1968), pp. 1-10. Sudisman, said to be the author of the *Otokritik*, produced a further critique at his trial before a special military tribunal in Jakarta in 1967. This defence speech has been published as *Analysis of Responsibility* (Works Co-operative, North Melbourne, 1975).The authenticity of the *Otokritik*, however, has sometimes been challenged by suggestions that it may be the work of PKI members in Beijing.

26. It is, in fact, somewhat questionable whether Tan Ling Djie actually held the revisionist views attributed to him. The campaign against him probably reflected, rather, a general desire by Aidit to refine party thinking on this question and to guard against revisionist tendencies, with a leavening, perhaps, of personal animosity and anti-Chinese prejudice. See Soerjono, 'On Musso's Return', translated by Ben Anderson, *Indonesia*, no. 29 (April 1980), p. 74.

27. See Helen Jarvis, *Partai Republik Indonesia (Pari), Was It 'the Sole Golden Bridge to the Republic of Indonesia'?* (James Cook University South East Asia Studies Committee, Occasional Paper no. 11, Townsville,1981), passim.

28. See Anthony Edward Lucas, 'The Bamboo Spear Pierces the Payung, the Revolution against the Bureaucratic Elite in North Central Java in 1945',

(Ph.D. thesis, Australian National University, Canberra, 1981), pp. 93-9.

29. Ibid., pp. 308-10.

30. See Donald Hindley, *The Communist Party of Indonesia 1951-1963* (University of California Press, Berkeley, 1966), pp. 106-9 for a careful consideration of the question; see Tarzie Vittachi, *The Fall of Sukarno* (Andre Deutsch, London, 1967) for a somewhat hysterical analysis.

31. See Hindley, *Communist Party of Indonesia*, pp. 78-9.

32. Soerjono, 'On Musso's Return', p. 73.

33. See Ruth McVey, *The Social Roots of Indonesian Communism* (Centre d'Etude du Sud-Est Asiatique et de l'Extrême Orient, Brussels, 1970), pp. 2-3 and passim.

34. McVey, *Rise of Indonesian Communism*, pp. 80-1.

35. Lucas, 'The Bamboo Spear Pierces the Payung', pp. 93-6

36. Soerjono, 'On Musso's Return', p. 80; Aidit, *The Indonesian Revolution and the Immediate Tasks*, p. 13; Ruth T. McVey, *The Soviet View of the Indonesian Revolution, a Study in the Russian Attitude towards Asian Nationalism* (Cornell University Modern Indonesia Project, Ithaca, N.Y., 1957), pp. 61-4.

37. Aidit, *The Indonesian Revolution and the Immediate Tasks*, p. 13. Emphasis in original.

38. Mortimer, *Indonesian Communism under Sukarno*, pp. 42-65; Hindley, *Communist Party of Indonesia*, pp. 39-45.

39. D.N. Aidit, 'Haridepan Gerakan tani Indonesia', *Bintang Merah* (July 1953), p. 34, quoted in Hindley, *Communist Party of Indonesia*, p. 41.

40. Verslag van het Buitengewoon Congres der P.K.I., *Het Vrije Woord*, 31 December 1920, p. 48, in McVey, *Rise of Indonesian Communism*, p. 75.

41. Tan Malaka, *Dari Pendjara ke Pendjara*, vol. 1 (Widjaya, Jakarta, n.d.), p. 151, in Jarvis, *Partai Republik Indonesia*, p. 3 (typographical error in original corrected). Tan Malaka also displayed minimal interest in the issues which were preoccupying Marxists elsewhere in the world. The 1927 Pari manifesto, as rendered by Dutch intelligence reports, contains the remark, 'The people of the Indies have enough to do without waiting around for the conclusion to the fight between Stalin and Trotsky', ibid., p. 9.

42. Soerjono, 'On Musso's Return', p. 73, and addendum, *Indonesia*, no. 30 (October 1980), p. 164.

43. D.N. Aidit, 'Revolusi Oktober dan Rakjat-Rakjat Timur' ('The October Revolution and the Peoples of the East'), *Bintang Merah* (October-November 1957), p. 383, quoted in Hindley, *Communist Party of Indonesia*, p. 30. See also Aidit, *The Indonesian Revolution and the Immediate Tasks*, pp. 103-4.

44. Antony Cominos, 'Indonesian Society and the Indonesian State, the Marxism of D.N. Aidit' (unpublished Honours dissertation, Griffith University, 1984).

45. See Ruth T. McVey, 'Indonesian Communism and China', in Tang Tsou (ed.), *China in Crisis*, vol. 2 (University of Chicago Press, Chicago, 1969), pp. 375-6. For a masterly statement in which M.H. Lukman, one of Aidit's closest colleagues, notes Khrushchev's promotion of the peaceful road to socialism without either rejecting it or suggesting that it should be applied to Indonesia, see Gerassi, *Towards Revolution*, pp. 164-5.

46. For Aidit's optimistic assessment, see *The Indonesian Revolution and the Immediate Tasks*, p. 42.

SELECT BIBLIOGRAPHY

Aidit, D.N., *The Indonesian Revolution and the Immediate Tasks of the Communist Party of Indonesia* (Foreign Languages Press, Peking, 1965). One of the works in which Aidit articulates most clearly his concept of the two aspects of the state. It is of course ironical that this work was published in Peking for international distribution while the philosophy it expounded was to be bitterly condemned by the Chinese only two years later.

Aidit, D.N., *Indonesian Society and the Indonesian Revolution* (Jajasan Pembaruan, Jakarta, 1958). The PKI's most important theoretical statement of the 1950's and early 60's, based on the decisions of the party's Fifth National Congress in March 1954.

Build the PKI along the Marxist-Leninist Line to Lead the People's Democratic Revolution in Indonesia, Five Important Documents of the Political Bureau of the CC PKI (Delegation of the CC PKI, Tirana, 1971). Includes the *Otokritik* of September 1966.

Hindley, Donald, *The Communist Party of Indonesia 1951-1963* (University of California Press, Berkeley, 1966). A systematic discussion of the party programme under Aidit.

McVey, Ruth T., 'The Enchantment of the Revolution, History and Action in an Indonesian Communist Text', in Anthony Reid and David Marr (eds.), *Perceptions of the Past in Southeast Asia* (Heinemann, Singapore, 1979). pp. 340-58. A sensitive study of Aidit's *Indonesian Society and the Indonesian Revolution*.

McVey, Ruth T., *The Rise of Indonesian Communism* (Cornell University Press, Ithaca, N.Y., 1965). The classic study of the party from its foundation to the uprisings of 1926-7.

Mortimer, Rex, *Indonesian Communism under Sukarno, Ideology and Politics, 1959-1965* (Cornell University Press, Ithaca, N.Y., 1979). A classic study of the party under Aidit.

Semaun, 'The Indonesian Movement in the Netherlands Indies', in R.T. McVey, (ed.) 'An Early Account of the Independence Movement', *Indonesia*, no. 1 (1968), pp. 46-75. One of the earliest analyses by an Indonesian Marxist of Indonesian society.

Soerjono, 'On Musso's Return', translated by Ben Anderson, *Indonesia*, no. 29 (April 1980), pp. 61-90, with addendum in *Indonesia*, no. 30 (October 1980), pp. 163-4. One of the few detailed participant accounts of PKI activity and ideology during the national revolution, 1945-9.

Sudisman, *Analysis of Responsibility*, translated by Ben Anderson (Works Cooperative, North Melbourne, 1975). The defence speech of the PKI General Secretary at his trial in July 1967. Sudisman, one of the five foremost leaders of the party in the 1950's and 60's, was the only one brought to trial; the rest were shot.

11

CONCLUSION: CONTINUITY AND CHANGE OF MARXISM- LENINISM IN ASIA
Nick Knight and Colin Mackerras

In the Introduction to this volume, we suggested the irony that a European system of thought which emphasised the role of the industrial proletariat in social change should have exercised such a dramatic political impact in the agrarian peasant-based societies of East and South East Asia. The irony becomes less apparent, however, when it is realised that European Marxism underwent a series of interpretations and reinterpretations to adapt its themes and ideas to a different social environment and changing world. Of these interpretations, the most important was Lenin's. Working within the general framework of the theory mapped out by Marx, Lenin supplied Marxism with a corpus of political strategies and organisational principles directly relevant to the task of waging revolution and seizing political power; and through his theory of imperialism, Lenin updated Marx's ideas on capitalism to explain its monopoly phase in which the struggle for colonies was the central feature. The Leninist interpretation of Marxism thus contained vital ideological ingredients of appeal to the activist temper of Asian revolutionaries, and provided a theory of revolution and social change directly relevant to pre-capitalist and colonial societies. Consequently, Asian Marxists from the 1920s onwards have generally claimed adherence to Marxism in its Leninist guise. They have not been just Marxists, but Marxist-Leninists.

While Leninism has become the orthodox form of Marxism for many Asian Marxists, there have been some important theoretical and practical departures from the theories and policies of Lenin. In other words, the process of the interpretation of Marxism has continued, either to cope with social problems and conditions unforeseen by Lenin or to suit the personal predilections of Asian Marxist leaders. There has thus been both continuity and change of important Marxist-Leninist tenets. In this concluding chapter, we will examine a number of themes of importance to Marxism-Leninism which have emerged in the various chapters of this book, noting areas of continuity and change, and drawing comparative generalisations where these appear warranted.

The differing views held by Asian Marxists on the nature and necessity of a dictatorship of the proletariat following the seizure of power constitutes a good example of the manner in which there have been variations on themes central to Marxism-Leninism. The concept of the dictatorship of the proletariat was derived from Marx by Lenin and transformed into an essential cornerstone of the Marxist theoretical edifice. Yet Asian Marxists have sometimes found it necessary to dilute their commitment to this form of state system, usually because their societies were insufficiently developed to warrant its immediate implementation. Prior to 1949, Mao Zedong recognised that the state system in post-revolutionary China would need to be constructed on a recognition of the important role played by classes other than the proletariat in Chinese society. Mao consequently recommended a 'people's democratic dictatorship' to accommodate the aspirations of other classes, especially the peasantry. Leadership of such a state system would nevertheless remain in the hands of the proletariat, and Mao believed that the industrialisation and modernisation of Chinese society would eventually create the social and economic conditions under which a dictatorship of the proletariat would be the appropriate state system. Indeed, during the Cultural Revolution of the late 1960s, Mao was to go further than Lenin had ever done in insisting that even during the socialist transition, the revolution had to be continued under the dictatorship of the proletariat to prevent a capitalist restoration. In Vietnamese Marxism, the concept of 'collective mastery' precluded an undiluted application of the dictatorship of the proletariat; the stress on 'the people' within Vietnamese Marxism necessitating a broader class base for the state system, 'a state of, by and for the people'. Similarly, while Korea has established a dictatorship of the proletariat, there has been a clear recognition that while the working class may constitute the vanguard of society, the peasantry remains its 'reliable ally'. The most notable departure from the Leninist concept of the dictatorship of the proletariat has emerged in Japan. It was argued in the 1932 theses that the revolution in Japan would be a two-stage process, the final stage being a socialist revolution under the dictatorship of the proletariat. However, since 1961 the Japanese Communist Party, in line with several Western European communist parties, has abandoned the concept altogether, removing reference to it from platforms and policies.

Lenin ascribed a central role to the party in leading revolution and directing socialist construction. Constituted of the most advanced and politically conscious section of the working class, the party would be led largely by revolutionary intellectuals and be a disciplined and hierarchical body founded on the organisational principle of democratic centralism. In general, this aspect of Leninism has persisted in the political thought of Asian Marxists, although again not entirely without adaptation and change. In prewar Japan, Fukomoto, in opposition to the more orthodox position of Yamakawa, stressed the overriding importance of 'theoretical correctness' of the party rather than its sociological links with the working class. In Korea, the party is recognised as the force which leads society, and is described as the 'General Staff of the revolution'; however, this deference to the leading role of the party is weakened by a belief that the party itself must be led, and that the party in its turn is created by the leader (Kim Il Sung). In Indonesian Marxism during the 1950s and early 1960s, the party was perceived as a reservoir of progressive ideas, its function being to disseminate and propagate these amongst the masses; the party was thus seen as an ideological as well as a political force. Perhaps the clearest departure from othodoxy occurred in China at the time of the Cultural Revolution. Mao Zedong had earlier indicated his willingness to permit an 'open-door' rectification of the party, and with the Cultural Revolution, the Chinese Communist Party was virtually demolished by non-party elements for allegedly pursuing a 'capitalist road'. Mao nevertheless moved quickly after 1969 to rebuild the party, and his successors since 1976 have strengthened the Leninist conventions of democratic centralism and collective leadership and have reasserted the central role of the party in directing the process of modernisation. Perhaps the most orthodox stance has been maintained in Vietnam where there has been a continued insistence on the leading role of the party and the necessity for organisation and centralism in political life.

Another important element of Leninist Marxism was the assertion that historical development involved the progression of society through a series of largely predetermined stages or modes of production. This schema has created a considerable impact on the way in which Asian Marxists have interpreted both the past and present. The concept of an Asiatic mode of production, which one might have expected to be of some relevance to Marxism in an Asian context, has in fact had very little influence, largely because it lay beyond the scope of the orthodox view of historical development espoused and enforced by Lenin and Stalin.

Considerable differences of opinion have emerged, however, when this orthodox framework has been employed in the interpretation of the historical development of Asian societies. One of the most vociferous debates was that between the Labour-Farmer faction and the Communist Party in prewar Japan. While both regarded Tokugawa Japan as a feudal mode of production, there was sharp disagreement over the historical significance of the Meiji Restoration. The Labour-Farmer faction argued that it constituted a bourgeois revolution which led Japan directly into capitalism, and that only a single-stage proletarian revolution was therefore necessary. The Japanese Communist Party, on the other hand, denied that the Meiji Restoration was a thorough-going bourgeois revolution, and because feudal elements persisted, a two-stage revolution (bourgeois-democratic, then proletarian) was necessary. Two very different strategies thus resulted from these opposed interpretations of the historical stage achieved by Japan.

A rather different interpretation emerged in Vietnam. While Vietnamese society was regarded as feudal, it was considered possible that a capitalist future might be avoided because of the particular position occupied by Vietnam within the international framework of French capitalism. What capitalism developed in Vietnam would be of a compradore variety, and little domestic capitalism could hope to survive. Vietnamese Marxists believed that socialism could thus be constructed directly on the basis of the small-scale production which characterised the indigenous economy without attending the emergence of a domestic capitalism whose development would be prejudiced by

French colonialism.

The Chinese and Indonesian examples are also instructive. While Mao believed that some development of capitalism was necessary, he argued that the industrialisation and modernisation which had accompanied the rise of capitalism in Europe could occur in China largely under the direction and control of a New Democratic government whose avowed aim was the transcendence of capitalism and the construction of socialism. Despite China's 'semi-feudal, semi-colonial' status, he did not advocate the unrestrained development of capitalism along European lines. Nevertheless, Mao remained within the framework of Leninist orthodoxy by insisting on a two-stage revolution, the first of which would be a bourgeois-democratic revolution. Indonesian Marxists, on the other hand, while conceding that their society remained 'semi-feudal and semi-colonial', tended to see a fundamental unity of interests between the national and proletarian revolutions; because the proletariat was exploited and oppressed by feudalism, it could lead a revolution against both feudalism and imperialism to achieve the twin goals of national independence and socialism. Perhaps the most audacious departure from orthodox Marxism-Leninism emerged with the assertion by the Communist Party of Kampuchea that Kampuchea had 'leapt over' both the semi-feudal and capitalist stages 'straight to a socialist society'.

Marxism was made more acceptable to Asian revolutionaries through Lenin's tendency to emphasise the political aspects of class struggle. While political conflict was inextricably linked to the antagonism between hostile economic class formations, the effectiveness of the struggle at the political level could, Lenin believed, determine the success or failure of a class in the prosecution of its interests. Lenin rejected the notion that it was necessary patiently to wait for the culmination of a lengthy process of evolutionary development during which the forces of production would mature and create the conditions for revolutionary change. Where conditions permitted, this process could be advanced through adroit political strategies. In other words, action within the realm of the superstructure could play a decisive role.

Asian Marxists have not only agreed with Lenin's estimation of the important and at times central role played by politics, they have gone further to emphasise the importance of such factors as ideology and consciousness in effecting historical change. The realm of the superstructure has thus assumed heightened emphasis within the theory of historical materialism as this has been interpreted by many Asian Marxists. Indonesian Marxism stressed the spread of progressive ideas as an important adjunct to political action; and in Kampuchea, emphasis on correct consciousness led to an unbridled voluntarism with tragic consequences. In post-revolutionary Korea and China, there emerged the belief that, despite a fundamental transformation in the system of ownership (a major component of the economic base), there had not been a commensurate transformation in the superstructure. The failure of the superstructure to conform to socialist changes within the economic base was thus blamed for hindering the consolidation and further development of a socialist economy, and the superstructure consequently became the target of political campaigns the aim of which was the elimination of conservative modes of thought and habits inherited from the old society. In Mao's China, the attempt to resolve contradictions in the superstructure resulted in intermittent and at times lengthy periods of struggle, a procedure repudiated by Mao's successors who have chosen to emphasise the primacy of the forces of production in historical development. While overt struggle has not been as pronounced in Korea, great emphasis has been placed on the importance of 'correct ideas' and forcing the superstructure to keep pace with the socialisation of the economy. In Vietnam, there has been a more orthodox assertion of the principal importance of the revolution in the economic base, but there has nevertheless been an insistence on the need for a revolution in culture and ideology to parallel and serve this revolutionary transformation of the economy.

Despite this emphasis on the importance of the superstructure in effecting historical change, Asian Marxists have generally still subscribed strongly to the belief that class analysis constitutes a central element of Marxism. Mao, for example, argued that class analysis represented 'the fundamental viewpoint of Marxism', and even a cursory reading of his writings reveals the importance of class analysis to his interpretation of history and society. Similarly, class analysis has provided Japanese Marxism with a framework for social investigation and interpretation, although some very different views of the nature of Japanese society were derived from such analysis. In Vietnam, a class analysis was mobilised to reveal the weakness of the domestic bourgeoisie, and this was to constitute an essential foundation for socialist and anti-imperialist strategies pursued by Vietnamese Marxists. Indonesian Marxism too utilised a class analysis to identify those forces which could be incorporated in an anti-imperialist, antifeudal united front.

One important difference which has emerged amongst Asian Marxists is over the extent to which class struggle persists during the socialist transition. Mao Zedong and his radical supporters believed that the seizure of political power and the initial socialist transformation of the ownership system did not signal the termination of class struggle. On the contrary, they were convinced that the bourgeoisie and counter-revolutionary forces remained a very real and persistent threat throughout the socialist transition, and that continued vigilance and revolutionary policies were consequently necessary. Socialist transition would thus be characterised by intermittent periods of overt struggle as the forces of reaction attempted to seize political power. Since 1978, Chinese Marxism has repudiated this view, arguing that while some class struggle does exist in socialist society it no longer represents the principal contradiction. Campaigns such as the Cultural Revolution are therefore regarded as wasteful and unnecessary, premised as they were on an exaggerated estimation of the intensity of class struggle during socialist transition. A similar view has characterised Vietnamese Marxism, which has admitted the existence of class struggle in socialist society while denying it to be as evident or intense as Mao believed. The most harmonious picture of the socialist transition emerges from Korean Marxism which asserts that class antagonisms have been eliminated forever.

Asian Marxists have also differed over the necessity of violent revolution for the seizure of political power. Since World War II, the Japanese Communist Party has rejected revolutionary theory, pinning its hopes for peaceful change on the parliamentary road to socialism; and this policy has led to a degree of political and electoral success for the Japanese Communist Party within the framework of Japanese capitalism. Similarly, during the 1950s and early 1960s, Indonesian Marxists believed that the state could be captured through peaceful means; the state possessed a 'dual nature' and its pro-people aspect could be enlarged through non-violent reforms. Many Asian

Marxists have, however, rejected a reformist or parliamentary road to socialism, opting instead for a strategy based on the seizure of political power through the violence of revolution. Such a choice has not been based solely on Marxist-Leninist theory, but on a pragmatic estimation of the dismal possibilities for reformist policies within dictatorial and repressive political systems; and this estimation has appeared justified by the success of revolutionary strategies pursued in Vietnam, Kampuchea, China and Korea.

Apart from isolated demurrals, Asian Marxists have agreed on the central role played by the masses and mass action in bringing about social change, and the consequent necessity for leadership to remain closely attuned to the aspirations and attitudes of the masses. The most articulate expression of this view emerged in China, and the leadership principle of the 'mass line' has persisted in its influence within Chinese Marxism. In Korea, the *juche* idea has placed great emphasis on collective action and allowing the masses to give play to their enthusiasm. However, this emphasis has been qualified by the insistence that the popular masses can make history only if properly led; hence, the importance attributed to Kim Il Sung. Vietnamese Marxism has also stressed the necessity of mobilising all sections of the community to resist imperialism and achieve social goals, and the concept of 'collective mastery' is predicated on mass mobilisation. Only in prewar Japan was there a tendency (on the part of Fukumoto) to perceive the theoretical correctness of the party as central, rather than the ability to mobilise the masses. However, this view was challenged by Yamakawa, and following World War II, the Japanese Communist Party has based its strategy on the need to build a mass party capable of attracting mass support.

An issue of vital concern to Marxism in Asia has been the relative roles of the working class and peasantry in leading revolution and building socialism. Although Marx's primary concern had been to critique the capitalist mode of production, he believed a major benefit brought by capitalism was the development of modern industry and the emergence of an industrial working class capable of initiating radical social change. In contrast, the peasants were, Marx suggested, backward and conservative, and lacking the ability and consciousness necessary to prosecute a modernising revolution. Lenin revised this verdict.

He perceived the importance of involving the peasantry as allies of the working class in the revolutionary endeavour in societies whose populations were predominantly peasant. While Lenin did not directly challenge Marx's view, it was he who formulated the concept of a 'worker-peasant alliance', a concept to be of crucial significance in the orthodox Marxism adopted by many Asian revolutionaries.

All of the Asian countries covered in this book, except Japan, have overwhelmingly peasant populations. However, apart from the case of Kampuchean Marxism, no Asian Marxist has overtly placed the peasants' revolutionary role above that of the workers. Indeed, Marxists in China, Korea, Vietnam, and Indonesia have declared repeatedly that the proletariat is the vanguard class, and that leadership of the revolution remains its prerogative. All of them have nevertheless subscribed to Lenin's formula of the 'worker-peasant alliance', and in practice Asian Marxist leaders have frequently focussed more attention on the revolutionary potential of the peasants than that of the workers. While the labour movements in China, Korea and Vietnam did make a significant contribution to their revolutions, Mao, Ho, and to a lesser extent Kim, depended more on peasant than proletarian support. It was only in Kampuchean Marxism between 1975 and 1979 that the orthodox relationship between proletariat and peasantry was reversed. As Kiernan notes, the Communist Party of Kampuchea 'did not rely on the forces of the workers'; the workers 'in concrete fact did not become the vanguard'. The peasantry was consequently attributed with a leading role in the Kampuchean revolution, a strategy at odds with orthodox Marxism-Leninism.

However, most Asian Marxisms have advocated a central role for industry in the construction of a socialist economy. Though the practical balance between industry and agriculture may have varied from place to place and time to time, the development of modern industry has served to expand the numerical size and the importance of the working class in the economies of these socialist societies. Again, the exception to this generalisation is the Kampuchean case. Under Pol Pot, cities were evacuated and the emphasis in socialist construction placed on the establishment of rural cooperatives.

The internationalist theme in Marx's writings has also created problems for Asian Marxists. Marx believed that the international character of capitalism would create the conditions whereby national differences would recede in importance and common class identification across national boundaries become a potent agent in laying the foundation for an international socialist order. While Lenin accepted this position, he argued that the achievement of an international order was a two-stage process, the first of which would witness national struggles by colonial and subject peoples to liberate themselves from imperialist oppression. Lenin did not condone nationalism of the narrow chauvinistic sort, but believed nationalism to be positive where it was employed to achieve liberation from imperialism and allow the consequent move to the second stage of merging nations and developing internationalism. While this may have been Lenin's position in theory, the practice of the Comintern under Lenin and later Stalin was directed primarily at enhancing the national interests of the Soviet Union in the realm of international relations.

Asian Marxists have generally subscribed to internationalism at the level of theory, and have clearly been influenced by Lenin's views on this matter. However, they have tended even more than Lenin to emphasise the role of nationalism and to exploit it to achieve revolutionary goals. There are two main reasons for this. The first is the importance of anti-imperialism as a constituent element of the revolutions which have occurred in colonial and semi-colonial countries. Neither Mao nor Kim found it difficult to convince the Chinese or Koreans of the evils of Japanese colonialism; the Vietnamese and Kampuchean people were readily convinced of the horrors of French, Japanese and American imperialism; and opposition to Dutch colonialism was a major theme of Indonesian Marxism. The espousal of anti-imperialist struggle and reconstruction of the nation free from the oppression of imperialism thus led to a frequent fusion of nationalist and Marxist goals. In effect, nationalism became a vital element in the appeal of Marxism to subject peoples in the colonial context.

Secondly, Marxist leaders in Asia have perceived that nationalism can assist them in gaining and holding power. Le Duan, for example, asserted that 'love of country means love of socialism', and his appeal to nationalism has been motivated in part by the need to rally support from the Vietnamese people. In Korea, the *juche* idea has stressed national independence and the importance of self-reliance, and there has been a strong tendency among other Asian Marxisms to point to the accomplishments of the socialist period to bolster national pride and consequently enhance the prestige of and support for Marxist leaders. Therefore, while most Asian Marxisms have not, at a theoretical level, rejected internationalism as a long-term goal, the more immediate needs of practical politics have usually necessitated an emphasis on nationalism.

Marx wrote very little about problems of socialist transition. However, in a famous passage in 'The Critique of the Gotha Programme', he did discuss impediments to the achievement of social equality during that stage of historical development. Bourgeois right (that is, inequalities left over from the past) would have to be tolerated initially, and during this stage the distributive principle of 'to each according to his labour' would operate. When society developed to the point at which there was material abundance and class differences had vanished, goods and services would be allocated on the principle 'to each according to his need'. This would be the higher phase of communist society.

Asian Marxists who have held power have generally desired a reduction in social inequalities, and have undertaken property reallocation to that end. All have faced the problems of entrenched privilege, and in particular the problem of the rich peasant class. Stalin attempted to resolve the problem posed by the *kulaks* through the use of terror, by physically eliminating them as a class. In so doing, he instituted inequalities favouring his own supporters. During the Cultural Revolution in China, Mao and his followers formulated a theory that bourgeois right should be restricted in order to facilitate the achievement of social equality and prevent the emergence of a 'new bourgeoisie'. However, after Mao's death this theory was decisively rejected. Chinese Marxism now argues that modernisation and rural development necessitate allowing the peasants to accumulate personal wealth and that growing disparities between rich and poor are an unfortunate byproduct of the modernisation drive. It is hoped that the poor will eventually catch up with the rich through a general increase in economic activity. In Korea, land reform was comparatively easy since the Japanese had taken over most of the land and their defeat left the country much freer of a landlord class than in China. Kim Il Sung has, however, never demanded the restriction of bourgeois right.

Asian Marxists have usually couched predictions of the arrival of the higher phase of communism in vague language. During the Yan'an period, Mao's view of the future was uncompromisingly optimistic, but by the time of the Cultural Revolution, his writings express a growing pessimism about the possibilities not only of achieving communism, but even of consolidating a socialist society. Ironically, his successors have become more optimistic as they have increasingly allowed the return of free enterprise. Deng Liqun predicted in 1982 that the higher stage of communism would arrive in 'several generations' hence. Kim Il Sung is even more optimistic about Korean social progress, although even he does not predict the achievement of communism in the immediate future.

Marx and Engels perceived the family in terms of exploitative property relationships and believed that the achievement of socialism would remove the necessity for domestic organisation such as the family. Mao echoed this sentiment in 1958 when he predicted with approval the disappearance of the family 'after maybe a few thousand years, or at the very least several hundred years'.

Considering the gross injustices of the feudal family system in Asian societies, especially in terms of discrimination against women, it is not surprising that Asian Marxists have denounced the family traditions of their own countries for relegating women to the position of virtual slaves. They have demanded the overthrow of the feudal family system, and advocated equality between the sexes. All have wished to make children a good deal more than articles of commerce and women more than mere instruments of production.

In practice, all Marxist governments in Asia have undertaken transformations in the feudal family and in relations between the sexes. Yet, except for the single exception of Pol Pot's Kampuchea, there has been no serious attempt to abolish the family. Sex roles may have declined in importance, and official policy has in most cases encouraged this trend, but in no country have they come close to disappearing. In Korea they remain especially important and Kim Il Sung seems quite happy to maintain them.

It is important to point out, however, that none of the Asian Marxist societies discussed in this book is half a century old. In this respect, it may be premature to belittle the significance of their family revolutions. Asia is renowned for the strength of its family traditions. Consequently, to expect Asian Marxist leaders to go beyond advocating thoroughgoing change in the nature of the family to calling for its total abolition would be quite unrealistic. Any who seriously attempted to implement such a doctrine would face an uphill and probably unwinnable battle.

Marx's materialist conception of history negates the role of the 'great man' in social and historical development. By implication Marx thus deplored any hero worship or cult of the individual, and he rejected it in practice. The personality cult of individual leaders would therefore appear to be unmarxist. However, Stalin encouraged his own personality cult and this reached monstrous proportions. Several Asian Marxist leaders have followed his example. The worst cases have been the Mao cult during the Cultural Revolution and that of Kim in Korea. Kim's cult of personality was already pronounced at the time of his accession to power in 1945 and it has become an all-consuming feature of Korean political and social life since then. Kim has even designated his own son Kim Jong Il as his heir and successor, and a cult of personality is being promoted around Kim Jong Il.

Despite these examples of personality cults among Asian Marxist leaders, there are also examples of collective leadership. Japanese Marxists have never produced a personality cult around any of their leaders, and in Vietnam, Ho Chi Minh assumed the persona of a popular folk hero but never dominated the party to the exclusion of others. Post-Ho leadership appears reasonably collective, with several influential leaders wielding power. Similarly, Mao's successors in China have stressed the collective nature of their leadership.

Personality cults have sometimes been justified through the need for national unity. Under some circumstances, such as invasion, the argument could carry conviction. However, it is striking that personality cults appear to be ephemeral, rarely surviving the death of the charismatic leader for long. Three years after Stalin's death he was debunked and his personality cult overthrown. The post-Mao leadership has reacted sharply against the cult of the individual leader and Mao's role has been reevaluated and downgraded. As for Kim Il Sung, the worst offender of all, we shall have to wait and see.

In surveying the record of the various interpretations of Marxism in Asia, one is struck by the continuity of important themes formulated originally by Marx. Concepts such as class struggle and the desire to establish socialism have characterised the thinking of all Asian Marxists. However, perhaps the most significant theoretical influence on Asian Marxism has been the interpretation of Marxism formulated by Lenin. Lenin revised and updated many of the major doctrines of Marx and in so doing formulated a system of thought which Asians could use effectively in bringing about a successful revolution. Asian Marxists have nevertheless needed frequently to adapt Lenin's views to the particular needs and characteristics of their own societies. There has consequently been a continuing process of interpreting and reinterpreting Marxism-Leninism in different social contexts and at different points in time. There has thus been both continuity and change in the development of Marxism in Asia, and the process is far from complete.

INDEX